ESSENTIALS OF COMMERCIAL LAW

Jeffrey A. Helewitz, JD, LLM, MBA

Copyright © 2002
All Rights Reserved.
Pearson Publications Company
Dallas, Texas

Website: Pearsonpub-legal.com

ISBN: 0-929563-67-0

Essentials of Commercial Law is designed as a textbook for classroom use. The information contained herein is intended only for educational and informational purposes.

KF889 .H46 2002
0134106188821
Helewitz, Jeffrey A.

Essentials of commercial
 law /
    c2002.

2003 11 12

FOREWORD

Essentials of Commercial Law is designed for the business student. Its objective is to acquaint the student with basic legal concepts that affect a commercial enterprise. It is not intended as a comprehensive analysis of each topic presented. For more detailed discussions on these areas, the student is referred to specific publications of Pearson Publications Company.

ACKNOWLEDGMENTS

The author gratefully acknowledges the kind and thoughtful assistance of Daniel Andre Alter, Esq., without whose comments and criticisms this text would not have been possible.

Jeffrey A. Helewitz

The publisher thanks the Pearson editorial team of Nancy Blanchette, Lance Cooper, Linda Furlet, Brenna Morgan, and Frances Whiteside as well as reviewers Eli Bortman, Dora Dye, William Goren, and Dr. Martha Troxell for contributing to the excellence of this work.

Enika Pearson Schulze

TABLE OF CONTENTS

Chapter One
The American Legal System 1

Chapter Two
Criminal v. Civil Wrongs 13

Chapter Three
Contracts and the Law of Sales..39

Chapter Four
Commercial Paper 65

Chapter Five
Real Property..81

Chapter Six
Personal Property...111

Chapter Seven
Law of Agency..127

Chapter Eight
Business Organizations..141

Chapter Nine
Employment Law..159

Chapter Ten
Bankruptcy..175

Chapter Eleven
Administrative Law..193

Chapter Twelve
Banking..205

Index..217

Chapter One

THE AMERICAN LEGAL SYSTEM

Introduction

In order to operate a business effectively in the United States, one must be familiar with a variety of legal concepts. **Jurisprudence**, literally defined as the "wisdom of the law," refers to the legal concepts under which a society operates. The law forms the framework within which a commercial enterprise must operate; any entity that goes beyond these boundaries risks incurring a legal sanction.

The entrepreneur is not expected to know all of the intricacies of American law—that is the function of the legal professional whose services and advice the entrepreneur should seek. However, the business person must have a basic understanding of the law to avoid legal problems when making and implementing business decisions. To this end, this text is designed to acquaint the business person with the essential elements of those legal principles that he or she is most likely to encounter in operating a business. This first chapter is intended to provide an overview of the legal structure of the United States.

When discussing the law, most lay persons assume that there is one all-encompassing source that provides immediate and conclusive answers to legal problems. However, the American legal system and structure is derived from several different sources. Rarely is the answer to a legal question immediate or absolute. American law is neither black nor white; it is, rather, varying shades of gray with the ultimate answer based on judicial decisions, legislative enactments, and the persuasiveness of the party seeking legal redress to a problem.

Most people are aware that the American legal system is referred to as a **common law system**, but usually are unaware of what that actually means. Common law refers to judicial precedent, law made by judges deciding how a particular legal problem should be resolved. The United States adopted this system from the British.

Most of the European countries, unlike the United Kingdom, operate under a different legal concept known as **civil law**, a legal system emanating from statutes enacted by a legislative body. This system of law evolved from ancient Roman law concepts. Even though the American legal system is called a common law system, statutory enactments have become so pervasive that the modern American system is actually a hybrid of both common and civil law.

The tremendous growth of administrative agencies created to regulate specific legislative enactments has created another source of American law known as **administrative law**. These are rules and regulations that persons and businesses must adhere to in order to reap the benefits or avoid the negative consequences of governmental enactments.

In order to interpret and administer these disparate laws, the United States has developed two separate but interrelated court structures, one on the federal level and the other developed by each of the individual states, the District of Columbia, and the U.S. possessions and territories. These courts try to apply the laws uniformly.

This chapter will examine the elements of case law, statutory enactments, administrative law, and the federal court structure. These concepts form the basis of all of the substantive laws that form the remainder of the text.

Case Law

As stated above, the American legal system is known as a common law system, meaning that American law is determined on a case-by-case basis as a legal problem is presented to a **judge** for **adjudication** (legal resolution of a problem). Once this decision is made, that decision is published. It becomes a legal **precedent**, which judges must follow when presented with similar problems to resolve. The concept of using a judicial decision as a legal precedent is known as *stare decisis*, the requirement that judges follow the legal application enunciated by other judges. If no other court has been called upon to decide a particular legal question, the question is deemed to be one of **first impression**, permitting the court to articulate its own legal precedent. Trial courts are called upon to make two decisions: one, based on the evidence presented—through witnesses, documents, and so forth—what actually happened (the facts) and, two, how judicial precedent must be applied to those facts (the law).

> *Example:* *Two farmers enter into an agreement for the sale of a horse. The buyer agrees to pay a certain amount of money, and the seller agrees to deliver to the buyer a two-year-old horse. The buyer gives the cash to the seller, but the seller delivers to the buyer an animal that the buyer insists is a mule. The seller claims that the animal is in fact a horse. The parties go to court to seek relief.*
>
> *Note that the parties have brought two problems to the court to be resolved. The first question is a* **question of fact***; i.e., is the animal in question a horse or a mule? The second question, which is dependent upon the answer to the factual one, is what the parties are legally entitled to under the terms of their agreement. If a person agrees to buy a horse but is given a mule instead, has he been legally injured? If a person receives what he has in fact bargained for but decides that he no longer wants it, can he back out of the deal without negative consequences?*
>
> *The answer to the first question, the question of fact, does not create a judicial precedent. It only concerns what has occurred. The second question, the* **question of law***, does create judicial precedent because it determines the legal rights of the parties based on the particular facts.*

Once a precedent has been established, judges in the same jurisdiction are required to apply that precedent to similar legal problems presented to them for resolution. However, if the precedent were applied indefinitely and inflexibly, it would be impossible to create new law to reflect a changing society. One of the benefits of a common law system is that the law can change. This change in the law can arise when later courts either **distinguish** former precedent, by which the court states that although the precedent is still intact, it is not applicable to the particular facts, or **overrule** a precedent, stating that the precedent is no longer the law because of societal changes.

> **Example:** Centuries ago, all travel was conducted on land or over water, and so a body of law developed to determine legal right involved in transporting goods by land and sea. In the last century air travel was created, and, because it was the result of new technology, there was no law covering such transportation. When called upon to decide cases involving air transport, the judges were able to adapt existing legal principles immediately to newly create legal problems.

Judicial precedent may also be changed by direct statutory enactment. The legislature, in response to society's dissatisfaction with a particular precedent, may by statute change the law. This aspect of the American legal system highlights the interplay between the common and the civil law.

> **Example:** Under common law, an employer was not legally responsible if one of its workers carelessly injured another worker while on the job. The purpose behind this precedent was to encourage business people to hire workers—if a business owner was held responsible for every accident that caused one of its workers to be hurt, there would be a chilling effect on an owner hiring workers. (Note that the employer would always be responsible for injuries that are caused by the owner's own fault.) This case law precedent existed for centuries.
>
> During the industrial revolution, when heavy machinery became more commonplace, many workers were injured by equipment that was improperly handled by their co-workers. This was especially true in the railroad industry where serious injuries were fairly typical. However, under judicial precedent, the injured worker could not sue the owner and could only seek recourse from the other worker, who had limited financial resources. As society became outraged by this result, the legislature, in order to rectify this injustice, enacted the original workers compensation statutes, laws that give the worker the ability to obtain financial relief if he or she is injured on the job by the action of a co-worker. In this manner, the common law was changed by legislative enactment.

In theory, under the American legal system, the primary source of the law is a recent judicial decision that can be used as a precedent to resolve a legal problem. In practice, the American legal system combines judicial precedent with legislative enactment.

Statutory Law

As illustrated above, in certain instances the common law concept of *stare decisis* may be disregarded by legislative enactment. The authority of the legislature to create laws overriding judicial precedent comes from the **United States Constitution**.

The United States Constitution is the supreme law of the land: no law—court, legislature or agency created— is valid if it violates the Constitution. Therefore, to be enforceable, all American law must be deemed to be constitutional—that which adheres to the Constitution. The Constitution further provides that Congress is empowered to enact laws, with certain prohibitions and limitations.

The power by which Congress enacts a law is known as the **legislative process**. This process starts with a member of Congress proposing a law in the form of a **bill**. This bill is then referred to a committee that refers it to a subcommittee to investigate the appropriateness of the proposed legislation. If the bill is approved by both the subcommittee and the committee, it is then sent to the chamber, either the House of Representatives or the Senate, from which it emanated. If that chamber passes the bill, it is referred to the other chamber for consideration.

The second chamber follows a similar process in determining the appropriateness of the bill. If it agrees that the legislation is warranted, it will pass its own version of the proposed statute. If there is any difference between the versions, the matter is referred to a **joint committee** for resolution. The eventual compromise is then submitted to both houses for consideration. If approved, the bill is sent to the President for signing. If the President refuses or fails to sign, known as a **veto**, the Congress may override the veto by a two-thirds vote. If the President signs the bill or Congress overrides the veto, the bill becomes a **public law**.

Public laws are printed and eventually organized by subject matter in a process known as **codification**. These laws are printed in a series of books called the **United States Code**. Statutes may create new law for legal issues that have no judicial precedent, may amend or change laws for which there is judicial precedent, or create a statutory statement of a judicial precedent. This system of statutory enactment operates in a similar fashion on the state level as well. All state statutes are required to meet the requirements of the U.S. Constitution and the constitutions of the state where the law is passed.

***Example:** Every state has enacted a version of the Uniform Commercial Code, a statute that will be discussed later in Chapter Three. The Uniform Commercial Code performs the following functions:*
- *It codifies judicial precedent by including the concept of custom and usage in its provisions, a concept long applied by the court.*
- *It changes the common law requirements for contract formation for situations in which both parties to the agreement are deemed to be "merchants," as defined by the statute.*
- *It creates law by specifying certain remedies for injured parties that did not exist under the common law.*

However, statutory enactment alone does not necessarily create a valid law. As indicated above, laws must be constitutional to be given legal effect. Therefore, once the legislature has enacted a law, a court may be called upon to determine that law's constitutionality. Furthermore, even if the court finds the statute to be constitutional, the judges are the ones who interpret and apply the law. This judicial interpretation and application may have the effect of changing or limiting the law's application. The right of a court to determine the constitutionality of a statute is known as **judicial review**. This right was firmly established as an integral part of the American legal system in the case entitled *Marbury v. Madison*, an opinion written by Chief Justice Marshall in 1803.

Consequently, if there is a statute on point, the law starts with the statute, but judicial precedent greatly affects the statute's application. However, if there is no statute on point, the law is determined by reference to judicial precedent.

Law is created by the integration of statutes and case law.

Administrative Agency Rules

Prior to the 1930s, administrative agencies were primarily organizations that assisted the executive in administering and applying the law that came within the purview of the cabinet (Treasury, State, etc., known as **executive agencies**) and those bodies created by Congress to administer specific laws that did not fall within the executive's authority, such as the Interstate Commerce Commission (**legislative agencies**). The agency was defined by the branch of government that created it and collectively was referred to as **administrative agencies**. (The judicial branch does not create agencies.)

In the 1930s, as a consequence of the Great Depression and the New Deal legislation, administrative agencies proliferated, both at the federal and state levels. Today, many typical legal problems encountered by commercial enterprises are regulated by the agency with the statutory authority, called **enabling statutes**, to see that a specific law is appropriately administered. For a complete discussion on the administrative rule-making process see Chapter Eleven, Administrative Law.

Just as with the courts and the legislature, administrative agencies are required to distribute their rules and procedures to the public in order to ensure that these regulations are uniformly applied. A body of law has developed, **administrative law**, which is exclusively concerned with the application of these agencies' rules to the American legal system. The general guideline for agency action appears in a statute called the **Administrative Procedure Act (APA)**. The federal government, and each of the states, has enacted a version of the APA to deal with agency rules, regulations, and procedures. Under the APA, administrative agencies have the ability to create rules that have the effect of a legislative enactment. Applying these rules has the effect of case law. To meet constitutional safeguards, all persons who are adversely affected by agency action are entitled to a fair hearing at the agency in question, and the agency must provide the party with a detailed statement of its findings and application of the law. If a person is dissatisfied with the agency action, the person may ask to have the agency decision overturned by seeking judicial review.

For many areas of law, administrative agencies provide a link between the legislature and the judiciary. The agencies must establish their own rules and regulations to apply the statute, but their determinations are still subject to judicial review.

Example: Congress enacted the Internal Revenue Code to establish laws with respect to taxing the public to provide income for the government. To administer these laws, the Internal Revenue Service was created.

A taxpayer deducts a certain item as a business deduction to reduce its tax liability for operating a business. It files an income tax return, but the IRS disallows the deduction. Under rules created by the IRS, the taxpayer has the right to challenge the IRS' position, first at the local level, then the regional level, and finally at the national office of the IRS in Washington, D.C. Only after the taxpayer has completed these internal review procedures established by the IRS can the taxpayer seek review of the IRS action in a court of law.

In this example, the taxpayer has become involved with all aspects of American law—the legislative, the Internal Revenue Code, the administrative agency established to administer that statute, and then the judicial, by seeking judicial review of the agency action.

The administrative process acts almost as a shadow legal system. Its authority is created by statute, but its ability to act is limited by judicial review. For the business person, the administrative process is frequently involved in the resolution of legal problems.

The American Court Structure

There are two distinct types of courts in the American legal system. The first, the **trial court**, is the tribunal that determines the facts in a given dispute. Once the facts are ascertained, it applies the law to those facts. The person or persons who decide the facts at trial, the **trier of fact**, may be either a judge, the official who presides over the court, or a **jury**, a selected group of lay persons. The trier of fact hears **evidence** in the form of **testimony** (sworn statements of witnesses and experts), documents, and other physical items that bear on the problem. The trier of fact then hands down its decision (called a verdict of given by a jury).

The judicial process in the United States is an **adversarial** one, meaning that in order to invoke the court's jurisdiction, the parties must have an actual legal dispute, referred to as a **case or controversy**. The courts generally will not give advisory opinions or rulings for questions that have already been resolved—the question is deemed to be **moot** if it is no longer a subject of controversy.

> *Example:* A job applicant has heard that a particular company never hires anyone who is a member of the applicant's religion. If true, this may be a violation of federal and state anti-discrimination employment laws. The applicant truly believes that the company will not hire her because of her religion and files suit in court against the prospective employer. The case would be disallowed because the applicant had not applied for the job, nor had she been rejected. She is filing suit merely on a supposition that she will be discriminated against. This case is not **ripe**—no injury or unlawful conduct has occurred. Prior to filing suit, the applicant must apply for the job, be rejected, and then follow certain administrative procedures before she may bring the matter before a court.
>
> If the applicant does apply and is rejected, and then follows all procedures, she may file a lawsuit against the employer.

The second type of court is the **appellate court**. The function of the appellate court is to review the decision of the trial court to determine that the law was appropriately applied to the proven facts. There are no juries at the appellate level, only judges. The decision of the appellate court creates judicial precedent.

The federal court structure is a three-tiered system. The lowest court, the trial court, is called the **district court**. The jurisdiction of the district court is geographic, and there is at least one federal district court in every state. (Several states have multiple district courts because of population.)

The second-tier courts of the federal court system are called **circuit courts**, often cited as the United States Court of Appeals for the ___ Circuit. The entire country is divided into 13 circuits, 12 of which are geographic. The 13th, the Federal Circuit, is in the District of Columbia, and it hears specified matters emanating from certain specialized federal district courts, which hear matters involving limited areas of law. The party who wishes to appeal the decision of the district court must file an appeal in the circuit court that has jurisdiction over the district court that originally rendered the decision.

The ultimate court of appeals in the federal system is the **United States Supreme Court**, the highest court in the land. Once the Supreme Court has decided a matter, it can be overruled only if the legislature enacts a specific statute or if the court later reverses it decision when it is presented with a similar legal question.

The state court system operates similarly with a trial court and at least one appellate court. Some states have a three-tiered system, mimicking the federal structure. The decisions of the highest state court may be appealed to the United States Supreme Court if the Supreme Court accepts the appeal. To initiate an appeal to the Supreme Court, the person seeking the appeal must file a document called a **writ of certiorari**, which requests the court to allow the petitioner to present his or her case. The Supreme Court does not automatically grant certiorari. It will only do so if the matter involves a federal statute or an interpretation of the United States Constitution. Its decision to accept a case is totally discretionary with the Court.

Chapter Summary

The American legal system is not a straightforward system; rather, it is a mélange of cases and statutes that weave together to create an ever-changing and evolving body of laws.

The historical basis of American law is judicial precedent. Judges make laws originating from decisions of appellate courts in deciding actual legal problems presented to them for resolution. Overlying this common law approach, the American system has interpolated the civil law concept of legislative enactment—those laws created by a legislative body that are framed prospectively, not in response to a particular dispute. In between both of these sources of law are the administrative agencies—those bodies created by the legislature or the executive to administer statutes—whose rules and regulations are subject to judicial review.

To apply these various laws to a given problem, the courts are divided into two distinct categories: trial courts, which determine the facts of a given problem, and appellate courts that review the decisions of the trial courts to ensure that the law was appropriately applied to the proven facts. The decisions of the appellate courts create judicial precedent, the basis of the common law.

To operate a business effectively, the entrepreneur must be aware that every business decision is subject to legal scrutiny, *i.e.*, all business decisions must adhere to the law.

Edited Judicial Decisions

Each chapter in this text includes two edited judicial decisions to demonstrate how the courts have applied the law discussed in the body of the chapter to a given legal problem. This is the way law comes into existence. In order to assist in interpreting these decisions, the reader should attempt to dissect the decision into the following component parts:
1. Facts
2. Procedure
3. Issue(s)
4. Decision
5. Holding(s)
6. Reasoning

Facts
This section provides the factual background that gave rise to the need for a judicial decision. When reading a case, the reader should try to avoid thinking of the litigants in terms of their actual names, but should attempt to refer to them by the legal roles they play in the situation, such as promissor, bailee, victim, and so forth. Because a judicial decision creates the law for the entire jurisdiction in which the decision is rendered, it is more important to note the legal situation that gave rise to the problem rather than the specific individuals involved. In this fashion, the reader can see the application the decision might have to a given legal problem.

Most cases recite the facts at the very beginning of the decision; however, the reader should be aware that not every fact mentioned by the court will eventually prove to be relevant to the ultimate conclusion. Therefore, the reader must analyze the entire decision to determine which are the operative facts used by the court in reaching its conclusion.

Procedure
The section on procedure is used to indicate to a reader exactly how this problem came before the court that rendered the decision. Because the majority of published decisions are appeals, the most typical procedure would be that the trial court found for one party, and the losing party appealed. However, under certain circumstances, the procedure may be more complex, and it is important to track the progress of the case through the judicial process.

Issue(s)
The issue is the question of law raised by the particular facts presented. In locating the issues in a case, the key is to look for words such as "the question presented to us" or "the issue is," or words to that effect. The courts are usually precise in alerting the reader to the points of law they will decide.

It is important for the reader to remember that courts may be required to decide multiple issues presented by a given set of facts. Rarely is there only one legal issue presented in each case.

Decision
The decision is the ultimate conclusion reached by the court indicating who wins. Because the decisions are all appeals, the options for the court are limited to the following:
1. Affirmed: the decision of the lower court is upheld.
2. Reversed: the decision of the lower court is overturned.
3. Affirmed in part, reversed in part: a portion of the decision of the lower court is upheld whereas a portion of the lower court's decision is overturned.
4. Remanded: the matter is sent back to the lower court to re-decide the case in accordance with the dictates of the court's reasoning; sometimes this decision will be entered as "reversed and remanded."
5. Dismissed: the court rejects the appeal, often for lack of jurisdiction.

Holding(s)
The holding is the rule of law for which the case stands. Appellate holdings create "the law," and so the holding is arguably the most important section of the decision. The holding is the declaratory statement for which the issue is the interrogatory. Generally the court will preface its ruling by stating that it is about to pronounce its rule of law. If the ruling is hard to discern, a good rule of thumb is to look for the issue phrased as a definitive statement.

Reasoning

The reasoning represents the court's analysis, indicating how it arrived at the holding from the issue. The bulk of the case will be the court's reasoning. The reasoning helps the reader understand how a different court, faced with a similar problem, might reach a similar conclusion as the court whose decision is the subject of the brief. The reasoning indicates the cases, statutes, and rules of law relied upon by the court rendering the decision to reach its ultimate conclusion.

GROVER, A/K/A GUILLERMO SALINAS, v. RAGAN
1999 Tex. App. LEXIS 6262

Opinion *Per Curiam*

Appellant, WILLIAM GROVER, a/k/a GUILLERMO SALINAS, perfected an appeal from a judgment entered by the 94th District Court of Nueces County, Texas, in cause number 97-2175-C. Appellees have filed a motion to dismiss the appeal. In the motion, appellees state that the parties have entered into a compromise settlement agreement. Appellant on or about July 6, 1999, executed the agreement. Appellees request that this Court dismiss the present appeal on the grounds that the cause is moot because it no longer presents a judicial controversy. On July 13, 1999, appellant filed a motion for voluntary dismissal of his appeal; however, appellant has now filed a motion to withdraw his motion for voluntary dismissal.

The existence of an actual controversy is essential to the exercise of appellate jurisdiction. If prior to the determination of the appeal the controversy is terminated, the appeal becomes moot. *Hallmark Personnel of Texas, Inc. v. Franks*, 562 S.W.2d 933, 935 (Tex. Civ. App. Houston [1st Dist.] 1978, no writ). When a cause becomes moot, an appellate court must dismiss the cause, not merely the appeal. *City of Garland v. Louton*, 691 S.W.2d 603, 605 (Tex. 1985). Having examined the documents on file, the Court is of the opinion that because the parties have settled the controversy between themselves, the issues are moot, and the cause of action should be dismissed. Appellant's motion for voluntary dismissal of appeal, motion to withdraw voluntary motion for dismissal, motion to withdraw settlement agreement, and motion for extension of time to obtain counsel and for mediation are dismissed as moot. Appellees' motion to dismiss is granted. The appeal and cause of action are hereby DISMISSED.

JOHNSON v. MORGESTER
1998 Conn. Super. LEXIS 100

In this matter, the plaintiff seeks an order that DNA testing be performed on himself, the defendant, and a child for the purpose of determining the paternity of the child. The defendant has moved to dismiss the plaintiff's request on the basis that the court lacks subject matter jurisdiction. Following oral argument of counsel, the court granted the defendant's Motion to Dismiss on December 17, 1997. This written decision is provided in response to the plaintiff's request for an articulation.

There are two general principles of jurisprudence relevant to the court's jurisdiction to hear this matter as presently framed. While it is axiomatic that the Superior Court, as a constitutional court of general jurisdiction, has the power to decide any controversy properly before it, such a controversy must be framed by a complaint that sets forth a cause of action. Practice Book 131 provides, in part: "The first pleading on the part of the plaintiff shall be known as the complaint. It shall contain a concise statement of the facts constituting the cause of action . . ." Secondly, the court will "decide a case only when it presents a live controversy which can be resolved by relief that is within the court's power to grant."

Schroeter v. Salvati, 6 Conn. App. 622, 623, 506 A.2d 1083 (1986); *Cumberland Farms, Inc. v. Town of Groton*, 46 Conn. App. 514, 699 A.2d 310 (1997).

In elucidating this notion, the Appellate Court, in Cumberland, stated, "Because courts are established to resolve actual controversies, before a claimed controversy is entitled to a resolution on the merits it must be justiciable . . . (citations omitted) . . . Justiciability requires (1) that there be an actual controversy between or among the parties to the dispute. . . (2) that the interests of the parties be adverse . . . (3) that the matter in controversy be capable of being adjudicated by judicial power . . . and (4) that the determination of the controversy will result on practical relief to the complainant (citations omitted)." *Cumberland Farms, Inc. v Town of Groton*, supra, 46 Conn. App. 517.

In reviewing the plaintiff's pleading, the court is not persuaded that it contains a cause of action or that it presents a controversy fit for the court's determination. The court notes that the plaintiff merely seeks DNA testing without a concomitant request that he be adjudicated the father of the child should the testing so indicate. Additionally, the plaintiff's pleading contains no request for orders should the plaintiff be adjudicated the child's father. Assuming that his prayer for relief were granted, while perhaps scientific evidence sufficient to determine that the plaintiff is or is not the child's biological father would be obtained, the testing itself would not necessarily determine the child's paternity. Thus, the pleading, as presently framed, does not present the issue of the child's paternity for the court's determination, but solely whether or not the plaintiff is the child's biological father.

In opposition to the Motion to Dismiss, the plaintiff asserts that the provisions of C.G.S. 46b-168 entitle him to the requested DNA testing. That statute, however, presupposes the existence of an underlying cause of action. In pertinent part, C.G.S. 46b-168 states, "In any proceeding in which the question of paternity is at issue the court or a family support magistrate, on motion of any party, may order genetic tests . . . to determine whether or not the putative father or husband is the father of the child." In this case, there is no underlying proceeding pending. By its own terms, the statute does not create a free standing right for a man, woman, or child, to seek genetic testing to determine paternity.

The plaintiff further argues that C.G.S. 46b-160, which entitles a mother or expectant mother to bring a paternity action, is discriminatory because it does not accord a parallel right to a man to bring such an action. The question of the constitutionality of 46b-160 is not properly before the court since the plaintiff has not, in fact, sought to bring a paternity action. While the plaintiff asserts that he seeks equal protection of the laws in bringing this action, by not seeking an adjudication of paternity and appropriate ancillary orders, the plaintiff's motion amounts to a request not available to either the child or the defendant. The plaintiff seeks no more than a requirement that he, the child, and the child's mother undergo genetic testing, presumably to leave the mother and child to their own judicial devices should the testing determine a high probability of his paternity. Such a request does not constitute a cause of action. Nor does his motion, as presently framed, constitute a case in controversy sufficient to invoke the court's jurisdiction.

For the reasons stated, the Motion to Dismiss is granted.

Glossary

Adjudication - The process of submitting a dispute to a court for resolution

Administrative agency - Organization created to administer specific statutes

Administrative law - Body of law dealing with administrative agencies

Administrative Procedure Act (APA) - Statute regulating the administrative law process

Adversarial - Having an actual legal dispute

Appellate court - Court that reviews the decision of the trial court and creates legal precedent

Bill - Proposed legislation

Case or **controversy** - Requirement that an actual dispute exist to invoke a court's jurisdiction

Circuit court - Federal court of appeals

Civil law – Statute-based law

Codification - Arranging statutes by topic

Common law - Law based on precedent; judge-made law

Distinguish - To argue that the rule in one appeals court decision does not apply to a particular case although there is an apparent similarity

District court - Federal trial court

Evidence - Every type of proof legally presented at trial that is intended to convince the judge or jury of alleged facts material to the case

Executive agency - Agency created by the executive branch of government

First impression - Subject that has never been presented to a court before

Joint committee - Legislative group that resolves differences in versions of a bill

Judicial review - The ability of a court to review agency and legislative action to determine legality

Jurisprudence - The wisdom of the law

Jury - Lay persons who are triers of fact

Legislative agency - Agency created by the legislative branch of government

Legislative process - Means by which a statute is created

Moot - Describes a matter that is no longer in controversy

Overrule - To reject an earlier judicial decision

Precedent - Case law

Public law - Statute that has been passed into law

Question of fact - Determination of the facts of a case

Question of law - Determination as to whether the law was properly applied to a given set of facts

Ripe - Describes immediate problem that can be resolved by a court

Stare decisis - Judicial precedent

Testimony - Sworn statement of witnesses at a trial

Trial court - Initial court that determines facts

Trier of fact - The judge or jury responsible for deciding factual issues in a trial

United States Code - Publication that prints all U.S. federal laws

United States Constitution - The fundamental, underlying document that establishes the supreme law of the land

United States Supreme Court - The ultimate court of appeals in the federal system

Verdict - The decision of a jury after a trial, which must be accepted by the trial judge to be final

Veto - Presidential refusal to sign a bill

Writ of certiorari - Document requesting the Supreme Court to review a matter

Exercises

1. Explain the difference between common law and civil law systems.

2. Indicate how a judicial precedent can be changed. Discuss why a given judicial precedent should, or should not, be changed.

3. How does a legislative enactment differ from a judicial precedent?

4. Indicate the significance of administrative agencies to the American legal system.

5. Go to a courthouse in your area and attend a trial and an appeal. Discuss how the processes differ.

Chapter Two

CRIMINAL v. CIVIL WRONGS

Introduction

Chapter One discussed the difference between civil and common law and described the different methods used to create the law. Another distinction in the law is made with respect to the nature of the wrong involved—whether the injury is to a private individual or to the society at large. If only the private rights of an individual are involved, the area of law is referred to as civil law. The term "civil law" applies to two distinct areas. It can refer to the differences between the methods used to create the law or to the nature of the injury. If the injury is to the population at large, the area of law is generally referred to as **criminal law**.

This chapter will focus on the distinction between civil and criminal law as they apply to commercial enterprises.

Commercial Enterprises and Tort Law

A **tort** is defined as a civil wrong in which an individual is injured as a result of the actions of another individual where such action is not covered by a different area of law such as contract law, property law, etc. Most legal professionals identify the tort in terms of a specific area that falls with the basic definition of tort law. These specific areas include vicarious liability, intentional torts, negligence, strict liability, product liability, defamation, and nuisance.

Vicarious liability

It is unlikely that an artificial entity itself could be physically responsible for committing a tort, and most commercial enterprises are artificial entities, such as corporations or limited liability companies. Because of this artificial nature of business enterprises, owners may be held liable if one of its agents or employees is the wrongdoer, or **tortfeasor**, and commits the act while engaged in the enterprise's business. The business owner's responsibility for the wrongs committed by its employees comes under the heading of **vicarious liability**, in which one person is deemed to be legally responsible for the actions of another. Under business law concepts, this vicarious liability is known as ***respondeat superior***, Latin for "let the master answer." In order for the commercial enterprise to be held liable, it must be proven that the employee committed the tortious act while the employee was furthering the employer's interest. If the employee was not furthering the employer's interest, but rather was on a **frolic of his own**, the employer will not be held liable.

> *Example:* *A manager employed by XYZ Corporation was driving his car when he negligently hit a pedestrian. If the manager was driving the car in order to attend a meeting for the corporation, the pedestrian could hold the corporation liable. However, if the manager was driving to lunch, the manager might be deemed to be on a frolic of his own, and the corporation may not be held vicariously liable.*

If the injury occurs to a third person while the employee was furthering the employer's business, this employer will be held liable for injuries caused by the negligent actions of its employees under the doctrine of *respondeat superior*. However, if the negligent action injures a co-worker, the employer will not be held liable due to an exception to the doctrine known as the **fellow servant exception**. This exception was originally formulated under the common law to encourage businesses to hire employees. To compensate the injured co-worker under these circumstances, the legislatures have enacted **workers compensation statutes,** which provide financial compensation to the injured worker based on the nature of the injury. The employer (and sometimes the employee) contributes to insurance that provides for this compensation.

As a general rule, an employer is only liable for the negligent actions or its employees and is not liable for their intentional torts, with the following exceptions:
- Force is an integral part of the employment relationship, such as a bouncer in a nightclub.
- The nature of the work is such that altercations with the public may be anticipated, such as bill collector.

Several states have enacted specific statutes that list additional exceptions.

If the commercial enterprise engages the services of an **independent contractor** (see Chapter Seven), an individual who is hired solely for the result to be accomplished, the enterprise will not be responsible for the independent contractor's actions. On the other hand, if the nature of the work is inherently dangerous, such as demolishing a building, or there is a duty imposed by law on the employer that cannot be delegated to another person, such as a duty to maintain a safe environment that is used by the public (a retail store) the enterprise will be held responsible.

In several states, a special law applicable to tavern keepers has been enacted known as the **dram shop act**. In these states, a tavern owner will be held liable for injuries caused by a customer's intoxication. Because this rule did not exist under the common law, each state's dram shop statute must be individually researched.

Be aware that an employer may be held individually, and not vicariously, liable if the employer did not exercise reasonable care in hiring the employee who caused the injury. This theory of liability is known as **negligent hiring**, whereby the employer is held responsible for poor judgment in hiring an employee who would be likely to injure third persons.

> *Example: A private school hires a teacher without checking his background. The teacher has several convictions for child molestation. Several months into the school year, the teacher molests one of his students. The school, as the employer, may be liable for negligent hiring because it did not check the teacher's background, and it placed him in a situation in which he caused injuries to others because of his history.*

If the commercial enterprise is sued and found liable for the injury under a theory of vicarious liability, the enterprise does not have to shoulder the entire financial responsibility. The financial liability may be shared or apportioned under three distinct theories:
1. **Contribution.** This permits the party who is held liable to sue to have a portion of the financial responsibility shared by someone who is deemed to be jointly liable. In a partnership, for example, each of the partners bears a share of the award to the third person (see Chapter Eight).
2. **Indemnification.** This permits the individual who bears the financial responsibility under a theory of vicarious liability to have the actual wrongdoer reimburse him or her for the amount that the employer had to pay.
3. **Comparative negligence.** In this situation, the injured party is in some way responsible for a portion of the injury and the award will be proportionately reduced, but total recovery will not be barred (see below).

> *Example:* In the earlier example of the corporation manager who hit a pedestrian, if the pedestrian was struck while she was jaywalking, ran into the street between two parked cars, or otherwise contributed to the accident, her own negligence is a factor in causing the accident. In jurisdictions that apply the doctrine of comparative negligence, the court would apportion the ultimate award between the manager and the pedestrian, based on the percentage of the injury that was caused by each person's conduct. Under the common law, the pedestrian's actions would be called **contributory negligence**, which would preclude her recovery entirely. Many states still apply the common law doctrine, so each state's statute must be individually analyzed.

Intentional Torts

An **intentional tort** is any injury that an individual causes another due to a voluntary act. In order to prove that an intentional tort has occurred, the injured party must establish the following elements:
- A volitional act on the part of the wrongdoer (tortfeasor)
- The intent to make that volitional act
- The act caused injury to the other party.

Intentional torts fall into five categories: assault, battery, false imprisonment, trespass to land, and trespass to chattels.

To determine whether a particular tort, or crime, has occurred, the injured party must be able to demonstrate that each element of the act has been met.

Assault is defined by the following elements:
- An act that creates a reasonable apprehension in the injured party
- Of an immediate harmful or offensive contact to his/her person
- Intent to perform that act
- Causation—the apprehension occurs.

A business may be responsible for assault if one of its employees' actions meets the above elements with respect to a third party.

> **Example:** *A restaurant manager becomes upset with a group of rowdy teenage customers. The manager comes over to the teens and threatens them with forcible removal if they do not quiet down. If, under the circumstances, it is reasonable for the teenagers to believe that the manager will forcibly eject them, the restaurant manager may have committed an assault. Note that actual touching does not have to take place, only the apprehension of such touching. Under the doctrine of vicarious liability, the owner of the restaurant may be liable to the teenagers in tort.*

Battery is defined by the following elements:
- Harmful or offensive touching
- To the injured party's person
- Intention to cause such touching
- Causation—injury to the person touched.

Assault is the apprehension of touching, and battery is the touching itself. The touching may occur with or without an assault. If the person was touched without warning, there is a battery but no assault. Also, be aware that the injury only has to be offensive touching, not actual or serious physical harm.

False imprisonment is defined by the following elements:
- An act that confines or restrains a person
- To a bounded area with no reasonable means of escape
- Intent to commit such an act
- Causation—the confinement of the person.

No specific time frame is necessary to constitute the restraint, only the fact that the person is prevented from moving. The injured party must also be aware of the confinement and there must be no reasonable means of escape available.

> **Example:** *A small commercial air carrier is flying a passenger when the plane is forced to make an emergency landing in a wooded area. The plane lands safely, but is badly damaged. The passenger wants to exit the aircraft, but the pilot refuses to let him leave because of the danger of exposure and getting lost in the woods. Even though the pilot was restraining the passenger for the passenger's own safety, it still may be considered a false imprisonment because the passenger was restrained in a bounded area.*

Trespass to land is defined by the following elements:
- Physical invasion of another's realty
- Intent to enter the other person's property
- Causation—actually entering the land.

The invasion may be by a person or by an object that the person places on another's real property. Real property includes not only the actual land, but also the airspace above the land and the subterranean space beneath the land (see Chapter Five).

> **Example:** A construction company is restoring an old house in a residential community. Because of space limitations, the company places some of its materials on the property of the homeowner's neighbor. If it was done without the neighbor's permission, this action constitutes a trespass to land.

Trespass to chattels is defined by the following elements:
- An act or taking that interferes with another's possessory right to a chattel (personal property such as a car, book, etc.)
- Intent to perform such an act
- Causation—interference with the right
- Damages, meaning actual pecuniary loss.

The act only involves a chattel and, in addition to causation, the injured party must show actual **damages**, a financial loss caused by the trespass.

> **Example:** The manager of a lakefront hotel needs to go into town for supplies. Other employees are using the hotel's car, and all of the hotel's boats are rented. To get to the town, the hotel manager takes the rowboat belonging to the homeowner of the house adjacent to the hotel without asking permission. If the boat is returned before the neighbor discovers it is missing, or during a period of time when the neighbor would not need the boat, there is no trespass to chattels because no damages have resulted. However, if the hotel manager damages the boat or the neighbor needs the boat during its absence, she could sue for trespass to chattels.

If the interference with the property owner's possessory right is considered severe, or the property is destroyed while in the hands of the tortfeasor (wrongdoer), the tortfeasor has committed a **conversion**, which is a trespass to chattel involving a very serious interference with the possessory right. In this instance, the property owner could sue for the entire value of the property.

> **Example:** Assume that in the previous example the hotel manager accidentally rammed the boat into the dock, destroying the boat. In this instance, the tort would be one of conversion.

If the tortfeasor can claim a legally valid reason for his or her action, the wrongdoer may be excused. For intentional torts, the following defenses are allowed:
- **Consent.** The injured party agreed to the act.
- **Self-defense.** If the tortfeasor reasonably believed that he or she had to act to defend him/herself or another person from harm, the action may be excused.
- **Privilege.** Under certain circumstances, often involving police action, certain torts are permitted. Privilege means that the party is legally permitted to commit the act that would otherwise be considered a tort.

- **Necessity.** The tortfeasor acts to protect him/herself or others from injury from an outside force. Necessity falls into two categories: **public necessity**, to protect the general public, and **private necessity**, to benefit a private individual. In private necessity, the trespasser must still compensate the owner for any actual damage to the property.
- **Discipline.** A parent or teacher may use reasonable force to discipline a child.

Negligence

Negligence actions are probably the most frequently litigated causes of action. **Negligence** is the failure of the ordinarily **reasonable person** to exercise reasonable due care under the circumstances. It is defined by the following elements:
- A duty of care imposed on the actor
- A breach of that duty of care
- The breach is the actual and proximate cause of an injury to a third person
- The third person suffered damages.

The duty of care requirement arises out of a standard of care imposed on a person either under the common law or by statute. These duties generally involve the imposition of an obligation of exercising care that would be exercised by the reasonable person with the same physical (not mental) characteristics of the actor in similar circumstances. Standards of care have been established for professionals, common carriers, innkeepers, owners and occupiers of land, manufacturers, etc. Furthermore, if a criminal statute exists that specifies a clearly defined standard of conduct and the statute was enacted to prevent the type of injury that occurred, the statute might be used as the basis of establishing the appropriate standard of care, such as speed limits for cars. Once the standard of care has been established, any facts indicating that the actor failed to meet that standard establishes a breach of the standard.

The element of causation has two requirements: actual and proximate cause. **Actual cause**, also referred to as **causation in fact**, means that, but for the tortfeasor's action, the injury would not have occurred. **Proximate cause**, or **legal cause**, means that the tortfeasor's actions were not only the actual cause of the injury but that the injury was a foreseeable consequence of the action.

> *Example:* A delivery van driver was making a delivery. In order to keep moving, he failed to stop at a red light and went through the intersection. A pedestrian had started crossing the street when the light changed and was hit by the van. The driver's actions were the actual and proximate cause of the injury. But for the driver not stopping at the light, the injury would not have occurred, and it was foreseeable that a pedestrian would be crossing the street in the crosswalk.

In addressing the element of causation, if it can be shown that another action, one that was not foreseeable, intervened between the tortfeasor's actions and the injury, and that action caused the injury, that action is referred to as an **independent supervening force** or intervening factor, which may relieve the tortfeasor of liability.

> **Example:** *A delivery van driver was speeding down a country road. Suddenly, a woman came hurtling out of the bushes and landed in the road. It is discovered that the woman was riding a bicycle that was defective and suddenly stalled, causing her to go careening over the hedge. It is arguable that the bicycle's malfunction, not the driver's speeding, was the proximate cause of the injury since it was not foreseeable that a person would go flying over a hedge on a deserted country road. On the other hand, the bicycle manufacturer could claim that the rider would not have been injured if the driver was not speeding.*

Finally, to proceed on a negligence claim, the injured party must demonstrate actual physical or financial injury as a result of the tortfeasor's actions.

Although almost any tort claim may involve a commercial enterprise, either as the tortfeasor or the injured party, two specific types of tort claims are directly related to business. **Tortious interference with contract** is based on one person, by word or deed, convincing a party to a contract to disaffirm the contract, thereby injuring the other contracting party. For example, a seller convinces a purchaser that its current supplier is untrustworthy, and the purchaser changes suppliers. This action caused a direct injury to the original supplier. **Negligent misrepresentation** occurs in a business or professional setting in which a misrepresentation is made regarding the profession or business. If that misrepresentation is relied upon by a third person and that person suffers financial injury, that person will have a claim of negligent misrepresentation. For example, a law firm falsely claims experience in particular area of law, causing a client to retain the firm. Because of the firm's lack of experience, the client loses a lawsuit and is thereby injured.

Defenses to Negligence

A person who is charged with negligence might be able to claim one of the following defenses:
- **Contributory negligence.** The injured party has him/herself been negligent, thereby contributing to the injury (such as a pedestrian crossing the street against a light). In jurisdictions that apply the doctrine of contributory negligence, negligence on the part of the injured party completely precludes that party's recovery.
- **Assumption of the risk.** The injured party was aware of the risk involved and knowingly placed him/herself in the situation in which the injury might occur, as the spectator who attends a hockey game is aware that he or she may be hit by a puck during the action. In jurisdictions that apply this doctrine, the action precludes the injured party from recovering from the tortfeasor.
- **Comparative negligence.** As discussed above, this is not a complete defense because it does not entirely excuse the tortfeasor. It does apportion the amount of damage between the tortfeasor and the injured party according to each one's actions, but complete recovery is not barred. This doctrine is statutorily based, and each jurisdiction's law must be analyzed to determine its applicability or scope.

Strict or Absolute Liability

Strict liability is imposed by law for certain types of actions regardless of the degree of care exercised by the tortfeasor. The elements of strict liability are
- an absolute duty of care imposed by law that cannot be avoided
- breach of that absolute duty

- the breach is the actual and proximate cause of injury
- damage to the injured party.

Strict liability is generally imposed for activities that are considered to be inherently dangerous (such as the use of explosives) and, importantly for commercial enterprises, for products liability. There is no defense to a claim based on strict liability.

Product Liability

Product liability refers to the legal obligation of a defective product's supplier to a person injured by the product. This obligation attaches to both the manufacturer and the retailer of the good. To maintain a lawsuit based on product liability, the injured party must prove that the product was defective, either in its design or in its manufacture. There are four theories of liability under the heading of product liability:

1. **Intent.** This theory is applicable when the supplier knowingly supplies a product to cause injury, such as selling a health tonic that the supplier knows is toxic. Anyone injured by the defect may be entitled to punitive damages as well as actual damages. The supplier may use the same defenses that are available for all intentional torts.
2. **Negligence.** This theory is based on a breach of a duty of care as discussed above.
3. **Strict liability.** For product liability cases, strict liability applies to commercial suppliers of a product. Any commercial supplier (not casual suppliers) may be liable to anyone injured by the product, provided that the injured party can prove actual physical or property damage.

Example: A woman purchases a toaster. When she goes to make her morning toast, the toaster explodes, causing her severe injuries. If the woman has used the toaster properly, there is no reason why it should have exploded. No matter how good the manufacturer's quality control was, the manufacturer would be held liable for her injuries.

4. **Breach of warranty.** A **warranty** is a guarantee or representation made by the supplier of a product that the product is fit for the ordinary purpose for which the product is generally used (**implied warranty of merchantibilty**), or the product is fit for a special use that the supplier knew or had reason to know that the buyer intends (**implied warranty of fitness for a particular use**). The law automatically imposes these two warranties in any sale of goods. Further, if the seller makes a direct representation to the buyer, either directly or in an advertisement, those express words also create a specific guaranty (**express warranty**).

Example: A homeowner is making some improvements to his home. He purchases tiles from a building supply store. When making the purchase, the homeowner tells the salesperson that he is planning to use the tiles for his roof, and the salesperson tells him that the tiles that have been selected will be fine. In fact, the tiles that were selected are designed for decorative uses only, and they disintegrate when they are exposed to the elements. If the homeowner uses the tiles for his roof, and the roof is damaged because of the tiles, the store will be liable for a breach of warranty.

Defamation

Defamation is defined by the following elements:
- defamatory language
- concerning the injured party
- published to a third person
- damage to the injured party's reputation.

Defamatory language is any language that has an adverse effect on a person or product's reputation. A commercial enterprise may be liable for defaming a person or for defaming another company's product. Also, certain types of commercial enterprises, primarily the media, may be liable if it reprints a defamatory statement made by someone else. If the person who is the subject of the statement is a public figure (someone who is well known or notorious) the public figure must also show that the statement was false and made maliciously.

Publication refers to the tortfeasor making the statement to a party other than the party being defamed.

Defamation falls into two categories: **libel**, which refers to written or printed defamatory statements, and **slander**, which is oral defamation. There are four defenses to a claim of defamation:
1. *Consent*. The person defamed permitted the defamation.
2. *Truth*. Truth of the matter is a defense.
3. *Absolute privilege*. Statements made during judicial or legislative proceedings are exempt from claims of defamation because the speakers are permitted by law to make such statements.
4. *Qualified privilege*. Statements made in defense of one's country or otherwise afforded protection by statute, such as marital communications (statements made between a husband and wife).

Nuisance

There are two types of nuisance:
1. **Private nuisance.** A substantial and unreasonable interference with another individual's use and enjoyment of property.
2. **Public nuisance.** An act that interferes with the health, safety, or property rights of the society as a whole.

A commercial enterprise may be the creator of a private nuisance, such as a business causing noxious odors to infiltrate adjacent property, or be the victim of a private or public nuisance. The injured party may be entitled to money damages to compensate for the interference with the possessory property rights and may also be granted an **injunction**—a court order requiring the tortfeasor to stop committing the tortious act.

Commercial Enterprises and Criminal Law

Criminal law is invoked whenever society as a whole, rather than just an individual, suffers. Tort and criminal law are often discussed together because many of the same theories apply to both concepts.

Criminal law consists of certain acts that are statutorily prohibited. An individual who is found to have committed a crime is deemed to be **guilty**, whereas the same person would be found **liable** for a similar act under tort law. Furthermore, the same act may engender two lawsuits, civil for the tort and criminal for the crime, because there are two victims—the private person and the society as a whole represented by the state.

Although criminal law is generally designed to punish individuals, commercial enterprises may also be held responsible for certain crimes. This section of the text will focus on those crimes for which a commercial enterprise, as distinguished from an actual person, may be found guilty.

Another classification of legal concepts should be mentioned here. The actual law and the rules of conduct are referred to as the **substantive law**, which concerns all legal theories involved with the specific areas of law that make up the body of jurisprudence. **Procedural law** concerns those rules and regulations that specify how the substantive law is to be applied and litigated. This distinction is important in addressing the concepts of criminal law.

Substantive Criminal Law

In order for an individual to be found guilty of a crime, the state, which prosecutes the offender on behalf of society, must prove that the individual
- performed a prohibited act
- had the requisite mental state to commit the act
- caused a convergence of the physical act and the mental state.

The first requirement demands that the individual, referred to as the **defendant**, perform a specific act or fail to perform an act if he or she is under a legal duty to perform the act. This omission to act will only satisfy the physical act element of a crime if there is a specific legal duty to act, the defendant has knowledge of the facts that give rise to the duty, and it is reasonably possible for the defendant to perform the act.

Example: A lifeguard is employed to protect swimmers at a pool. One day a child begins to drown, and the lifeguard simply stays at his station and does nothing. Because the lifeguard was under a duty to act and could have acted, but did nothing, the lifeguard may be held guilty of a crime.

There are certain crimes that are strict liability crimes, similar to strict liability in tort, but the only major strict liability crime that is applicable to a commercial enterprise is the selling of liquor to a minor.

Commercial enterprises are criminally liable for actions of an employee performed within the scope of the employee's office or employment, actions performed by a corporate agent in a sufficiently high position to presume that his/her actions reflect corporate policy, and vicarious liability for an employee committing a regulatory offense under which punishment is limited to a fine.

The crimes that will be discussed that apply to commercial enterprises fall into the following categories:

- inchoate crimes
- offenses against the person
- property offenses
- offenses against habitation
- offenses against judicial procedure.

Be aware that there are more categories of crimes than those listed above, but they are generally not applicable to business.

Inchoate crimes

An **inchoate crime** is one that is deemed to be punishable even though no actual injury has occurred. There are three inchoate offenses:

1. **Solicitation** is the inciting, counseling, or convincing another to commit a crime with the intent that the person solicited commits the crime. The person so solicited need not agree to commit the crime.

> *Example:* *A business is losing money and the owner asks someone to burn down the building so that she can collect on the insurance. The owner's action is considered to be solicitation.*

2. **Conspiracy** is an agreement between two or more persons with the intent to enter into the agreement to commit a crime. In addition, the state must show some overt act in furtherance of the conspiracy, regardless of how insignificant the act might be.

> *Example:* *Assume that in the previous example two people own the business. The two owners meet and agree to hire someone to burn down the company's building. To further this agreement, they buy a book of matches. The business owners may be convicted of conspiracy even though no fire actually takes place.*

Note that a corporation cannot conspire with one of its agents, but two corporations may combine to commit a conspiracy.

3. **Attempt** is any act done with the intent to commit a crime that falls short of actually committing the crime. The act must be more than mere preparation and must be dangerously close to a successful completion of the crime.

> *Example:* *Assume that in the previous example the owners decide to burn the building themselves. They meet at the building at night and enter the building, but then change their minds. These actions will constitute an attempt even though they fail to complete the crime.*

Offenses against the person

Most of the crimes against the person are also civil torts. In addition, offenses against the person also includes the crime of **homicide**, the unlawful taking of a human life. Commercial enterprises, as distinct from natural persons, are not held culpable for homicide. Also, **kidnapping**, which is generally defined as false imprisonment with any movement of the person so confined, falls under the category of crimes against the person, and a commercial enterprise through its agents may be held so responsible. These crimes include the same elements as their tortious counterparts and are deemed crimes as well as torts because of their impact on society, even though a private person is the actual victim.

Property offenses

Larceny is defined as a taking and carrying away of tangible personal property of another by trespass with the intent to deprive that person permanently of his or her interest in the property. Larceny is similar to the tort of conversion discussed above; it must be proven that the defendant intended to deprive the property owner of the property permanently.

Example: A deliveryman brings a package to a company and must wait for an officer's signature on the receipt. While in the waiting area, the deliveryman sees a calculator that he picks up and puts in his pocket. When he leaves the office, he has committed larceny against the company.

Embezzlement is defined as the fraudulent conversion of personal property of another by a person in lawful possession of the property. Embezzlement is distinguishable from larceny in that the property owner has given the defendant possession of the property.

Example: A bank teller is given a calculator by her employer to assist her in her duties. One day the bank teller decides to slip the calculator into her purse for her own use. Because the teller has been given possession of the calculator, her action is now considered embezzlement.

False pretenses are defined as obtaining title to another's personal property by intentionally making a false statement of fact with the intent to defraud. To be considered false pretenses, the wrongdoer must acquire title to the property, not mere possession of it.

Example: On a Saturday morning, two men ring a homeowner's doorbell. When a man answers, the men tell him that his wife had their company clean the homeowner's rugs and they were there to get paid. The two men lied—they had never spoken to the wife. If the husband believes them and gives them cash, they obtained title to the cash by false pretenses.

Robbery is the taking of another's personal property from the property owner's person by force or threats of force with the intent to deprive that person of the property permanently. Basically, robbery is larceny committed in the presence of the property owner with threats of force or violence. If the property is merely taken from the person without the element of force, the act is larceny.

Receipt of stolen property consists of receiving possession and control of stolen personal property known to have been obtained in a manner constituting a criminal offense by another person with the intent to deprive the owner of the property permanently.

> *Example:* *A man enters a pawnshop to obtain money for a diamonds necklace. The shop owner gives the man $100 for the necklace that is obviously worth many times that amount. If the owner of the shop knew, or had reason to know, that the necklace was stolen, he is now guilty of the receipt of stolen property.*

Forgery is the making or altering of writing with legal significance so that it is false with the intent to defraud.

> *Example:* *A disgruntled secretary in a corporation goes into her boss' office and takes the company checkbook. She types out a large check to herself and signs her boss' signature to the check. She then cashes the check. The secretary is guilty of forgery.*

Offenses against habitation

This offense applies to any structure, including a commercial enterprise. The major offenses within this category are burglary and arson.

Burglary is defined as the breaking and entering of a structure of another with the intent of committing a crime therein. Some jurisdictions require that the intended crime be a **felony**, a crime punishable by at least one year imprisonment or a larceny. The wrongdoer must intend to commit the crime at the time of the entry; if the intent to commit the crime occurs after entry, it is not a burglary.

> *Example:* *A man breaks the lock on a warehouse door and enters so that he can steal electronic equipment stored inside. This is an example of a burglary.*

> *Example:* *A man breaks into a warehouse to escape a severe snowstorm. Once inside, when he sees electronic equipment, he decides to steal some. The man has not committed burglary because the intent to commit the crime came about after the entry. However, he has committed larceny.*

Arson consists of the malicious burning of another's dwelling. Under current law, any structure, not just a dwelling, satisfies this requirement. To qualify as arson, the building must be at least charred but does not have to be completely burnt.

> *Example:* A business owner decides to burn down his competitor's factory. He actually goes to the building and starts a fire. If the building is even charred, he will be found guilty of arson.

Offenses against judicial procedure

These offenses include actions that hinder the judicial process. Commercial enterprises may be found guilty of these crimes through the authorized actions of their agents. The major offenses within this category are:
- **perjury.** Intentionally making of a false statement under oath in a judicial proceeding.
- **subornation of perjury.** Inducing another to commit perjury.
- **bribery.** Offering something of value to an official in order to persuade the official to exercise his or her office in a particular way.
- **misprision of a felony.** The failure to stop the commission of a felony.

In addition, under federal law, commercial enterprises may be found guilty of racketeering under the **Racketeering Influenced Crime Organization Act (RICO)**. This statute encompasses any enterprise that is involved with organized crime.

Procedural Criminal Law

The foundation of all criminal procedure is the United States Constitution, which provides certain safeguards against state action with respect to the rights of individuals.

Regardless of the nature of the crime involved, all criminal prosecutions follow the same general format. The **complaint** is the formal allegation that the accused has committed a crime and is the starting point of a criminal proceeding. Once a complaint has been properly filed, the accused is **arrested**, or detained by the police. Federal and state statutes require that the accused be brought before a magistrate without undue delay for an initial hearing to be informed of the charges against him or her, be informed of his or her constitutional rights, and to set bail. An **indictment** is a charge brought by a grand jury. Grand jury hearings are secret and designed only to determine whether **probable cause** exists to continue the prosecution. The grand jury does not determine guilt or innocence. For lesser crimes, an **information** is considered sufficient. An information is a document signed by the public prosecutor, the official charged with bringing the suit on behalf of the state. After the indictment or the information is filed, there is an **arraignment**. The accused is brought before the court to answer the charges and to enter a plea. **Preliminary hearings** are frequently used to permit the accused to challenge the charges against him or her before any other process occurs. The accused must enter one of the following pleas:
- **Not Guilty.** He or she did not commit the crime; this plea requires a trial.
- **Guilty.** The accused committed the crime, and therefore no trial is necessary, only a hearing for the purpose of sentencing the defendant.
- **Nolo Contendere.** Rarely permitted, the accused does not admit nor deny the charge but states that he or she is willing to accept punishment; a hearing is set to determine the punishment.

At the **pretrial** stage the prosecution discloses the evidence that the state intends to produce at the trial. The parties can make **motions** to the court, requests that the court take certain action, typically with respect to permitting certain evidence to be introduced at the trial. At the **trial**, which is usually before a judge and jury, evidence is presented, and the defendant is determined to be guilty or not guilty of the charges. If the defendant is found guilty, the court must determine the **sentence** to be imposed, which may be a fine, imprisonment, community service, or a combination of punishments. Occasionally, the defendant is sentenced but then placed on **probation**, by which the defendant does not go to jail but must make regular reports to a **probation officer** to make sure that he or she is no longer engaging in criminal activity. If the defendant is found guilty, he or she has the right to **appeal** the decision to a higher court; if the defendant is found not guilty, the state does not have the right to appeal.

Chapter Summary

There are two areas of law that have a direct impact on a commercial enterprise: tort and criminal law.

A tort is a civil wrong in which the injured party is a private person who is injured in his or her private capacity. The injury could be physical, in which the person's body is affected, financial, in which the person suffers a pecuniary loss, or possessory, in which the person's right to possess property has been infringed.

A crime may involve many of the same aspects and elements of a tort, but with a crime, society as a whole is deemed to be the injured party (society being represented by the particular victim). When involved with criminal law, the U.S. Constitution demands that certain safeguards be imposed to protect the rights of the individual who is alleged to have committed the crime.

A commercial enterprise may become involved in both these areas of law either as the perpetrator or as the victim.

Edited Judicial Decisions

ILLINOIS v. JOHNSON
305 Ill. App. 3d 102, 711 N.E.2d 787 (1999)

The petitioner, Tracy E. Johnson, broke into the home of the victim, Sterns Crapnell, with the intent to commit a theft. During the course of the crime, Crapnell returned home and the petitioner killed him. The petitioner was convicted of felony murder based on burglary, burglary and residential burglary. Ill. Rev. Stat. 1989, ch. 38, pars. 9--1(a)(3), 19--1(a), 19--3(a). He was sentenced to a 70-year term of imprisonment for felony murder and a concurrent 15-year term of imprisonment for residential burglary. No sentence was imposed on the burglary conviction.

On appeal, this court affirmed his convictions and sentences. *People v. Johnson*, 223 Ill. App. 3d 169, 584 N.E.2d 515, 165 Ill. Dec. 336 (1991). The petitioner then filed a post-conviction petition, which the trial court dismissed at the first stage of proceedings. On appeal from that dismissal, the petitioner argued for the first time that his conviction for felony murder should be vacated because he could not have been convicted of that offense as a matter of law. The petitioner noted that at the time of the crime, felony murder could be predicated upon burglary but not residential burglary. Since the time of his direct appeal, our supreme court had ruled that burglary and residential burglary are mutually exclusive and that one could not be convicted of burglary of a residence. See *People v. Childress*, 158 Ill. 2d 275, 633 N.E.2d 635, 198 Ill. Dec. 794 (1994). Therefore, the petitioner argued, his conviction for residential burglary precluded a finding that he committed burglary, the predicate crime for his felony-murder conviction. In addition, he alleged that both trial and appellate counsel were ineffective for failing to attack the felony-murder charge on this ground. We remanded the petition to the trial court to allow the petitioner to amend his petition to include this contention and allow the trial court to rule on its merits. *People v. Johnson*, No. 3--93--0293 (1995) (unpublished order under Supreme Court Rule 23). On remand, the trial court again dismissed the petition. The petitioner appeals, and we reverse.

On appeal, the petitioner argues that his rights to due process and the effective assistance of counsel were denied when he was convicted of felony murder based upon burglary when the record conclusively establishes that, as a matter of law, he could not have been guilty of burglary. See *People v. Childress*, 158 Ill. 2d 275, 633 N.E.2d 635, 198 Ill. Dec. 794 (1994).

In response, the State argues that the holding in *Childress* is inapplicable to this case. In the alternative, the State contends that even if this court is bound by the holding in *Childress*, it need not be applied retroactively to the petitioner's case because *Childress* created a new rule of law.

At the time of the offense, the burglary provision stated that, "a person commits burglary when without authority he knowingly enters *** a building *** with intent to commit therein a felony or theft. This offense shall not include *** the offense of residential burglary as defined in Section 19--3 hereof." Ill. Rev. Stat. 1989, ch. 38, par. 19--1. Based on this provision, our supreme court found that residential burglary and burglary are two separate offenses that are mutually exclusive. *People v. Childress*, 158 Ill. 2d 275, 302, 633 N.E.2d 635, 647, 198 Ill. Dec. 794 (1994). Residential burglary can be committed only in dwelling places, while simple burglary cannot occur in a dwelling place. *Childress*, 158 Ill. 2d at 302, 633 N.E.2d at 647.

Here, at the time the petitioner murdered Crapnell, residential burglary was not a predicate offense of felony murder. See Ill. Rev. Stat. 1989, ch. 38, par. 9--1(a)(2), 2--8. Therefore, the petitioner's felony murder conviction can only be upheld if the petitioner could have been convicted of felony murder predicated upon burglary. However, a defendant cannot commit a burglary in a dwelling place. *Childress*, 158 Ill. 2d at 302, 633 N.E.2d at 647. Since the crime occurred in the victim's home, a dwelling place, the petitioner could not have been guilty of burglary as a matter of law. Therefore, the petitioner's conviction for felony murder predicated upon burglary must be vacated.

The State, argues, however, that we should not vacate the petitioner's felony murder conviction because we need not apply the ruling in *Childress* retroactively to the petitioner's case. Specifically, the State contends that a decision that announces a new rule of law is not to be applied retroactively to cases pending on collateral review. *People v. Moore*, 177 Ill. 2d 421, 686 N.E.2d 587, 226 Ill. Dec. 804 (1997).

We do not believe that *Childress* announced a new rule of law. Instead, it merely applied the statutory law to the facts of this case and held that the offenses were mutually exclusive. *Childress*, 158 Ill. 2d at 302, 633 N.E.2d at 646; cf. *People v. Moore*, 177 Ill. 2d 421, 686 N.E.2d 587, 226 Ill. Dec. 804 (1997) (a decision does not announce a new rule of law if it merely applies precedent to a similar set of facts). We need not reach the petitioner's remaining contentions regarding the effective assistance of trial and appellate counsel based upon our resolution of the foregoing issue.

Accordingly, the judgment of the circuit court of Rock Island County is reversed, and the petitioner's conviction for felony murder is vacated.

Reversed.

WALLS v. LOMBARD POLICE OFFICERS
2000 U.S. Dist. LEXIS 6579

Plaintiffs Brian Walls (Walls) and Nadine Blake-Walls (Blake-Walls) (collectively Plaintiffs) filed a 12 count Second Amended Complaint against the following members of the Lombard Police Department: Officer Jay Jerome (Jerome); Officer William Marks (Marks); Sergeant Richard Montalto (Montalto); Officer Jeffrey Virene; Officer Clark (Clark); Officer John Latronica; Officer Daniel Marciniak (Marciniak); Officer James Schrepferman (Schrepferman); Lieutenant Scott Watkins (Watkins) and Other Unknown Lombard Police Officers (Other Unknown Officers) (collectively Defendants), alleging, among other things, defamation under Illinois law (Counts VIII and XII) and intentional infliction of emotional distress under Illinois law (Count XII). Defendants have moved to dismiss Counts VIII and XII of the Second Amended Complaint pursuant to Fed. R. Civ. P. 12(b)(6). For the reasons set forth below, the Court grants defendants' motion to dismiss Count VIII and denies defendants' motion to dismiss Count XII.

I. BACKGROUND

The complaint alleges the following facts that, for the purposes of ruling on this motion, are taken as true. *Hishon v. Kemp & Spalding*, 467 U.S. 69, 73, 81 L. Ed. 2d 59, 104 S. Ct. 2229 (1984). On May 4, 1998, the Plaintiffs and their child were in the car when Blake-Walls had a panic attack and asked Walls to stop the car. She exited the car, removed her child from the car seat and sat on the sidewalk.

Defendants Jerome, Marks, Clark, Marciniak and Schrepferman approached Blake-Walls and one of them asked her if she was ok. She said that she was fine. (Compl. P 20.) When Walls approached, some of the defendants began questioning him about what, if anything, had transpired between him and Blake-Walls. Walls stated that everything was ok, and Blake-Walls stated that she wished to go home. The defendants then told Walls not to stay with his wife and child at home and if they were to find him there "it would not be good for him." (*Id.*) The defendants then took the names, address, telephone number, license number and car registration of the Plaintiffs. Walls dropped Blake-Walls and their child off at their apartment, packed a bag and left, per the defendants' instructions.

That night, defendants Jerome, Watkins and Other Unknown Officers arrived at the apartment demanding entry. Defendants told Blake-Walls that they had been summoned on complaints of noise. Blake-Walls explained to the defendants that there was no noise coming from her apartment and there must have been a mistake. The defendants ignored her and demanded to know the whereabouts of her husband. She explained to the defendants that she and her child were alone in the apartment.

Eventually, the defendants forcibly entered the apartment knocking Blake-Walls into a compact disc case and injuring her back. She inquired about a warrant, to which the defendants stated, "We don't need a warrant." (*Id.* P 55.) The defendants searched the entire apartment, scattering and damaging its contents and ignoring Blake-Walls's request that they leave. Defendants kept her in the apartment against her will, physically abused her and verbally threatened her.

Blake-Walls reported the incident by calling 911. The 911 operators advised her to file a complaint at the police station. Blake-Walls, accompanied by Walls's aunt and uncle, went to the police station and attempted to file her complaint. One of the defendants refused to allow her to file the complaint and called her drunk. Montalto stated to the aunt, uncle and others present at the police station "that the defendant officers had to go to the apartment of Mr. Walls and Ms. Blake-Walls on a frequent basis because they were always fighting." (*Id.* P 96.) Montalto knew that this was untrue. In fact, neither of the plaintiffs had experienced any contact with the Lombard Police Department or its officers. On that same day, defendants also "reported to the Department of Children and Family Services that Nadine Blake-Walls was abused by Brian Walls." (*Id.* P 139.) Plaintiffs allege that defendants did so to conceal their own wrongdoing despite the fact that they had no information to indicate that Walls had battered Blake-Walls.

Plaintiffs' Second Amended Complaint alleges, among other claims: (1) defamation in violation of Illinois law; and (2) intentional infliction of emotional distress in violation of Illinois law. In response, Defendants have filed the present motion seeking to dismiss these claims (Counts VIII and XII).

II. DISCUSSION

A. Standard for a Motion to Dismiss (deleted)

B. Defamation

Despite the liberal pleading requirements of Federal Rule of Civil Procedure 8, "courts generally have continued to require that [defamation] be pleaded with some specificity." *Betten v. Citibank* F.S.B., 1995 U.S. Dist. LEXIS 8924, No. 94 C 5460, 1995 WL 387802, at *3 (N.D. Ill. June 28, 1995); see also *Doherty v. Kahn*, 289 Ill. App. 3d 544, 682 N.E.2d 163, 172, 224 Ill. Dec. 602, (Ill. App. Ct. 1997) (holding that under Illinois law, the allegedly defamatory statement itself must be set forth with specificity). Thus, it is clear that "vague and general assertions will not sustain a claim for defamation; neither will mere conclusory allegations." *Richardson Electronics, Ltd. v. Video Display Corp.*, 1989 U.S. Dist. LEXIS 11441, No. 89 C 3588, 1989 WL 117980, at *3 (N.D. Ill. Sept. 26, 1989) (citations omitted). However, where "the substance of the defamatory statements is adequately identified," plaintiffs have been able to plead less specifically. *Jones v. Sabis Educ. Systems, Inc.*, 1999 U.S. Dist. LEXIS 19449, at *11, No. 98 C 4252, 1999 WL 1206955, at *4 (N.D. Ill. Dec. 13, 1999) (citations omitted).

The Illinois courts have not created "a general rule defining what words are defamatory, [thus] each case must be decided based upon its own facts." *Heerey v. Berke*, 188 Ill. App. 3d 527, 544 N.E.2d 1037, 1040, 136 Ill. Dec. 262 (Ill. App. Ct. 1989). Generally, "[a] statement is considered defamatory if it tends to cause such harm to the reputation of another that it lowers that person in the eyes of the community or deters third persons from associating with him." *Van Horne v. Muller*, 185 Ill. 2d 299, 705 N.E.2d 898, 903, 235 Ill. Dec. 71 (Ill. 1998). The two forms of defamation recognized in Illinois are: defamation *per se* which includes statements so obviously defamatory that it is unnecessary to allege or prove special damages; and defamation *per quod* which include statements for which allegation and proof of special damages is necessary. *Rosner v. Field Enters*, 151 Ill. Dec. 154, 564 N.E.2d 131, 143 (Ill. App. 1st 1990).

1. Defamation *Per Se*

The Court first analyzes whether the defendants' statements constitute defamation *per se*. Under Illinois law, "Certain limited categories of defamatory statements are deemed actionable *per se* because they are so obviously and materially harmful to the plaintiff that injury to the plaintiff's reputation may be presumed." *Van Horne*, 705 N.E.2d at 903. Illinois law recognizes five categories of words as defamatory *per se* for which special, or pecuniary, damages are presumed: (1) words imputing the commission of a criminal offense; (2) words imputing infection with a loathsome communicable disease; (3) words imputing an inability to perform or want of integrity in the discharge of duties of office or employment; (4) words that prejudice a party, or impute lack of ability, in his or her trade, profession or business; and (5) words imputing adultery or fornication. *Id.*

a. Count VIII

In Count VIII, plaintiffs contend that defendants defamed them when Montalto stated to Walls's aunt and uncle and others that Lombard Police Officers "had to go to the apartment of Mr. Walls and Ms. Blake-Walls, on a frequent basis because they were always fighting." (Compl. P 96.) Although the plaintiffs have sufficiently pleaded the speaker, audience and content of the statement, this statement does not constitute defamation *per se*. The only recognized category of defamation *per se* that this could arguably be related to his statements imputing commission of a crime. However, this statement is simply insufficient.

A statement involving the imputation of a criminal offense need not state the commission of a crime with the particularity of an indictment to qualify as defamatory *per se*. *Weber v. Village of Hanover Park*, 768 F. Supp. 630, 638 (N.D. Ill. 1991) (citations omitted). While it is true that a statement involving the imputation of a criminal offense is actionable as defamation *per se*, the crime imputed must be an indictable one, involving moral turpitude and be punishable by death or by imprisonment, and not merely a fine. *Id.*

The fact that officers were called to plaintiffs' apartment often because of fighting does not, on its face, accuse the plaintiffs of committing a crime, much less an indictable crime, involving moral turpitude, punishable by death or by imprisonment, and not merely a fine. At best, this statement implies that on a few occasions the plaintiffs had loud arguments that disturbed neighbors. Without more, this statement cannot be considered defamatory under Illinois law. Thus, plaintiffs have failed in Count VIII to state a cause of action for defamation *per se*.

b. Count XII

In Count XII, plaintiffs allege that defendants defamed them when one of the defendants "reported to the Department of Children and Family Services that Nadine Blake-Walls was abused by Brian Walls." (Compl. P 139.) This statement, unlike the previous statement, clearly accuses Walls of abusing his wife. Domestic Battery is a crime in Illinois punishable by imprisonment. 720 ILL. COMP. STAT. 5/12-3.2 (West 1993) (defining Domestic Battery as a Class A Misdemeanor); 730 ILL. COMP. STAT. 5/5-8-3(a)(1) (West 1997) (defining the sentence for a Class A Misdemeanor as any term of imprisonment less than one year). Therefore, this statement meets the requirements for defamation *per se* under Illinois law.

The analysis does not end here, however, since in Illinois all allegedly defamatory statements are subject to the "reasonable innocent construction rule." This standard is set forth in *Chapski v. Copley Press*, 92 Ill. 2d 344, 442 N.E.2d 195, 65 Ill. Dec. 884 (Ill. 1982):

[A] written or oral statement is to be considered in context, with the words and the implications there from given their natural and obvious meaning; if, as so construed, the statement may reasonably be innocently interpreted or reasonably be interpreted as referring to someone other than the plaintiff it cannot be actionable *per se*.

Id., 442 N.E.2d at 199. The complaint clearly alleges that the defendants "reported to the Department of Children and Family Services that Nadine Blake-Walls was abused by Brian Walls." (Compl. P 139) It is impossible for this Court to see how such a statement could be innocently constructed. There is no indication from the context of this accusation of domestic battery that it should be interpreted innocently. Quite the contrary, this statement is an accusation by law enforcement officers to the governing state department regarding spousal abuse. There is also no indication that defendants were referring to anyone other than the plaintiffs. Thus, the innocent construction rule cannot be employed to defeat the claim for defamation. As such, Count XII states a claim for defamation *per se*.

2. Defamation *Per Quod*

Having found that Count VIII does not state a claim for defamation *per se*, the Court next must decide whether it sufficiently states a claim for defamation *per quod*. Statements where "extrinsic facts are required to explain the defamatory meaning," are considered defamation *per quod. Kolegas v. Heftel Broad. Corp.*, 154 Ill. 2d 1, 607 N.E.2d 201, 206, 180 Ill. Dec. 307 (Ill. 1992). In order to state a cause of action for defamation *per quod*, one must plead special damages. *Brown & Williamson Tobacco Corp. v. Jacobson*, 713 F.2d 262, 270 (7th Cir. 1983). The pleading of special damages is governed by Federal Rule of Civil Procedure 9(g) which states that "when items of special damage are claimed, they shall be specifically stated." *Id.* A complaint must do more than allege that the injury suffered was the natural result of the alleged defamation. *Id.* At the very least, the allegation of special damages must be "explicit." *Id.* Thus, under Illinois law, "general allegations as to damages, such as, damage to one's health, emotional distress, damage to reputation and economic loss, are insufficient to state a cause of action for defamation *per quod*." *Heerey*, 188 Ill. App. 3d at 532-33.

In Count VIII, plaintiffs have failed to plead with specificity the specific damages required to support a claim [*14] of defamation *per quod*. The only reference to damages in Count VIII states, "Defendant officers defamed and injured the reputation of Ms. Blake-Walls and Mr. Walls." (Compl. P 101.) Because plaintiffs merely allege damage to their reputations, this Court cannot characterize this description of damages as specific. Rather, this is a general allegation of damage to reputation. See *Heerey*, 544 N.E.2d at 1041. Accordingly, the Court dismisses Count VIII, since that count fails to state a claim for either defamation *per se* or defamation *per quod*.

In sum, defendants' motion to dismiss is granted with respect to Count VIII and is denied with respect to the defamation claim of Count XII.

C. Intentional Infliction of Emotional Distress

In Count XII of their Second Amended Complaint, plaintiffs also assert a claim for intentional infliction of emotional distress under Illinois law. The pleading standard for intentional infliction of emotional distress in Illinois is heightened "to state an action for intentional infliction of emotional distress, the complaint must be specific and detailed beyond what is normally considered permissible in pleading a tort action." *Welsh v. Commonwealth Edison Co.*, 306 Ill. App. 3d 148, 713 N.E.2d 679, 684-85, 239 Ill. Dec. 148 (Ill. App. Ct. 1999) (quoting *McCaskill v. Barr*, 92 Ill. App. 3d 157, 414 N.E.2d 1327, 1328, 47 Ill. Dec. 211 (1980)). The necessary elements to plead a cause of action for intentional infliction of emotional distress are: 1) conduct which is truly extreme and outrageous; 2) intent that the conduct inflict severe emotional distress or knowledge that there is a high probability that the conduct would cause severe emotional distress; and 3) the conduct caused severe emotional distress. *McGrath v. Fahey*, 126 Ill. 2d 78, 533 N.E.2d 806, 809, 127 Ill. Dec. 724 (Ill. 1988).

Defendants contend that plaintiffs have failed to allege conduct that rises to the level of extreme or outrageous. The "extreme and outrageous" nature of conduct is judged objectively. *Doe v. Calumet City*, 161 Ill. 2d 374, 641 N.E.2d 498, 507, 204 Ill. Dec. 274 (Ill. 1994). "Mere insults, indignities, threats, annoyances, petty oppressions or trivialities," are not "extreme and outrageous" conduct. *Public Finance Corp. v. Davis*, 66 Ill. 2d 85, 360 N.E.2d 765, 767, 4 Ill. Dec. 652 (Ill. 1976). Furthermore, "liability has been found only where the conduct has been so outrageous in character, and so extreme in degree, as to go beyond all possible bounds of decency." *Id.*

The Court recognizes that the "application of the 'outrageousness' requirement is necessarily difficult due to its vagueness." *McGrath*, 533 N.E.2d at 809. Nonetheless, courts have focused on certain factors that make a finding of outrageousness more likely. One such factor is "the degree of power or authority that a defendant has over a plaintiff... The more control which a defendant has over the plaintiff, the more likely that defendant's conduct will be deemed outrageous." *Id.*, 533 N.E.2d at 809. n4 Where an abuse of power is found, "the extreme and outrageous nature of conduct may arise not so much from what is done as from the defendant's actual or apparent ability to damage the plaintiff's interests by his exercise of power or authority." *Welsh*, 713 N.E.2d at 683.

In the present case it is alleged that defendants knowingly made a false report to the Department of Children and Family Services that Walls was physically abusing Blake-Walls. A false accusation of domestic abuse from anyone in the community rises above the category of mere insults or annoyances. Furthermore, when this statement is made by a law enforcement officer who has a great deal of power and authority, particularly in dealing with criminal charges and investigations, this Court considers such an abuse of power "extreme and outrageous" conduct. Thus, plaintiffs have sufficiently stated a claim for intentional infliction of emotional distress. Accordingly, the Court denies defendants' motion to dismiss Count XII.

III. CONCLUSION

For the reasons set forth above, the Court grants defendants' motion to dismiss Count VIII and denies defendants' motion to dismiss Count XII. The Court dismisses Count VIII without prejudice.

Glossary

Actual cause (causation in fact) - But for the tortfeasor's action, the injury would not have occurred

Appeal - To ask a higher court to reverse the decision of a trial court after final judgment or other legal ruling

Arraignment - Criminal proceeding in which the accused is informed of the charges against him or her

Arrest - To take or hold a suspected criminal with legal authority, as by a law enforcement officer

Arson - The malicious burning of a dwelling

Assault - Words or actions that place another person in fear of a harmful or offensive touching

Attempt - Any action in preparation of a criminal activity

Battery - A harmful or offensive touching of another

Burglary - The breaking and entering of a dwelling with the intent to commit a crime

Causation in fact - But for the action the injury would not have occurred

Complaint - Document that initiates a legal proceeding

Conspiracy - Two or more persons agreeing to commit a crime

Contributory negligence - Theory that prohibits an injured person whose actions added to the injury from recovering on a negligence claim

Conversion - Permanently depriving a person of his or her personal property

Criminal law - Body of law that deals with injuries to society as a whole

Damages - The amount of money that a plaintiff may be awarded in a lawsuit

Defamation - Making a defamatory statement about another person that causes damage to that person's reputation

Defamatory language - Any language that has an adverse effect on a person or product's reputation

Defendant - The party sued in a civil suit or the party charged with a crime in a criminal prosecution

Dram shop act - State statute that holds a tavern keeper liable for injuries caused by a patron who became intoxicated at the tavern keeper's establishment

Embezzlement - Conversion of personal property by a person who was given possession of the property by the owner

Express warranty - Guarantee on a product that is explicitly stated

False imprisonment - Restraining a person against his or her will

False pretenses - The crime of knowingly making untrue statements for the purpose of obtaining money or property fraudulently

Fellow servant exception - An employer is not vicariously liable for actions of one of its employees that injure another of its employees

Felony - Crime punishable by imprisonment in excess of one year and a day

Forgery - The crime of creating a false document, altering a document, or writing a false signature for the illegal benefit of the person making the forgery

Frolic of his own - Theory that relieves an employer from liability for his employee's actions if the employee was not furthering the employer's business at the time the action takes place

Guilty - Having been convicted of a crime or having admitted the commission of a crime by pleading "guilty"

Homicide - The unlawful taking of a human life

Implied warranty - Product guarantee that arises by operation of law

Inchoate crime - Conspiracy, attempt, and solicitation

Independent contractor - Person hired for the result to be accomplished

Indictment - Document filed by the grand jury so that a criminal prosecution may proceed

Information - Document filed by the public prosecutor so that a criminal prosecution may proceed

Independent supervening force - an unforeseeable action that intervened between the tortfeasor's actions and the injury, causing the injury

Injunction - A writ issued by a court ordering someone to do something or prohibiting some act after a court hearing

Kidnapping - False imprisonment with moving of the person

Larceny - The unlawful taking of another person's property

Liable - Responsible or obligated

Libel - To publish in print, writing or broadcast through radio, television or film, an untruth about another which will do harm to that person or his or her reputation, by tending to bring target into ridicule, hatred, scorn or contempt of others

Motion - A formal request made to a judge for an order or judgment

Negligence - Failure to meet a duty of care that results in injury to another person

Negligent hiring - An employer may be held individually, and not vicariously, liable if the employer did not exercise reasonable care in hiring the employee who causes an injury

Negligent misrepresentation - Making false statements to induce someone to act

Nuisance - Tort of interference with another's use and enjoyment of his or her property

Preliminary hearing - In criminal law, a hearing to determine if a person charged with a felony should be tried for the crime charged, based on whether there is some substantial evidence the he or she committed the crime

Pretrial - The stage in a trial in which the prosecution discloses the evidence that the state intends to produce at the trial

Private necessity - Protecting a private individual from an outside force

Probable cause - Reasonable belief that a crime has been committed

Probation - Criminal sentence in which the defendant must report to a probation officer rather than go to jail

Probation officer - Official who oversees probation

Procedural law - Law dealing with the judicial process

Product liability - Tort dealing with defective goods

Proximate cause (legal cause) - Action that is the immediate reason the injury occurred

Public necessity - Protecting the general public from an outside force

Racketeering Influenced Criminal Organizations (RICO) - Federal statute that prohibits organized criminal activities

Reasonable person - Standard of care that would be exercised by the reasonable person with the same physical (not mental) characteristics of the actor in similar circumstances

Receipt of stolen property - Crime of accepting goods that the person knows or has reason to know are stolen

Respondeat superior - Theory that holds an employer liable for its employee's negligent actions that injure third persons

Robbery - Larceny coupled with threats to the property owner

Sentence - The punishment given to a person convicted of a crime

Slander - Oral defamation, in which someone tells one or more persons an untruth about another, which will harm the reputation of the person defamed

Solicitation - Inducing someone to commit a crime

Strict or absolute liability - Theory in which a person is held liable regardless of the degree of care exercised

Substantive law - Law that defines legal theories and standards of conduct

Tort - A civil wrong

Tortfeasor - Person who commits a tort

Tortious interference with contract - Unlawful interference with another person's contract rights

Trespass to chattels - Interference with rightful possession of personal property

Trespass to land - The entry onto, above, or below the surface of a land owned by another without the owner's permission or legal authorization

Trial - The examination of facts and law presided over by a judge with authority to hear the matter

Vicarious liability - Attachment of responsibility to a person for harm or damages caused by another person in either a negligence lawsuit or criminal prosecution

Warranty - A written statement of good quality of merchandise, clear title to real estate or that stated in a contract is true

Warranty of fitness for a particular use - Guarantee as to the appropriateness of a good for a certain use made known to the seller prior to the sale

Warranty of merchantability - Guaranty that a good is fit for normal use

Workers compensation law - Statute that provides remedies for workers injured by the negligence of fellow workers

Exercises

1. Determine whether your state follows a contributory or comparative negligence theory. What difference would it make for a commercial enterprise?

2. Discuss how you would determine whether an employee was acting within the scope of his employment or was on a frolic of his own when an accident took place. Give some examples of each situation.

3. Discuss your opinion of an employer being held liable for the actions of its employees. Do you believe that this would have a chilling effect on employment? Discuss.

4. What is your opinion of a person being tried civilly and criminally for the same act? Explain.

5. Indicate instances in which a commercial enterprise would be held criminally liable for the different crimes indicated in the chapter. Use examples from your local newspaper.

Chapter Three

CONTRACTS AND THE LAW OF SALES

Introduction

The law of contracts as it is applied to commercial enterprises provides an excellent illustration of the distinction between common and civil law as discussed in Chapter One. Possibly no other area of law has more impact on commercial enterprises than the law of contracts, and in no other area of law has common law precedent been more expanded and superseded by statutory enactment. The provisions of Article 2 of the Uniform Commercial Code, as applied to merchants today, primarily regulates the law of contracts for the sale of goods. Contracts for services or for the sale of goods by nonmerchants depend upon the common law.

The **Uniform Commercial Code (UCC)** originated as a model act proposed in 1952 by the American Law Institute and the National Conference of Commissioners on Uniform State Laws. Since that date, every state, including the District of Columbia, has enacted some or all of the provisions of the model statute, thereby making the UCC universal if not exactly uniform. The UCC is not a federal statute; it is a state enactment. Consequently, each state's version of the UCC must be analyzed for the applicability of a given provision in a given jurisdiction. Regardless, the UCC forms the basis of the law of sales for most commercial enterprises in the country.

The UCC, Article 2, applies to all contracts for the sale of goods valued over $500, provided that at least one of the contracting parties is a merchant. The term **merchant**, as defined by the UCC, is one who regularly deals in goods of the kind sold or who otherwise by his profession or through an agent holds himself or herself out as having knowledge and skill particular to those goods. **Goods** are defined as all items that are tangible, moveable, and identified by the contract. Article 2 of the UCC does not apply to services, real estate, or intangibles. If the item in question involves both goods and services, such as custom-made clothes, the item's predominant category—good or service—will prevail and determine the applicability of the UCC. For all items not deemed to be goods, the common law of contracts, not the UCC, applies.

This chapter will focus on the general law of contracts, with special attention placed on the sale of goods as applied to merchants. Whenever differences exist between the common law and the UCC, such distinctions will be explained. It is important to bear in mind that the law of contracts forms one of the backbones of the U.S. legal system, and its application to everyday life is more predominant than any other area of law.

Elements of a Contract

In order for a contract to exist, the following elements must be present: offer, acceptance, consideration, legality of the subject matter, capacity of the parties, and contractual intent. All six requirements must be met for the contract to be valid.

An **offer** is defined as a proposal by one party to another manifesting intent to enter into a valid contract. Under the common law, for the offer to be effective, the **offeror**, the one making the proposal, must manifest a present intent to enter into a valid contract and communicate the offer to the **offeree**, the one to whom the offer is made. Further, the offer must be certain and definite with respect to the essential terms of the proposed contract. The manifestation of present intent must appear in the terms of the offer itself by the use of words of present intent. If the offeror uses words that indicate a future intent, no contract can be formed by the terms of this proposal.

> *Example:* *The owner of a factory states that he is thinking of retiring and may be willing to sell his business for a stated amount if he still feels this way in six months. This does not create a valid offer. The owner is indicating a possible future intent, not a present intent to enter into a contract.*

To initiate the contractual process, the offer must be communicated to an **offeree**, someone who has the legal ability to accept the offer and thereby create a valid contract. The offeror may make the proposal to a particular individual, to a group, or to the general public by means of an advertisement or a brochure. Be aware, however, that should the offeror place the proposal in a newspaper of general circulation, the advertisement will be deemed to be a valid offer only if it is explicit in its terms; the less precise the terms of the proposal in an advertisement, the more likely it is that the courts will construe the advertisement to be an invitation to the public to make an offer to the advertiser.

> *Example:* *A retail store places an ad in the newspaper advertising a sale on winter coats for $99 and up. This ad will not be a valid offer. The advertisement merely invites the public to view the retailer's merchandise.*

Finally, the proposal itself, under the common law, must be certain and definite with regard to price, subject matter, parties to the contract, and time of performance. For contracts that are governed by the common law, the court may interpret the terms to be a reasonable price and a reasonable time of performance if the offeror failed to include those terms in the offer. However, if the parties attempt to include one of these terms, but do so in a manner that is imperfect under the law, the court cannot rewrite the terms, and the contract will fail.

> *Example:* *A woman offers to sell her house for a price to be determined at a later date. At this point, there is no valid offer. The woman has failed to specify a price and has indicated that the price will be filled in at a later date, which negates the element of present intent. Because the woman has indicated some reference to the price, the court cannot assume a reasonable price to make the offer valid, which they might have been able to do if no mention of price had been made at all.*

For merchants, the UCC has drastically changed the common law requirements. Under Article 2, merchants need only state the quantity of the goods that form the subject matter of the agreement. All other terms are left up to the merchants themselves, who, pursuant to the statute, are deemed to be the best suited, based on custom and usage in the industry and the past dealings of the parties, to complete the contract terms. The major stated objective of the UCC is to promote commerce, and so most of the provisions of Article 2 are designed to foster contract formation under commercially reasonable expectations and with the requirement that the merchants trade in good faith.

It should be noted that there is a special type of contract in which quantity, even for merchant traders, is not expected to be specified. These agreements are known as Seller's **output contracts** or Buyer's **requirements contracts**. For example, a farmer agrees to sell his entire crop (output) to a food manufacturer at a specified price per unit, or a factory agrees to purchase all of its energy needs from a particular supplier at a specified price per unit (requirements). However, even under these types of agreements, there is a caveat—the output or requirement cannot substantially exceed the historical output or requirements of the parties. To permit otherwise would create a situation in which the actual fulfillment of the contract could be contrary to the expectations of the parties when the contract was formed.

Acceptance is defined as the manifestation of assent in the manner required or authorized by the offeror. Under the common law, the offeree was not permitted to vary the terms of the offer. The **mirror image rule** requires that the acceptance mirror the terms of the offer. Any variance, except for items that are implicit in the offer, such as the offeror having good title to sell the item, is considered to be a **counter-offer** or a **cross-offer**, which terminates the original offer and creates a new offer in which the roles of the parties are reversed.

> *Example:* *A homeowner offers to sell her house for $300,000. The offeree says that he accepts and agrees to buy the house for $250,000. The change in price is not an implicit term and substantially changes the terms presented by the homeowner. The potential buyer, by his words, is now the offeror, offering to purchase the house for $250,000, and the homeowner's offer is terminated. She now has the power of accepting the buyer's offer.*

For contracts covered by the UCC, mirror image acceptance is not required. Merchants are not bound by the terms of the original offer unless the offer is specifically stated to be **ironclad**, take it or leave it, in which case the common law rules apply. Merchants are free to vary the terms of the original offer, and a contract can still be formed. If the offeror fails to object to the change within ten days of the acceptance, the contract is formed with the changes included. This legal ability to change contract terms for merchants is sometimes referred to as the **battle of the forms**. Each merchant forms the parameters of the agreement by varying the contract terms and making changes.

In order to create a valid contract, the offeree must accept in the manner requested by the offeror, such as in writing, by e-mail, etc. Certain rules have developed under the common law with respect to the manner of acceptance utilized by the offeree, known as the **mailbox rule**. Under this doctrine, acceptance of an offer is effective when it is properly dispatched in the manner authorized by the offeror: when the acceptance is mailed the contract is formed. As a corollary, the **rejection** of an offer is only effective when actually received by the offeror. These rules can create unintended consequences.

> **Example:** *An offeree mails a rejection at 11 a.m., then changes his mind and mails an acceptance at 2 p.m. Pursuant to the mailbox rule, the contract was formed at 2 p.m. even though the offeror was unaware of that fact. If the offeror receives the rejection first, he or she would assume that no contract exists and might sell the subject matter of the contract to someone other than the initial offeree. However, since the contract was formed at 2 p.m. the offeree could maintain a claim for a breach of contract, meaning that the offeror did not fulfill the contractual obligation.*

To avoid this result, the modern trend is to determine the moment of creation of the contract, under these circumstances, based on the reasonable expectations of the offeror. If the offeror receives the rejection first, no contract is formed if the offeror relies on that rejection to change his or her position. If the offeror does not rely on the rejection, then a contract will be formed at the time the acceptance was mailed.

Until a contractual offer is accepted, the offeror has the power to **revoke** or **renounce**, meaning that he or she can stop the offeree from having the power to accept and no contract will result. If the offeree attempts to accept after the offeror has revoked, that acceptance is deemed to be an offer to the original offeror, and the roles of the parties are now reversed.

For merchants, acceptance may take the form of fulfilling the contractual obligation, such as shipping the goods that have been ordered, without any specific mailed or worded acceptance. It should be noted, however, that under both common and statutory law, silence is never considered to be an acceptance unless the offeree is under some legal duty to speak.

At this point, it should be noted that contracts fall into two broad categories with respect to the manner of their formation. The most prevalent type of contract is a **bilateral contract**, which is a promise for a promise (I promise to sell you my car for $3,100 if you promise to pay me $3,100 for the purchase of my car). The second category of contract is a **unilateral contract,** which is a promise for an act in which the offeror does not request a mutual exchange of promises but instead requests the offeree to perform some act, which is the contract obligation and the manner of acceptance (I promise to pay you $500 if you paint my house on Tuesday). Historically, unilateral contracts could only be accepted if the offeree completed the requested act; currently, acceptance occurs once the offeree has substantially performed, has made a substantial beginning on performance, or has changed his position in reliance on the offer. However, unilateral contracts are generally disfavored, and the court will attempt to find the contract to be bilateral whenever possible because parties are generally presumed to be bargaining for an exchange of promises. The difference between the two types of contracts is essential to determine the rights of the parties. A bilateral contract comes into existence when the promises are exchanged. Either party's failure to fulfill those promises gives rise to an action for breach of contract. A unilateral contract only comes into existence when the performance is completed, and therefore the party's nonperformance does not give rise to an action for breach.

> **Example:** *An entrepreneur promises to pay an interior designer $5,000 if she delivers decorating plans to his office in one week. The designer buys paper, obtains sample fabrics, paint chips, and begins to draw up plans. The entrepreneur then tells her that he has changed his mind about redecorating his office. In this instance, because the designer made a substantial beginning on the project, the entrepreneur will not be allowed to revoke.*

Consideration is the bargain element of the contract. Consideration is generally defined as a benefit conferred or a detriment incurred at the request of the other party. It is a bargained-for exchange. In order for a valid contract to exist, both parties must give and receive legally sufficient consideration (**mutuality of consideration**). Consideration does not have to be money—any legal benefit or detriment will suffice.

> **Example:** *In a contract for the sale of a book, the seller receives $50 and gives up a book; the buyer receives a book and gives up $50. Each party has given and received consideration.*

> **Example:** *As part of an employment contract, an employee agrees not to work for a competing company if and when she terminates her employment. The employer gives a salary and receives the employee's work and forbearance to work for a competing company; the employee receives a salary and gives up her right to work for her employer's competitors. Each side has given and received consideration.*

It is not considered to be legally sufficient consideration if one of the parties agrees to perform a duty that he or she is already legally required to perform. For instance, a crime victim may offer a reward for the capture of the criminal, but the police officer who catches the criminal cannot accept the reward because the officer was already obligated to perform that duty. This is known as the **pre-existing duty rule**. However, there are certain exceptions to this rule:
- More or different consideration is performed.
- The promise is used to ratify a voidable contract (see below).
- The pre-existing duty is owed to someone other than the promisor.
- There is a valid dispute with respect to whether such a duty exists.
- Unforeseen circumstances exist that would discharge the obligated party.

Not only is consideration necessary to create a contract, additional or new consideration is needed in order to modify an existing contract. Because the parties are already legally bound, there is no reason why one of the parties would relieve the other of a contractual duty unless the party receives consideration for such a release. However, if the contracting parties are merchants, the UCC does not require additional consideration to modify an existing contact; it only requires that the modification be made in good faith.

> **Example:** *Two merchants agree to buy and sell lead pipe for $1 per foot. Because of unforeseen circumstances, the cost to the seller has increased, and he now needs to sell the pipe at $1.25 per foot. If the buyer agrees, which he does not have to do, the contract may be modified without any additional consideration.*

The court will not inquire into the sufficiency of the consideration, provided that it can be demonstrated that the parties did in fact bargain for the consideration in good faith. The courts do not insure contracts nor relieve parties of a bad bargain, provided that a bargain does in fact exist. However, the courts will not sanction **sham consideration**, that which has no value, or **illusory promises** in which the parties provide no consideration at all. Also, **nominal consideration**, consideration far beneath the true value of the bargain, always raises the spectre of a sham transaction.

The law will not enforce agreements that are illegal. Therefore, in order for the agreement to be considered valid, the subject matter of the contract may not violate the law.

There are two general categories of illegality with which contract law is concerned. Acts that are *malum in se*, morally reprehensible, such as an agreement to commit homicide, are totally void and unenforceable. The second category includes those acts that are *malum prohibitum*, acts that are prohibited by statute, such as violating usury or licensing laws. Although these contracts are unenforceable, the courts may permit some relief to prevent one party from being unjustly enriched by the other. For example, it would be unfair to permit a person to keep funds she borrowed just because the interest rate charged was usurious; the borrower may be required to return the funds and pay the lawful interest rate. In this instance, the relief granted by the court is known as **quasi-contractual**, meaning that it is almost like a contract, to avoid unfairness to one or both of the parties. However, bear in mind that the agreement is not thereby considered to be a valid contract; the relief just looks like a contractual remedy.

One of the most frequently encountered statutes that may appear under a claim of *malum prohibitum* is the **Statute of Frauds**. To be enforceable, the Statute of Frauds requires that certain types of contracts must be in writing. Note that a contract, even if oral, may still be valid, but the courts may not *enforce* it. The contracts that fall within the Statute of Frauds are:
- contracts for an interest in realty
- contracts that are not to be performed within one year
- contracts in consideration of marriage
- **guarantees** (promises to pay the debts of another)
- contracts for the sale of goods valued at more than $500 (now part of Article 2 of the UCC)
- executors' promises to pay the decedent's debts from his or her personal funds.

However, if the parties actually perform under the agreement or if the contract is for custom-made goods and production of those goods has started, the parties are deemed to have taken the contract out of the Statute of Frauds by their own actions, and the agreement is enforceable in the courts. For contracts between merchants under the UCC, any memorandum signed by the party to be charged is considered sufficient writing to take the contract out of the Statute of Frauds.

To enter into a valid contract, both parties must have **contractual capacity**, the legal ability to contract. Contractual capacity involves two distinct areas: age and mental ability.

All persons over the age of 18 are automatically deemed to be old enough to enter into a valid contract. **Minors**, persons between the ages of 14 and 18, although able to contract are permitted to avoid their contractual obligations by renouncing the contract up to their 18th birthday. These contracts entered into by minors are called **voidable** because one, or both, of the parties may legally avoid his or her obligation if he or she so chooses to fulfill those obligations. The only contracts for which a minor cannot avoid responsibility are those to supply the minor with **necessaries**—food, clothing, shelter, education, healthcare, and military service.

The person's mental ability to enter into a contract is determined at the moment of contracting. Persons who are under guardianship or are residents of mental institutions are deemed incapable of contracting, but persons with mere mental lapses still may contract, provided that they understand the nature of the contract when it is entered into. Also, persons who are under a temporary incapacity brought on by drugs or alcohol may avoid the contract once they regain capacity or may then ratify the agreement and fulfill their contractual obligation. As with minors, these persons' contracts are voidable.

The final element for contract formation is the intent of the parties. The court will not enforce agreements that have been entered into without the intent of the parties to be contractually bound as measured by an objective standard. If one or both of the parties did not mean to enter into a contract, there can be no mutual assent. Aside from the situation in which the parties are merely joking with each other, the courts look into those situations in which a lack of intent may result: fraud, duress, and mistake.

Fraud is defined as the misrepresentation, with the intent to deceive, of a material fact that is relied upon by the other party to his or her detriment. If the speaker did not intend to deceive but misstated a fact that he or she should have known might be inaccurate, it is considered **misrepresentation** instead of fraud. However, the recipient of the information, in either instance, cannot be said to have intended to enter into the contract because he or she does not have the true facts regarding the contractual terms. The fraud negates the knowledge necessary for a knowing assent.

> *Example:* *A man buys a watch that the salesman says is a Molex, but it is not. The man has paid a large sum for the watch, and when it breaks in one week, he discovers that it is not a Molex but a knockoff. In this instance, the salesman committed a fraud, and there is no contractual intent.*

Duress involves a form of coercion that forces one of the parties to agree to a contract. Duress can take the form of physical, emotional, or financial threats used to induce agreement. Also, in situations in which one side has an unfair bargaining position (because of his or her presumed expertise or lack of competition) the party with the lesser bargaining position may avoid such agreement. These agreements are called **adhesion contracts** and are voidable.

> *Example:* *The owner of a health club physically intimidates a prospective customer into taking a three-year membership. The customer may avoid this contract because of the owner's intimidation.*

Mistake involves an error with respect to the subject matter of the contract. Note that the law, as stated above, does not provide relief simply because one of the parties made a bad bargain; however, if it can be demonstrated that the parties were in error with respect to an essential term of the contract, the court may permit them to avoid the contact.

> *Example:* *Two parties agree to the sale of a factory, unaware that the factory was destroyed by fire the day before. Under these circumstances, the contract will not be enforced because the parties were mistaken about the availability of the subject matter.*

The law distinguishes between mutual mistakes and unilateral mistakes. **Mutual mistake**, as in the example above, arises when both of the parties are under a misconception regarding the subject matter of the contract. **Unilateral mistake** arises when only one party is under a misconception. For unilateral mistakes the court will generally enforce the contract according to the expectations of the innocent party. Note, however, there are some exceptions to these rules. If the innocent party should have known that a mistake existed, the contract will not be enforced.

> *Example:* *A construction company asks for bids from suppliers. One bid is $30,000 less than the next lowest bid, and all of the other bids are within $2,000 of each other. The bidder made a mathematical error in computing his costs. This mistake should be obvious to the construction company, and the court will not let it take advantage of the bidder's innocent error.*

Rights and Obligations of Third Parties

Generally, contracts involve just two parties, the promisor and the promisee. The **promisor** is the party who has a contractual duty to perform, and the **promisee** is the recipient of that obligation. Note that in all valid contracts each side performs both roles in fulfilling the requirement of mutuality of consideration. However, there are certain circumstances in which third persons have some rights or duties even though they are not direct parties to the contract.

Third-Party Beneficiaries

A **third-party beneficiary** is a person who the original contracting parties intended, at the time of contract formation, to receive some benefit from the contract. To be considered a third-party beneficiary, that person's rights must be identified in the original contract.

Historically, the law identified two types of third-party beneficiaries—creditor beneficiaries and donee beneficiaries. A **third-party creditor beneficiary** is a creditor of one of the original contracting parties, and the purpose for the contract was to extinguish the debtor's obligation to the creditor. A **third-party donee beneficiary** is a person to whom one of the contracting parties wishes to receive the contractual consideration as a gift. Modern trends simply refer to both types of third-party beneficiaries as the **intended beneficiary**.

> **Example:** *A manufacturer owes his supplier several thousand dollars but lacks the cash to pay the obligation. The manufacturer enters into a sales agreement with a retailer to purchase some of the manufacturer's product and specifies in the contract that the retailer is to pay the purchase price to the supplier. The supplier is the intended beneficiary of the contract between the manufacturer and the retailer because one of the purposes of the contract was to extinguish the manufacturer's debt to him.*

> **Example:** *A man wishes to send his mother a gold necklace for her birthday. He buys a gold necklace from a television-shopping channel and instructs the seller to ship the necklace to his mother. The mother is the intended beneficiary of the sale between the man and the shopping channel because the purpose of the sale was an agreement to provide the mother with a gift.*

Any other person who benefits tangentially from the contract, such as the shipper of the goods, is called an **incidental beneficiary** and has no enforceable rights.

A third-party beneficiary has the right to enforce the contract even though he or she was not a party to the contract once his or her rights **vest** (become legally enforceable). Such rights vest when the intended beneficiary manifests an assent to the contact, the intended beneficiary brings suit to enforce the contract, or the intended beneficiary materially changes his or her position in reliance on the contract.

The third-party intended beneficiary can sue the promisor for enforcement of the contract, and the promisor can defend by asserting any defense he or she has against the promisee, such as failure of consideration, duress, etc. A creditor beneficiary may also sue the promisee under the original debt, but a donee beneficiary may only sue the promisee if he or she had detrimentally relied on the contract.

Assignment

An **assignment** is a transfer of contractual rights. Unlike a **third-party beneficiary contract**, the purpose of the original contract is not to benefit an outside third person; rather, after the contract has been formed, one of the contracting parties decides to have someone else receive the contractual rights. The transferor/promisee is called the **assignor**, and the recipient of the right is called the **assignee**.

Generally, all contract rights are assignable with the following exceptions:
- any transfer of rights that would substantially change the promisor's obligation
- contracts for personal services or based on personal confidence
- future rights that will arise only from future contracts
- rights that are nonassignable by law, such as the assignment of Social Security benefits
- rights that the parties themselves have specifically stated are not assignable, appearing in contractual **nonassignment clauses**.

Assignments may be gratuitous (a gift) or may be for consideration. All assignments for consideration are irrevocable, whereas gratuitous assignments are revocable by the assignor except if the promisor has already performed, a token has been delivered to the assignor to memorialize the assignment, the assignment is in writing, or the assignee detrimentally relied on the assignment.

Generally, assignments need not be in writing, and every assignment, if properly effectuated, creates enforceable obligations on the promisor to the benefit of the assignee. The assignee is entitled to the promise for contractual performance and may sue the promisor for non-performance. Further, the assignee can sue the assignor if the assignor wrongfully revokes the assignment or the promisor successfully defends against a suit by the assignee by asserting defenses the promisor has against the promisee/assignor.

If an assignor has made successive assignments of the contractual rights, the first in time prevails unless a later assignee has a greater claim in equity.

> *Example:* A manufacturer enters into a sales agreement with a retailer. After the contract is signed, the manufacturer asks the retailer to send the payment not to the manufacturer but to a supplier to whom the manufacturer owes a sum of money. Because the transfer of rights occurred after the contract was formed, the manufacturer has effectuated an assignment of its contractual rights.

Delegation

Similar to an assignment, a **delegation** occurs after the formation of the original contract. Unlike an assignment, a delegation is an agreement whereby the **delegator** has someone (the delegate) assist him or her in fulfilling his or her duties under the contract. With an assignment, the promisee transfers the contractual rights; with a delegation, the promisor transfers a contractual duty.

Basically all contractual obligations may be delegated except for:
- contracts for personal services
- transfers that would change the promisee's expectations, such as an output contract where the delegate produces more or less product than the promisee had intended
- situations in which the promisor is in a position of trust with respect to the promisee (see Chapter Eight)
- contracts that specifically state that they are nondelegable.

With a delegation, the promisor/delegator remains liable under the contract for any malfeasance or nonperformance on the part of the delegatee.

Novation

A **novation** is a complete substitution of contractual parties; it is both an assignment and a delegation. With a novation, the original party to the contract is totally removed from the contract and a new person is substituted for all rights and duties. The contract will now read as though the original party was never a party to the agreement. Novations are very rare and must be specifically stated and intended by the parties.

Contract Provisions and Rules of Construction

All contracts are composed of clauses that define the parties' rights and obligations. These clauses, except for introductory and definitional paragraphs, are divided into two categories: covenants and conditions.

A **covenant** is an absolute, unconditional promise to perform. It is the basic obligation intended by the parties to the contract, and a failure to fulfill a covenant gives rise to an immediate action for **breach** of the contract (failure to fulfill contractual obligations).

A **condition**, by contrast, is the timing element of the contract; it specifies the moment when the parties are obligated to perform the covenants. Conditions are classified according to their relationship to the covenant performance.

A **condition precedent** is a fact or event that gives rise to the obligation to perform.

Example: A land developer agrees to purchase a tract of land conditioned upon its ability to acquire financing within 30 days. The condition with respect to the financing must occur before it is obligated to complete the purchase.

A **condition subsequent** is a fact or event that extinguishes the absolute duty to perform.

Example: A retailer purchases a quantity of goods from a manufacturer with the agreement that the retailer may return the goods if unacceptable within ten days of delivery. The ability to return the goods is a condition that extinguishes the retailer's duty to pay for the merchandise.

A **condition concurrent** is a fact or event that arises at the same time as the covenant, such as a cash purchase in which the exchange of cash for goods occurs at the same time.

The failure of a condition generally does not cause a breach of contract but may extinguish the contractual covenants.

The parties may excuse conditions in one of the following manners:
- A party wrongfully prevents a condition from occurring, therefore it should not benefit from the action.

Example: A construction contract specifies that payment will be made only if an architect approves the completed building. If the promisor causes the architect to refuse to issue the certificate, the promisor cannot be allowed to escape payment, and the conditional requirement becomes moot.

- The condition will be excused if the other side makes an anticipatory repudiation. An **anticipatory repudiation** is an unconditional statement that either party will not fulfill

its contractual obligations. Anticipatory repudiation relieves the other party of performance, and that party may sue for breach of contract.
- A condition will be excused when a party indicates that it may be unable to perform. Note that a prospective inability to perform differs from anticipatory repudiation because the prospective inability only raises uncertainty of performance but does not indicate a refusal to perform. For contracts between merchants under Article 2 of the UCC, a prospective inability to perform gives the other party the right to demand **written assurances** from the uncertain party. If the uncertain party does not respond to the demand within 30 days, the party seeking the assurance may consider the contract as breached. For contracts under the common law, the innocent party may suspend performance until the uncertain party's inability to perform becomes definite.
- The condition is excused if a party substantially performs even though the condition has not occurred.
- The party entitled to the condition may **waive** the right to the condition.
- The condition will be excused if it becomes impossible to perform.
- If the contract is **divisible** (capable of being viewed as separate, identical, small contracts grouped into one agreement, such as a rental agreement for one year with rent to be paid in monthly installments), the failure of a condition for this mini-contract will not be considered a breach of the entire agreement. Also, under the UCC, **installment contracts**, those in which delivery is required to be made in separate deliveries, may only be declared a breach of the entire contract if the failure of the delivery substantially impairs the entire agreement.

In interpreting contract provisions, the courts have formulated certain **rules of construction**, doctrines used to interpret contracts. The most typical rules of construction are:
- Handwritten provisions prevail over typed provisions.
- Ambiguities in the contract are viewed against the party who drafted the contract.
- Words are given their ordinary meaning unless a different definition is specified.
- Contracts are construed according to business custom and usage.

As a corollary, the common law as well as the UCC has adopted the **parol evidence rule**, which states that oral testimony may not be used to vary the terms of a writing except
- To show fraud, duress, mistake, or failure of consideration.
- To explain ambiguities.
- To show the existence of a contemporaneous oral agreement.
- To evidence a condition precedent to the contract.
- To show a subsequent modification.

Discharge of Contractual Obligations

Not every contractual obligation is fulfilled, nor does the failure to fulfill such obligation necessarily give rise to a lawsuit for breach of contract. Both the common law and the UCC recognize eight methods whereby a party's contractual liabilities may be discharged without engendering a breach of contract. The eight methods are:
1. excuse of conditions
2. performance
3. agreement of the parties
4. impossibility of performance
5. supervening illegality
6. death or destruction of the subject matter

7. frustration of purpose
8. breach of contract.

1. Excuse of conditions is the timing element of the contract; a contacting party's obligation to perform is created or extinguished by this timing factor. If the condition has not been met for conditions precedent, no contractual performance is required. Conversely, if the conditional element is a condition subsequent, the contractual obligation is extinguished if the condition occurs. Therefore, the happening or nonhappening of the conditions specified in the agreement can excuse the parties' covenants.

2. Fortunately, the overwhelming majority of contractual obligations are met by the actual performance of the obligations by the parties. Once the contractual duty is completed, no further obligation is required.

3. There are several types of agreements that the parties to a contract may reach that have the effect of excusing the original contractual obligation. These agreements are
   - **Mutual rescission**, which occurs when both parties decide that they do not wish to fulfill the contract and they agree to rescind, or take back, the original contract. To be valid, the mutual rescission may only occur if the contract is **executory**—both parties have yet to perform the contractual obligations.
   - A **release**, which is an agreement in which one side agrees to let the other party out of the contractual duty. Usually a release requires that the nonperforming or released party provide the other party with some consideration.
   - An **accord and satisfaction**, which is a special type of agreement in which the parties to a disputed contract agree to settle the dispute by changing the obligations of the contract for a new contract incorporating all the new terms. To be valid, there must be a legitimate dispute and the consideration for the accord and satisfaction is the new agreement and the relinquishment on both sides of the ability to take the other side to court to seek judicial relief. For merchants, the UCC permits contracts to be modified upon a showing of good faith on the part of the party who is seeking the contractual change (see above).
   - **Substituted agreements** are new contracts that incorporate the terms of the original contract in the new agreement. Once agreed to, the new contract assumes all of the provisions of the old contract, which is legally merged into the new agreement.
   - Novation, a substitution of parties, which has been discussed above, excuses contractual duties because the new party to the agreement has assumed those duties.

4. A contract will be excused if it becomes impossible to fulfill. To meet the legal requirements of impossibility of performance, the impossibility must not have been contemplated at the time the contract was entered into or assumed as part of the obligations when the contract was formed. Events that simply cause delays in performance, such as a transit strike or labor dispute, do not meet this requirement.

5. A supervening illegality comes about because a change in the law makes the reason for which the contract was formed incapable of being fulfilled because it has now become unlawful. An example would be an agreement to open a retail store in a specific location that has been rezoned for residential purposes only.

6. Death or destruction of the subject matter only applies for unique subject matter that is described as such and cannot be replaced by one of the parties.

7. Frustration of purpose requires a supervening act that was not reasonably foreseen at the time the contract was formed, which destroys the purpose of the contract and was understood by both parties. Frustration of purpose differs from impossibility; with the former, the contract could still be completed although it would be meaningless, whereas with the latter the contract could not be completed. The most famous example of frustration of purpose occurred in England at the end of the last century when rooms were rented for the day of Edward VII's coronation to view the procession. On coronation day, Edward was taken ill and the coronation was postponed. Although the rooms could still be rented, the reason for the rental no longer existed, and all parties knew of the purpose for the rental when the contract was formed.

8. As previously stated, a breach of contract is the failure of one or both of the parties to fulfill its contractual duties. If one party to the contract fails to perform, the nonbreaching party is excused from performing its obligation. Remember, a contract is a bargain with a mutual exchange of consideration; if one side does not receive consideration, the other side does not have to provide consideration.

If one party to the contract breaches, the other side is excused from performance. This is the reverse of complete performance and is permitted because of the concept of mutuality of consideration.

Contractual Remedies

If the contractual obligations are neither fulfilled nor excused, the party to whom the performance was due may seek judicial relief to remedy the breach. To determine the extent of the relief to be awarded, the court must first determine whether the breach was a material or a minor breach. A **material breach** occurs when the innocent party does not receive the substantial benefit of the bargain and excuses its performance. A **minor breach** means that the innocent party is receiving substantially all of what was promised but not the complete bargain. To be able to recover for a minor breach, the nonbreaching party must perform its contractual obligation. To determine the extent of the breach the court looks at the following factors:
- the amount of the benefit received by the nonbreaching party
- the adequacy of the relief to the nonbreaching party
- the extent of the performance by the breaching party
- hardship to the breaching party
- negligent or willful actions of the breaching party
- the likelihood that the breaching party may still perform.

In seeking contractual remedies, the nonbreaching party may seek relief in both law and equity. In law, legal remedies involve money, known as damages; in equity the equitable remedies provide for nonmonetary relief.

Legal Remedies

There are five types of damages available for a breach of contract.

1. **Compensatory damages**, which is the standard measure of damages, are designed to put the innocent party in the same financial position that it would have been in had the contract been fulfilled. The monetary amount must be readily ascertainable; the court will not award damages for injuries that are uncertain or speculative.

For merchant traders under the UCC, damages are measured by the difference between the contract price and the market price when the seller tenders the goods or the buyer discovers the breach. If the buyer breaches, the seller may withhold delivery or stop delivery, resell the good and recover the difference, or receive ordinary contract damages.

If the seller breaches, the buyer may reject nonconforming goods, cancel the contract, seek **cover**, which involves buying goods in substitution from another seller and suing the original seller for the difference in the buyer's costs, recover damages, recover goods that have been specifically identified, or seek specific performance (see below).

2. **Consequential damages,** which are damages in addition to the standard measure, are permitted if a reasonable person could have foreseen that the nonbreaching party would suffer additional injury if the contract were breached. The nonbreaching party has the burden of proof of the foreseeability of these damages.

3. **Punitive damages** are intended as a punishment for certain breaches that involve action in addition to a mere breach of contract. To be awarded punitive damages, the injured party must demonstrate not only a breach of contract but also a breach of trust. Also, by statute, certain types of breaches automatically entitle the nonbreaching party to punitive damages. Punitive damages are generally not permitted for contractual disputes.

4. **Nominal damages** are permitted if there is an actual breach, but the nonbreaching party suffers no actual financial injury.

5. **Liquidated damages** appear as a provision of the contract that specify that in the event of a breach, the nonbreaching party will be entitled to a specific dollar amount in compensation. These provisions are available only if actual damages would be difficult to determine at the time the contract is formed, and the amount specified is reasonable and not intended to disguise a punishment for the breaching party. Under the UCC, the courts can consider actual damages to determine whether a liquidated damages provision should be given effect.

In all instances of breach of contract, before the nonbreaching party may seek legal remedies, it has a duty to **mitigate damages**, which means it must lessen the financial injury suffered by using reasonable efforts to seek relief from other sources. The injured party needs only exert reasonable efforts in good faith to mitigate its damages.

Equitable Remedies

When monetary damages would be insufficient, the nonbreaching party may seek specific performance, injunctions, rescission and restitution, quasi-contractual remedies, *quantum meruit*, or *quantum valebant*.

In **specific performance**, a court will order the breaching party to perform the contractual obligations. This remedy is always available if land or unique goods are involved but is never permitted for service contracts. If the goods in question are fungible or readily substituted, specific performance will not be granted.

Injunctions, which are court orders requiring the breaching party to do or to stop doing something, are available in certain contractual situations in which the breaching party has contractually agreed to forego certain actions, such as an employee's noncompetition clause as mentioned above.

In **rescission and restitution**, the court rescinds (see above) the contract, and the nonbreaching party may recover any benefit it had transferred to the breaching party prior to the breach.

Quasi-contractual remedies is available under circumstances in which no actual contract existed, but one party had conferred a benefit on another under circumstances in which no gift was intended. To avoid having the recipient be unjustly enriched, the courts permit for two quasi-contractual remedies ("quasi" means "like"): *Quantum meruit*, the dollar value of services the innocent party performed for the other and *quantum valebant*—the dollar value of the goods the innocent party transferred to the other.

Special UCC Issues

Pursuant to Article 2 of the UCC, when a merchant trader sells goods, either to another merchant or a nonmerchant customer, certain warranties, or guarantees, with respect to those goods are imposed. Under the UCC, there are four types of warranties:
1. **warranty of title** and **against infringement**
2. **implied warranty of merchantability**
3. **implied warranty of fitness for a particular use**
4. **express warranties.**

Warranty of title and against infringement guarantees that the seller has a title to the goods sufficient to pass title to the buyer and that the goods sold are free of any patents, trademarks, copyrights or similar claims.

Implied warranty of merchantability attaches automatically for every good sold by a merchant and guarantees that the goods sold are fit for the ordinary purpose for which such goods are used.

Implied warranty of fitness for a particular use attaches, by law, when the seller has reason to know that the goods are going to be used for a specific or particular purpose, and the buyer is relying on the seller's judgment in making the purchase.

Express warranties are specifically agreed to by the seller and are not automatically implied by law. These warranties arise by express statements of the seller (oral or in writing), by a description of the goods in an ad or brochure, or by means of a sample used to entice the buyer to make the purchase.

The seller may avoid liability under the above warranties by means of a disclaimer. A **disclaimer** is a statement in which the seller specifically states that it is not giving the indicated guarantees. For implied warranties, the disclaimer must be in writing and be conspicuous. The implied warranties may also be disclaimed if the goods are sold as is or sold with all faults. For express warranties, the courts limit disclaimers only to the extent that they are consistent with the warranty given. Furthermore, many jurisdictions impose a standard of strict liability on all merchants for goods that cause injury due to internal defects (see Chapter Two).

Chapter Summary

The area of law having the greatest impact on the day-to-day operations of a business is contract law. Commercial enterprises operate by entering into contracts, and consequently, contracts form the basis of all modern business. Not only does contract law involve basic common law principles, but also the provisions of the Uniform Commercial Code now govern many agreements, especially for merchants.

To be valid under common law, all contracts must have the following elements: offer, acceptance, consideration, capacity of the parties legality of the subject matter, and contractual intent. If any one of these elements is missing, it is unlikely that a contract can be found. However, in contracts for the sale of goods involving merchants, the UCC has formulated rules that permit the parties to create a contract even if many of these elements are missing as long as the quantity of the goods is specified.

In certain situations, persons who are not parties to the agreement may have rights with respect to the contract. Third-party beneficiaries are persons for whose benefit the contract was formed and who are capable of enforcing the contract against the promisor. Assignees are persons to whom the promisee of a contract has transferred its rights, and delegates are persons who agree to assist the promisor in fulfilling the contractual obligations.

Contracts are composed of two distinct elements: covenants, which are the contractual promises, and conditions, which are the timing elements indicating when the covenants must be performed. Failure to fulfill a condition may excuse the covenant, but failure of a covenant is a breach of the contract.

If a contract is breached, the injured party may seek redress by asserting legal remedies, which are money damages, if money will compensate for the injury, or equitable remedies in situations in which money would be insufficient.

Edited Judicial Decisions

Lorbrook Corp. v. G & T Industries, Inc.
162 A.D.2d 69, 562 N.Y.S.2d 978 (1990)

Plaintiff is a domestic corporation whose principal plant is located in Columbia County where it manufactures vinyl goods. Defendant is a Michigan corporation that, in 1988, purchased goods from plaintiff for resale under its trade name to customers who installed them in their marine products.

Plaintiff brought this action for some $288,000, allegedly representing the agreed purchase price for its goods sold and delivered to defendant. Defendant moved to dismiss the complaint on the basis of forum non-conveniens [incorrect couthouse]. The principal support for defendant's motion was a printed provision set forth on the reverse side of defendant's purchase orders for the goods in question stipulating that "[t]his transaction shall be governed by and interpreted under the laws of, and any legal disputes resolved in, the State of Michigan." Plaintiff opposed the motion, contending that, under UCC 2-207, the foregoing "choice of forum" clause in the purchase order never became a part of the parties' agreement. That section of the UCC provides that a timely expression of acceptance or written confirmation "operates as an acceptance even though it states terms additional to or different from those offered or agreed upon, unless acceptance is expressly made conditional on assent to the additional or different terms" (UCC 2-207 [1]). The additional terms are deemed to be "proposals for addition to the contract" and, if the contract is "[b]etween merchants," the terms become part of the contract unless, inter alia, "they materially alter it" (UCC 2-207 [2] [b]).

Plaintiff's submission in opposition included three letters from plaintiff's management to defendant's management purporting to be in confirmation of an oral agreement between the parties reached during several meetings and telephone conversations that took place in 1987. In a letter dated July 23, 1987, it is recited that the agreed selling price of "marine seating vinyl" of a certain type would be $1.90 per 54-inch yard for colors and $2 for the same quantity in reds with a minimum run of 1,500 yards per color, terms "net 45 days F.O.B. Hudson, New York." And in a letter dated November 3, 1987, plaintiff's representative recites that "[s]ince the handshake has taken place between us, the following are my understandings which outline our agreements," among which was that "[defendant] will insure that the vinyl production allocated to [plaintiff] will average 25,000 to 30,000 yards weekly." Plaintiff averred that the foregoing writings were in confirmation of an oral agreement entered into between the parties before any purchase order for the covered products was sent by defendant. Therefore, according to plaintiff, the provision contained in the purchase orders fixing Michigan as the forum State for any legal dispute was, under UCC 2-207, an "additional term" which did not become part of the contract because it "materially alter[ed] it." Supreme Court agreed, and defendant appeals from the denial of its motion.

[1] On appeal, defendant does not dispute that the transactions that are the subject matter of this action were "between merchants," as that phrase is defined under the UCC (see, UCC 2-104 [1], [3]). Nor is it contested that, if UCC 2-207 applies, the addition of a provision in an acceptance or confirmation designating a forum for legal disputes between the contracting parties would materially alter the agreement and, thus, not become part of the sales agreement without an additional expression of assent by the other party (see, *Pacamor Bearings v. Molon Motors & Coil*, 102 AD2d 355, 358). Defendant's primary contention on appeal, however, is that no sales contract was ever formed here by virtue of any verbal discussions or exchanges of correspondence between the parties. Rather, each purchase order containing the forum selection clause sent to plaintiff constituted a separate offer to purchase by defendant, which was then accepted in all of its terms by plaintiff's delivery of the goods requested therein (citing UCC 2-206 [1] [b]). Thus, according to defendant, UCC 2-207 never came into play, and the forum selection provision of each purchase order was a binding term of the parties' series of agreements. We disagree. From our review of the parties' evidentiary submissions, we conclude that, on any factual version of the parties' transaction supported by the evidence, the forum selection provision of defendant's purchase orders never validly became incorporated in their agreement.

First, it can be inferred from the evidence, as plaintiff contends, that plaintiff and defendant reached an oral agreement, confirmed by plaintiff's letters previously described, which adequately covered the essential terms of a valid requirements contract as to price, identity of the goods sold, minimum quantity, delivery, and time and method of payment (see, UCC 2-204; cf., *Kleinschmidt Div. v. Futuronics Corp.*, 41 NY2d 972, 973). Had such a prior oral agreement been reached, defendant's purchase orders would be nothing more than a request to ship a portion of the goods covered by that agreement, and the insertion of the forum selection clause would then be an unsuccessful ploy by defendant unilaterally to add a term not covered by the preexisting binding contract (see, *LTV Aerospace Corp. v. Bateman*, 492 SW2d 703 [Tex]; see also, *Matter of Marcus Bros. Textiles v. Avondale Mills*, 78 AD2d 800, appeal dismissed 54 NY2d 833; 2 Anderson, Uniform Commercial Code §2-207:5, at 273 [3d ed]). Alternatively, under the same scenario, defendant's purchase orders could readily be considered as confirmations of the preexisting contract (see, *Foley Co. v. Phoenix Eng'g & Supply Co.*, 819 F2d 60, 61; *M.K. Metals v. Container Recovery Corp.*, 645 F2d 583, 591; 2 Anderson, Uniform Commercial Code §2-207:26, at 285 [3d ed]). As such, however, the additional term fixing Michigan as the forum State for litigation never became part of the contract, because it materially altered the prior agreement and plaintiff never expressly assented to it (see, UCC 2-207 [2] [b]; *Foley Co. v. Phoenix Eng'g & Supply Co.*, supra, at 63-64; see also, *Matter of Marlene Indus. Corp. [Carnac Textiles]*, 45 Y2d 327, 332-333).

[2] Another possible version of the parties' transaction, also reasonably inferable from the evidence, is that plaintiff's letters collectively instituted an offer to enter into an agreement for the sale of its products to defendant, which was accepted by defendant's purchase orders. Again, however, the choice of forum clause in defendant's purchase order acceptances never became part of the sales agreement because it was an additional term materially altering the contract and was not expressly assented to by plaintiff (see, UCC 2-207 [2] [b]; *Daitom, Inc. v. Pennwalt Corp.*, 741 F2d 1569, 1575, 1577; *Mead Corp. v. McNally-Pittsburg Mfg. Corp.*, 654 F2d 1197, 1203-1204; *Idaho Power Co. v. Westinghouse Elec. Corp.*, 596 F2d 924, 925-927; see also, *Matter of Marlene Indus. Corp. [Carnac Textiles]*, supra).

[3] Finally to be considered is defendant's factual hypothesis that no bilateral contract was entered into by the parties as a result of their oral discussions or exchange of writings; instead, the operative events in the parties' transactions were defendant's offers communicated through the purchase orders, which were accepted according to all of their terms by plaintiff's deliveries of the ordered goods. The fatal flaw in this argument, however, is that it ignores the uncontested fact that there was an exchange of writings between the parties setting forth the essential terms of their proposed deal. Plaintiff's letters constituting, at the least, an offer to enter into a contract, preceded defendant's purchase orders. Clearly, a valid bilateral agreement could then have been formed on its terms by a simple expression of defendant's assent to plaintiff's offer. It necessarily follows that defendant's purchase orders were either acceptances of plaintiff's offer, or they were counteroffers. In either event, because of these exchanges between the parties, UCC 2-207 controls as to contract formation and content, rather than common-law mirror image rules of offer and acceptance, or other provisions of the UCC (see, *Matter of Marlene Indus. Corp. [Carnac Textiles]*, supra, at 332-333; UCC 2-207, Comments 1, 2; 2 Anderson, Uniform Commercial Code secs. 2-207:3, 2-207:4, at 269-272 [3d ed]).

As we have already discussed, if the purchase orders are deemed to have constituted an acceptance of the offer contained in plaintiff's letters, the additional choice of forum term relied upon by defendant is unavailing because it never was validly incorporated into the parties' agreement.

[4] The only remaining possibility under defendant's version of the facts is that its purchase orders were counteroffers. As counteroffers, concededly, plaintiff never expressly accepted the purchase orders, however. Therefore, the parties' writings (plaintiff's offer and defendant's counteroffers) did not establish a contract. Nonetheless, the parties' conduct over a period of months clearly manifested mutual recognition of the existence of a sales contract and, under UCC 2-207 (3), such conduct "is sufficient to establish a contract for sale although the writings of the parties do not otherwise establish a contract." But, UCC 2-207 (3) also modifies the common-law rule whereby the other party's performance following the counteroffer is considered an acceptance of the terms of the counteroffer. "A major consideration of [UCC 2-207] is the prevention of the imposition of harsh conditions upon one party merely as a result of his accepting a price quotation of a purchase order form" (2 Anderson, Uniform Commercial Code §2-207:4, at 272 [3d ed], quoting *Falcon Tankers v. Litton Sys* 355 A2d 898 [Del]). Instead, the terms of the contract "consist of those terms on which the writings of the parties agree, together with any supplementary terms incorporated under any other provisions of this Act" (UCC 2-207 [3]). Thus, the UCC dispenses with the advantage defendant might otherwise have obtained at common law because its counteroffer was the last writing before performance. "At common law, the offeree/counterofferor gets all of its terms simply because it fired the last shot in the exchange of forms. Section 2-207 (3) does away with this result by giving neither party the terms it attempted to impose unilaterally on the other. * * * Instead, all of the terms on which the parties' forms do not agree drop out, and the UCC supplies the missing terms" (*Diamond Fruit Growers v. Krack Corp.*, 794 F2d 1440, 1444).

Therefore, even if we accept defendant's position that the parties never entered into a binding bilateral sales agreement through their writings and oral discussions, it cannot succeed in enforcing the choice of forum provision in its purchase orders. Since the writings exchanged between the parties do not agree regarding the designation of Michigan as the forum for any legal dispute between them, that provision in the purchase orders never became part of their agreement. Apart from that provision, defendant clearly has not established any basis for dismissal of plaintiff's suit on the ground of forum non-conveniens. Accordingly, the Supreme Court was correct in denying defendant's option.

KMART CORP. v. BALFOUR BEATTY, INC., et al.
994 F. Supp. 634 (D.V.I. 1998)

This matter is before the Court on motion of defendant Balfour Beatty incorporated [BBI] to dismiss on the basis that plaintiff, KMART Corporation [KMART], is not an intended third-party beneficiary of a construction contract [contract] between BBI and the plaintiff's landlord, Tutu Park Ltd. [TPL]. In the event this Court denies the motion and holds that plaintiff is a third-party beneficiary of the contract, BBI has requested that the action be stayed pending enforcement of the contract's arbitration clause. The Court has diversity jurisdiction in this case pursuant to §22 Revised Organic Act of 1954, 48 U.S.C. §1612, and 28 U.S.C. §1332.

I. FACTS

In January of 1992, BBI entered into a contract with TPL for the design and construction of a shopping center in St. Thomas. In September of 1995, the roof of the shopping center was damaged by the winds accompanying Hurricane Marilyn.

KMART was one of the tenants of the shopping center. Contending that it is a third-party beneficiary of the construction contract, plaintiff instituted this action in August, 1997, alleging breach of contract and negligence.

For its part, KMART points out that a number of provisions in the relevant documents indicate that the parties intended to convey a benefit to KMART. The specifications for the construction as described in defendant Bentley Engineers & Architects documentation [Bentley Specifications] call for the construction schedules to comply with KMART's requirements. (Bentley Specifications, P1.04A3). The drawings made in the design phase of performance were to be submitted to KMART. (*Id.* P1.04A4.) Warranties of work performed by defendant and its subcontractors were to be executed in KMART's favor and submitted directly to KMART. (*Id.* P2.01B.)

II. APPLICATION OF LAW AND FACT

BBI asserts that, because it is not a party to the construction contract, KMART may not claim relief under the agreement and moves to dismiss for failure to state a claim under Fed. R. Civ. P. 12(b)(6). In considering such a motion, the Court is constrained to view all factual allegations in KMART's amended complaint as true and to give it the benefit of every reasonable inference. *Kelly v. Borough of Sayreville*, New Jersey, 107 F.3d 1073, 1075 (3d Cir. 1997), citing *Schrob v. Catterson*, 948 F.2d 1402, 1408 (3d Cir. 1991). BBI further prays that, if the Court should find KMART to be a party to the contract, the instant litigation should be stayed pending arbitration as mandated in the contract. The Court will address each of defendant's motions in turn.

In sum, the Court finds that KMART is indeed a third-party beneficiary to the contract and that, as such, KMART is bound by the contract's terms to submit its claims to arbitration.

A. KMART's Standing As A Third-Party Beneficiary

Section 302 of the Restatement (Second) of Contracts [Restatement] provides a blueprint for determining whether or not a party is an intended third-party beneficiary.

(1) Unless otherwise agreed between promisor and promisee, a beneficiary of a promise is an intended beneficiary if recognition of a right to performance in the beneficiary is appropriate to effectuate the intention of the parties and either:

(a) the performance of the promise will satisfy an obligation of the promisee to pay money to the beneficiary; or

(b) the circumstances indicate that the promisee intends to give the beneficiary the benefit of the promised performance.

(2) An incidental beneficiary is a beneficiary who is not an intended beneficiary.

An intended beneficiary acquires a right under the contract. *Id.* §304 ("A pomise in a contract creates a duty in the promisor to any intended beneficiary to perform the promise, and the intended beneficiary may enforce the duty"). An incidental beneficiary does not. *Id.* §315 ("An incidental beneficiary acquires by virtue of the promise no right against the promisor or the promisee"). Promises to render performances other than the payment of money require some expression of intent by the parties to give the benefit of performance to the beneficiary. *Id.* §304 cmt.

In a 1985 case construing the Restatement (First) of Contracts, a Maryland court found that "one is an [intended] beneficiary when 'performance of the promise will satisfy an actual or supposed or asserted duty of the promisee to the beneficiary.'" *District Moving & Storage Co., Inc. v. Gardiner & Gardiner, Inc.*, 63 Md. App. 96, 492 A.2d 319, 322 (Md. Ct. Spec. App. 1985) citing *Weems v. Nanticoke Homes, Inc.*, 37 Md. App. 544, 378 A.2d 190 (Md. Ct. Spec. App. 1977). In *District Moving*, the landlord owed a contractual duty under a lease to provide the putative third-party beneficiary with a building. Just as the Maryland court had no difficulty finding the tenant was a third-party beneficiary to the construction contract, so does this Court find that KMART was a third-party beneficiary of the construction contract between BBI and TPL. The contractual duty of performance owed by BBI to its promisee, TPL, would satisfy TPL's duty to its beneficiary, KMART. KMART, then, is a third-party beneficiary to the construction contract between BBI and TPL.

Continuing to bear in mind the requirement to construe factual issues in favor of the non-movant, the language of the contract at issue here also conveys intent among the contracting parties to bestow a benefit upon KMART. The contract's specifications call for construction schedules to comport with KMART's requirements. The drawings to be used were to be submitted to KMART and all warranties were to be executed in KMART's favor. All of these facts support a conclusion that BBI and TPL entered into the construction contract to erect a building for the benefit of KMART.

BBI asserts that the following contract provision specifically excludes KMART as a third-party beneficiary:

2.2.9 The Design/Builder warrants to the Owner . . . that the Work will be of good quality, free from faults and defects, and in conformance with the Contract Documents (emphasis added).

The contract defines "owner" as TPL. Even if this paragraph could be read as BBI urges, the inclusion of provisions in the contract specifications contemplating KMART's active participation in design and construction of the building creates an ambiguity that, at this stage of the litigation, must be resolved in the plaintiff's favor.

Other common law courts have applied different standards, principally two, to determine whether or not the parties to a contract intended to benefit one claiming third-party beneficiary status. Some attempt to determine if the performance of the contract runs to the putative third-party beneficiary. (See, *John D. Calamari and Joseph M. Perillo*, Contracts, §17.3 at 695 (3d ed. 1987).)

Others, and the increasingly more modern view, hold that it is enough that the promisor (here, BBI) understood that the promisee had intent to benefit the third-party (here, KMART). (See, *Id.* at 696, citing *Lucas v. Hamm*, 56 Cal. 2d 583, 364 P.2d 685, 689, 15 Cal. Rptr. 821 (Cal. 1961).)

Under either formulation, the result is the same. Given the lease plaintiff had with TPL, and the extensive involvement of KMART in the specifications for the construction of the space, there is little question but that the performance in this case, construction of the building, ran directly to the benefit of the plaintiff. The promisor, BBI, clearly had notice that its promisee, TPL, had intent to benefit KMART.

For all these reasons the Court concludes that KMART is an intended third-party beneficiary to the BBI-TPL contract. KMART can enforce such rights as it may have under that contract per Restatement §304.

Glossary

Acceptance - Manifestation of assent to create a contract

Accord and satisfaction - Special type of contract used to settle a legitimate dispute

Adhesion contracts - Contract written for the benefit of the dominant party

Anticipatory repudiation - Definitive statement or action indicating that a contracting party does not intend to fulfill the contract

Assignee - Transferee of contract rights

Assignment - Transfer of contract rights

Assignor - Transferor of contract rights

Battle of the forms - UCC concept for contracts between merchants; the last indication of terms of the contract prevails

Bilateral contract - A promise for a promise

Breach - Failure to fulfill contractual obligations

Compensatory damages - The standard measure of legal remedy

Condition - A timing element of a contract

Condition concurrent - Fact or event that occurs at the same time as the covenant

Condition precedent - Fact or event that gives rise to an absolute duty to perform

Condition subsequent - Fact or event that extinguishes an absolute duty to perform

Consequential damages - Monetary relief above the standard measure for foreseeable financial injury caused by the contractual breach

Consideration - The bargained element of the contract

Contract - Legally enforceable agreement supported by consideration

Contractual capacity - The legal ability to enter into a contract

Counter- or cross-offer - Offer made by the offeree

Covenant - Absolute and unconditional promise to perform

Cover - UCC remedy to acquire goods in substitution

Delegation - Having someone assist the promisor in fulfilling the contractual obligation

Delegator - One who delegates his or her duties under a contract to another

Disclaimer - Statement that a merchant will not be bound for warranties

Divisible contract - Agreement that can be divided into equal parts, creating separate smaller contracts

Duress - Any force used to negate contractual intent

Executory - Something not yet done or performed

Fraud - The misrepresentation of a material fact made with the intent to deceive relied upon by another person to that person's detriment

Goods - Personal property that is tangible and moveable at the time the contract is formed

Guarantee - Promise to pay the debt of another

Illusory promise - Promise that is not in fact supported by consideration

Incidental beneficiary - Person who benefits from a contract only tangentially

Installment contracts - Under the UCC, a contract that requires or authorizes delivery in two or more separate lots to be accepted and paid for separately

Intended beneficiary - Third-party beneficiary to a contract

Ironclad - Under the UCC, a contract that cannot be altered

Liquidated damages - Contract provision providing for damages in case of breach

Mailbox rule - An acceptance is valid when properly dispatched in the manner authorized by the offeror

Malum in se - Bad in and of itself

Malum prohibitum - Statutory wrong

Material breach - Breach of contract that goes to the heart of the agreement

Merchant - Under the UCC, a person who regularly deals in the goods of the kind in question

Minor - Someone under legal age, which is generally 18

Minor breach - Breach of contract that is basically insignificant

Mirror image rule - Under the common law, the acceptance must exactly match the terms of the offer

Misrepresentation - Fraud without the actual intent

Mistake - Error that negates contractual intent

Mitigation of damages - Nonbreaching party's obligation to lessen the damages suffered

Mutuality of consideration - In a contract, both parties must give and receive legally sufficient consideration

Mutual mistake - Mistake made by both parties, negates the contract

Mutual rescission - Both parties take back the contract; only permitted for executory contracts

Necessaries - Food, clothing, shelter, education, healthcare, and military service

Nominal consideration - Insignificant consideration

Nominal damages - Monetary relief granted for insignificant breaches of contract

Nonassignment provision - Contract clause prohibiting assignment

Novation - Substitution of parties to a contract

Offeree - A person or entity to whom an offer to enter into a contract is made by another

Offer - Proposal to enter into a valid contract

Offeror A person or entity who makes a specific proposal to another to enter into a contract

Output contract - Agreement to purchase all products manufactured

Parol evidence rule - Oral testimony may not be used to vary the terms of a writing

Pre-existing duty rule - A contract cannot be supported by an agreement to do what one is already legally bound to do

Promisee - A person whom is to be the beneficiary of a promise, an obligation, or a contract

Promisor - The party who has a contractual duty to perform

Punitive damages - Monetary relief used as a punishment

Quantum meruit - Equitable remedy granting money for services rendered

Quantum valebant - Equitable remedy granting money for goods transferred

Quasi-contract - Noncontracts that are treated as though they were contracts

Rejection - Not accepting a contract

Release - An agreement to relieve someone of a contractual duty

Requirements contract - Agreement to buy or sell all of the goods needed

Rescission and restitution - Equitable remedy permitting the contract to be voided

Revocation - The offeror taking back the offer before acceptance

Revoke or **renounce** - The offeror can stop the offeree from having the power to accept and no contract will result

Rules of construction - Doctrines used to interpret contracts

Sham consideration - Consideration that is insufficient to support a contract

Specific performance - Court order making a person fulfill a contractual duty, used for unique goods

Statute of Frauds - Law in every state which requires that certain documents be in writing

Third-party beneficiary - Person not a party to a contract for whose benefit the contract was created

Third-party beneficiary contract - Contract formed to benefit a person not a party to the contract

Third-party creditor beneficiary - Intended beneficiary who is owed a debt by one of the contracting parties who uses the contract to extinguish the debt

Third-party donee beneficiary - Intended beneficiary who is to receive a gift because of the contract

Uniform Commercial Code (UCC) - Statute that regulates contracts between merchant traders for the sale of goods

Unilateral contract - Promise for an act

Unilateral mistake - Error made by one side to a contract

Voidable - Contract that can be avoided without being in breach

Waiver - Giving up a contract right

Warranty against infringement - Guaranty that the goods are not subject to patents, copyrights, claims, etc.

Warranty of title - Guaranty that the transferor has a title sufficient to transfer the goods

Written assurances - The UCC provides that if one of the parties in a contract has reasonable grounds to believe that the other party will not perform as contracted, he or she may in writing demand adequate assurance of due performance form the other party

Exercises

1. Discuss the differences between an assignment, a delegation, and a novation. Obtain a copy of each type of provision from the library or the Internet.

2. Locate an advertisement in your local newspaper that indicates express warranties.

3. Give two examples of unilateral contracts.

4. If your school terminated your program before you graduated, what, if any, relief could you be afforded in the courts? Discuss.

5. Create a bilateral contract that does not involve the exchange of money. To complete this exercise, obtain samples of this type of agreement and use those samples to draft your own format.

Chapter Four

COMMERCIAL PAPER

Introduction

The stated purpose of the Universal Commercial Code, as it appears in Article 1, is to facilitate commerce. To this end, the statute encompasses various aspects of commercial activities. This chapter will focus on Article 3, which deals with commercial paper. This text will later discuss the banking provisions of the UCC and their effect on commercial enterprises.

Commercial paper can be traced back to the Renaissance and the increasing amount of foreign trade that took place at that time. In order for merchants from one geographic area to trade with merchants in a different location, a system was needed to permit sales to take place over large regions without the necessity of traders carrying huge amounts of gold to effectuate the purchase. One of the methods that developed to deal with this problem, and thereby promote commerce, was commercial paper, also referred to as **negotiable instruments**. Specifically, **commercial paper** is any document that may be transferred from one person to another and is used as a substitute for cash. There are two types of negotiable instruments, notes and drafts. **Notes** are two-party instruments in which one party, the **maker**, promises to pay another party, the **payee** or **bearer**, a sum of money. In common parlance, variations of this instrument are referred to as IOUs. **Drafts** are three-party instruments in which one party, the **drawer**, orders another party, the **drawee** (often a bank), to pay a sum of money to a third person, the payee or bearer. A typical example of a draft is a bank check.

Almost every large commercial transaction is effectuated by the **negotiation**, or transfer, of commercial paper in payment for goods or services sold and, therefore, is the primary method of fulfilling a contract obligation to pay money in the financial world. This chapter will discuss the requirements relating to the use of commercial paper as contained in Article 3 of the UCC.

Requirements for Negotiation

In order for a document to be deemed legally negotiable (capable of being transferred), the instrument must be in writing, be signed by the maker or drawer, contain an unconditional promise or order to pay a sum certain, be payable either on demand or at a specified date, and be payable to order or to bearer.

Under the UCC, any intentional reduction to a tangible form is considered to be a writing. Note that this is a far more liberal interpretation of that term than is generally found in the law, either statutorily or under the common law, and may include tapes, disks, videos, etc.

Anything that the parties intend to constitute a signature will satisfy this requirement, such as a stamp, a seal, or a symbol used by the maker or drawer to evidence his or her acquiescence to the document. However, if the signature was unauthorized by the person who is presumed to be the maker or the drawer, that person is not liable under the instrument, but the unauthorized signer is held personally liable as though he or she was the maker.

> *Example: A corporate president has had a stamp made with a facsimile of his signature to be used to sign certain documents that he is called upon to approve. One day, while he is out of the office, his secretary takes a check out of the corporate checkbook, types out a check payable to her cousin, and then uses the seal as the president's signature. In this instance, the president will not be held liable for the amount of the check, but the secretary will be liable.*

An unconditional promise to pay a sum certain must be divided into several parts in order to comprehend its implications. **Unconditional** means that all of the terms of the payment must appear on the face of the instrument itself. If the instrument is **subject to** another document, it is not deemed to be an unconditional promise. Despite this general rule, a promise is still considered to be unconditional if it refers to another document but does not attempt to incorporate its terms into the instrument, indicates that the promise is secured, states that it was conditional payment for another agreement, refers to another document to determine certain pre-payment or acceleration rights, or states the condition that gave rise to the creation of the instrument. If the instrument contains any express conditions (see Chapter Three), it is nonnegotiable; however, implied or constructive conditions do not affect the instrument's negotiability.

A **promise to pay** is an unconditional obligation to perform. An **order to pay** is a specified direction to a third party to do something; it is more than a mere request or desire that the third person perform some act at the director's request. Promises appear in notes, and orders appear in drafts.

Sum certain requires the amount of money represented by the instrument (remember that commercial paper is a cash substitute) to be specified. It may include a specified rate of interest without affecting the requirement of being a sum certain, because the amount of the interest appearing in the instrument can be readily determined. The following items do not negatively affect the requirement of being a sum certain: stated interest or stated installment payments, different rates of interest if the specified difference is spelled out, stated discounts, explicit exchange rates if the instrument is for foreign currency, and the requirement that the cost of arbitration or attorneys' fees be added in the case of default. To meet this requirement, the instrument must be for the payment of money in currency; promises to pay property instead of money destroy the instrument's status as a negotiable instrument.

An instrument is considered to be **payable on demand** if it so states or says nothing about the time of payment. To be **payable at a definite time**, a stated date must appear on the document or a fixed period of time after a stated date. If the instrument calls for payment after the happening of a conditional event, such as the death of a person, the instrument is not negotiable. Further, acceleration or extension clauses do not affect this requirement if the option also includes a specified date (see below).

To be **payable to order**, the instrument must use the word "order," "assign," or "exchange" and indicate a specific person or persons. To be **payable to bearer**, the instrument must say it is "payable to bearer" and may be negotiated by anyone who has actual possession of the instrument. If an instrument indicates it is payable to both order and to bearer, it is considered to be an order instrument.

Negotiating Commercial Paper

In order to negotiate, or transfer, commercial paper, the transferor must be a holder. A **holder** is anyone who has good title to the instrument and has possession of the instrument. In order for the holder to have good title, all requisite parties must sign the instrument. Anyone who has possession of a bearer instrument is deemed to be a holder, but for order instruments, only the named payee is a holder unless he or she has **indorsed** the instrument (signed the instrument indicating a transfer of the rights to the instrument) to either order or bearer. To be valid, all indorsements must be authorized.

> *Example: An employee receives a paycheck and wishes to give the check to her daughter as a present. On the back of the check, the employee signs her name and writes that the check is payable to her daughter, which acts as an indorsement, or transfer, of the instrument.*

Indorsements are used to transfer title to the instrument. The indorsement must appear either on the instrument itself or on a special document used exclusively for indorsements known as an **allonge**. The UCC provides for four types of indorsements:
1. **Special indorsement.** The **indorser** names a specific person as **indorsee**.
2. **Blank indorsement.** The indorser simply signs his or her name and the instrument becomes payable to bearer.
3. **Qualified indorsement.** The indorser uses the words "without recourse," which limits the indorser's potential liability (see below).
4. **Restrictive indorsement.** The indorser limits the further use of the instrument, such as using the words "for deposit only."

In order for commercial paper to be usable as a cash substitute, the payee must be given some assurance that he or she will actually be given cash when the instrument is presented for payment. All holders have the right to seek such payment, but their actual ability to collect may be limited by legal defenses the parties to the instrument may have. In order to ensure negotiability, the UCC has identified some persons who have superior rights to those of a mere holder. These persons are known as **holders in due course (HDC)**, who are holders for value, in good faith, without notice of any claim against the instrument. To qualify as an HDC, the holder must give something of value to acquire the interest in the instrument. The value does not have to qualify as contractual consideration—almost anything of value, including antecedent debts, will suffice. Nor does the value have to be equal to the face amount of the instrument; a person may become an HDC for a portion of a negotiable instrument.

Good faith is determined by a subjective, not an objective, test. A subjective test considers the peculiarities of the particular individual; an objective test uses the standard of the average person in the community. Did the specific individual act in good faith? To acquire the instrument without notice, the person must lack both actual and constructive notice of any claim or other problem with the instrument.

A transferee acquires all of the rights of the transferor pursuant to a doctrine known as the **shelter rule**. This means that once a person qualifies as an HDC, he or she can transfer that status to all subsequent transferees except for a transferee with notice or who participates in a fraud or illegality with respect to the instrument.

Once a person qualifies as an HDC, he or she takes the instrument free of all personal defenses and claims on the instrument, and is only subject to real defenses and claims. The real defenses are: duress, alteration of the instrument, fraud, forgery, illegality, discharge in bankruptcy, incapacity of the parties, and statute of limitations.

The personal defenses are the general contract defenses that include: mistake, unconscionability, failure or consideration, fraud in the inducement, impossibility, and nondelivery.

Liability of the Parties

As a general rule, a party's liability with regard to a negotiable instrument is limited to the capacity in which he or she signed the instrument. In order for the potential liability to arise, the instrument must be presented for payment and be dishonored. **Presentment** means bringing the instrument to the drawee, or maker, on the date that the payment is due and request money in exchange for the instrument. **Dishonor** means that the person obligated to pay on the instrument refuses to do so; however, if the instrument is presented prior to its due date, it is not dishonor.

To indicate the party's liability, the following list of potential parties to a negotiable instrument is presented:
- **Maker**. This person is primarily liable on the instrument to the payee or the bearer, and this liability accrues regardless of whether he or she has any notice of the dishonor.
- **Drawer**. The drawer is secondarily liable on the instrument—it is the drawee who must make the payment.
- **Indorser**. The indorser is secondarily liable if the maker or drawer fails to pay and must have notice of such dishonor before the liability attaches.
- **Drawee**. The drawee has no liability to the payee; he or she is only liable to the drawer.
- **Transferor**. A transferor is anyone who transfers the instrument for consideration, and as such warrants to the validity of the instrument to all subsequent holders if the transferor signed the instrument. If the transferor does not sign the instrument, his or her warranty (or liability) is only to the immediate transferee who gave the consideration. The transferor's warranties are: good title, all signatures are genuine, the instrument has not been materially altered, he or she knows of no defense against the instrument, and he or she knows of no insolvency proceeding again parties to the instrument. Remember, the transferor is anyone who accepts consideration for the instrument, regardless of his or her other status as a holder, HDC, payee, etc.
- **Accommodation party**. An accommodation party is anyone who adds his or her signature to the instrument as surety. The accommodation party is only liable in the capacity in which he or she signed, except that he or she is not liable to the party so accommodated.
- **Guarantor**. A **payment guarantor** guarantees payment on the instrument and is primarily liable. A **collection guarantor** agrees to guarantee payment only if the holder sues on the instrument and receives a judgment in his or her favor and therefore is only secondarily liable.
- **Acceptor**. The acceptor is a drawee of a draft who signed it thereby becoming liable in the same fashion as the maker of a note. An example would be a bank certifying a check drawn by one of its depositors. As such, the acceptor becomes primarily liable on the instrument.

In order for a party to the instrument to become liable on the instrument, the instrument must be presented for payment. Anyone who presents an instrument, by law, makes the following warranties to the party to whom the instrument is presented:
- The presenter has good title to the instrument.
- The presenter has no knowledge of any claim against the instrument.
- The instrument has not been materially altered.

In order to obtain payment, the holder first presents the instrument to the party who is primarily liable for its payment, either the drawee or the maker. If the party who is primarily liable dishonors the instrument, the holder may seek redress from the other parties to the instrument in the reverse order in which they signed.

Example: John executes a check on his First National Bank account to Jean as a birthday gift. Jean indorses the check to Evan in payment for a sweater she bought from Evan. Evan indorses the check to his landlord in payment for his rent. The landlord then presents the check to the First National Bank, which dishonors the check because John had insufficient funds in his account. The landlord is an HDC who must seek payment from Evan. Evan is an HDC who seeks payment from Jean. Jean is not an HDC because she gave no value for the instrument and must seek payment from John. If John did in fact have sufficient funds in his account, he may have recourse against the bank if it charged him a fee for dishonoring the check.

Forgery, Alteration, and Discharge

Forgery

If the signature appearing on a negotiable instrument is forged, it is the forger who is liable on the instrument. The person whose signature has been forged is not liable unless there is
- *a fictitious payee.* This arises if the person who creates the instrument knows that the payee does not exist or gave the instrument to a person without determining the identity of the person who acquires possession of the instrument.

Example: A land developer contacts a surveyor to survey the land she has just purchased. Someone appears at the developer's office pretending to be the surveyor and has the developer make out a check to him. The developer will be liable on this instrument because she did not check to be sure that the person who appeared was who he pretended to be.

- *negligence.* If the person contributes to the forgery, he or she will be liable on the instrument.

Example: A woman leaves a blank signed check on her desk. A visitor to the office finds the check and puts his own name on it and then cashes it. The woman will be liable because her own negligence contributed to the forgery.

- *a bank statement rule.* The UCC imposes a duty on a bank customer to check his or her bank statement for any inaccuracies, including forged instruments charged to the customer's account. If an inaccuracy is not reported within a reasonable time, the customer is estopped from denying liability.
- *certification.* Certification by a bank estops the bank from denying liability.

Material Alteration

Any alteration to a negotiable instrument is considered material if it changes the obligations of the parties under the instrument in any way. If the instrument is altered by a **meddling stranger**, a third party who is not a party to the instrument, that alteration has no effect on the instrument's negotiability and the instrument is read as originally written. If a holder makes the alteration, and the alteration is found to be fraudulent and material, all prior parties are completely discharged of any liability under the instrument. If the alteration was caused by a party's negligence, that party is not discharged.

Discharge

Parties to commercial paper are discharged from their obligations under the instrument in one of the following ways:

- *Payment in satisfaction.* Once the party has paid, he or she is discharged to the extent of that payment.
- *Tender of payment.* If payment is offered but refused, the party tendering such payment is discharged.
- *Cancellation and renunciation.* A holder may voluntarily cancel any instrument gratuitously.
- *Impairment of recourse.* A party is discharged if a holder imposes any condition on the instrument without the party's consent and without justification. A surety is discharged if the creditor releases the primary debtor, or the creditor extends the time for payment without the surety's consent.
- *Reacquisition.* If a prior party reacquires an instrument, all intervening parties are discharged.
- *Any act that operates to discharge a simple contract.*
- *Delay in presentment.* If the instrument is not presented on time without a valid reason, such as the presenter being physically incapable on the day of presentment, the indorsers are discharged. A drawer who has funds deposited with the drawee, however, is not discharged.
- *By the fraudulent or material alteration of the instrument.*

Chapter Summary

The law and rules with respect to commercial paper are extremely structured because of the importance of these instruments to the commercial world. Commercial paper is used as a cash substitute and to facilitate commerce. It is the primary medium for payment of large commercial transactions. To ensure that these instruments will be freely negotiable and accepted, the UCC has very specific requirements with respect to their creation and use.

In order to qualify as commercial paper, the instrument must be in writing, signed by the maker or drawer, containing an unconditional promise to pay a sum certain to bearer or to order upon demand or at a specified time. Any document not meeting these requirements or intended as a cash substitute does not qualify as a negotiable instrument.

Commercial paper is divided into two broad categories: notes, which are two-party instruments, and drafts, which are three-party instruments. The objective of commercial paper is to have a document that can be freely negotiated, or transferred. Anyone who has a negotiable instrument and has a good title is deemed to be a holder of the instrument, capable of further negotiating the instrument. If the transferee takes the instrument for value, in good faith, and without notice of any claim against the instrument, he or she qualifies as holder in due course, who takes the instrument free of all personal defenses against the instrument and has a good title superior to all others.

Parties to a negotiable instrument are only liable on the instrument in the capacity in which they have signed it. Makers are primarily liable on the instrument, as are acceptors and payment guarantors. All other parties are only secondarily liable if the person with primary liability defaults by failing to pay on the instrument. Liability only arises if the instrument is dishonored on presentment. A party will be discharged of liability on the instrument if the party actually pays, tenders payment, the instrument has been cancelled, or the note fails under general contract principles.

Edited Judicial Decisions

ONE VALLEY BANK OF OAK HILL, INC. v. BOLEN
188 W. Va. 687 (1992)

The Circuit Court of Fayette County asks us to determine to what extent an assignee of a note is liable to the payor of that note for a fraud committed by the assignor (original payee). Specifically addressed in this certified question is the way the West Virginia Consumer Credit and Protection Act affects the general holder in due course rules. At issue is the ready availability of credit to consumers.

On September 12, 1988, Robert Bolen, Sr., and Judith Bolen, defendants/counterclaimants in this action, purchased a used 1988 Cadillac DeVille from Derald Rollyson, Inc. for $22,900. The Bolens purchased the car for $2,889.77, traded in their 1984 Cadillac El Dorado (valued at $1,583.24), and financed the rest of the purchase price. The Bolens promised to pay 60 monthly installments of $486.36, which is the remainder of the purchase price financed at an annual interest rate of 10.9%.

Allegedly, the DeVille was described by the salesman as a factory official car. On May 16, 1989, the Bolens assert that they discovered that, in fact, the car had been owned by Hertz and used as a rental car in Florida from February through June of 1988. The Bolens claim that this was a material difference, and they would not have bought the car had they known it had been a rental car.

On the same day the car was sold, Derald Rollyson, Inc., sold the Bolen's credit obligation to One Valley Bank of Oak Hill (Bank). Bank received Rollyson's formal written assignment of its rights, title, and interest under that credit agreement. When the Bolens discovered the alleged fraud, they stopped making payments on the note. Bank then brought suit to repossess the DeVille and to establish what amount remained on the obligation after the repossession. The Bolens countersued Bank, asking for the damages they suffered as a result of the alleged fraud on the part of the Bank.

To help resolve this claim, the Circuit Court of Fayette County certified the following questions:

1. Does West Virginia Code 46A-2-102 limit the amount of compensatory or punitive damages that a consumer may recover from an assignee that holds an instrument, contract or writing that was induced by fraud on the part of the seller occurring prior to July 1, 1990?

2. If the provisions of West Virginia Code 46A-2-102 allow a consumer to recover damages from an assignee that exceed the amounts paid by that consumer with respect to the consumers credit obligation, are these provisions

a. Preempted by the FTC Notice of Claims and Defenses Regulation (16 C.F.R. 433.2); or

b. In violation of the West Virginia or United States Constitutions.

Credit, for better or worse, is the lifeblood of our consumer economy. The need to make credit more readily available was a driving force behind the creation of the Uniform Commercial Code as well as the great strides made earlier by Lord Mansfield at the end of the 18th century and transplanted wholesale into our law in the 19th century. The ability of negotiable commercial paper to flow nationwide without regard to local conditions allows all business, no matter how small or remote, access to nationwide capital markets.

The main reason for this free flow of commercial paper is the holder in due course provisions contained in W.Va. Code 46-3-305 [1963] that permit a purchaser who, in good faith, purchases a negotiable instrument and gives value for it without notice of any defense against it or claim to the instrument, to take the instrument free from virtually all defenses.

Although this rule worked well to increase available credit, it also created some harsh results. Consumers, it was discovered, lacked adequate bargaining power to protect themselves from slick operators in the retail business. For example, a woman might buy a television set on credit from Slick Willie's Appliance Shoppe and sign a promissory note for the balance. After the woman gets home and plugs in the television, the set blows up. Furious, she may bring the television set back to Slick Willie's the next day only to find that Willie has assigned her note to the Last National Bank and headed for Rio. The bank, as holder of the note, could still demand payment on the note, and the woman would be obligated to pay. Meanwhile, Slick Willie has gone underground and cannot be found. Now the consumer has no television, no useful cause of action, but the consumer is still liable to pay for the television.

Indeed, this very scenario occurred frequently in door-to-door sales transactions, most notoriously the sale of storm windows, storm doors, and aluminum siding. Thus, by the early 1970s, the Supreme Court of New Jersey began to look behind the claim of holder in due course status to determine whether a bank was actually part of the scheme. In *General Investment Corp. v. Angelini*, 58 N.J. 396, 278 A.2d 193 (1971), the New Jersey court found that the good faith requirement to be a holder in due course has a significant meaning.

In the field of negotiable instruments, good faith is a broad concept. The basic philosophy of the holder in due course status is to encourage free negotiability of commercial paper by removing certain anxieties of one who takes the paper as an innocent purchaser knowing no reason why the paper is not as sound as its face would indicate. It would follow, therefore, that the more the holder knows about the underlying transaction, and particularly the more he controls or participates or becomes involved in it, the less he fits the role of a good faith purchaser for value; the closer his relationship [sic] to the underlying agreement which is the source of the note, the less need there is for giving him the tension-free rights considered necessary in a fast-moving, credit-extending commercial world. (quoting *Unico v. Owen*, 50 N.J. 101, 109, 232 A.2d 405, (1967)) [Emphasis added]

General Investment, 58 N.J. at 403, 278 A.2d at 196. As the New Jersey Supreme Court was taking this approach toward banks that tried to hide behind the holder in due course doctrine, the court noted that the New Jersey Legislature had taken steps to prevent the continuation of this problem.

The Legislature settled this problem for the future by L. 1969, c. 237, §2, which provides that, "No home repair contract shall require or entail the execution of any note unless such note shall have printed the words 'CONSUMER NOTE' in 10-point bold type or larger on the face thereof. Such a note with the words 'CONSUMER NOTE' printed thereon shall be subject to the terms and conditions of the home repair contract and shall not be a negotiable instrument within the meaning of chapter 3 (Commercial Paper) of the Uniform Commercial Code, N.J.S. 12A:3-101 *et seq.*" N.J.S.A. 17:16C-64.2

New Jersey stripped all notes based on underlying home repair contracts of their holder in due course status in order to protect consumers from this unfair situation. Similarly, the West Virginia Legislature, looking to mitigate the harshness of the holder in due course rules on consumers, enacted the West Virginia Consumer Credit and Protection Act. W.Va. Code Chap. 46A [1974]. See *Clendenin Lumber and Supply Com. v. Carpenter*, 172 W.Va. 375, 379-380, 305 S.E.2d 332, 336-337 (1983).

Part of the West Virginia Legislature's plan for mitigating the harsh effects of the UCC also included stripping assignees of consumer commercial paper of most of the benefits of being holders in due course, although the West Virginia statute was far more comprehensive than the early New Jersey statute quoted above. W.Va. Code 46A-2-102(5) [1974] provided:

The following provisions shall be applicable to instruments, contracts or other writings, other than negotiable instruments, evidencing an obligation arising from a consumer credit sale or consumer lease, other than a sale or lease primarily for an agricultural purpose . . . Notwithstanding any term or agreement to the contrary or the provisions of article two [§46-2-101 *et seq.*], chapter 46 of this code or section 206 [§46-9-206], article nine, of said chapter 46, an assignee of any such instrument, contract or other writing shall take and hold such instrument, contract or other writing subject to all claims and defenses of the buyer or lessee against the seller or lessor arising from that specific consumer credit sale or consumer lease of goods or services, but the total of all claims and defenses which may be asserted against the assignee under this subsection or subsection (7) of this section shall not exceed the amount owing to the assignee at the time of such assignment, except (i) as to any claim or defense founded in fraud and (ii) for any excess charges and penalties recoverable under section one hundred one [§46A-5-101], article five of this chapter. [Emphasis added]

In 1990, the Legislature renumbered this section and added a provision that clearly expresses a limitation on the amount of recovery "provided that as to any claim or defense founded in fraud arising on or after the first day of July, 1990, the total sought shall not exceed the amount of the original obligation under the instrument, contract or other writing."

W.Va. Code 46A-2-102(1) [1990]. The Bolens argue that we can infer from the adoption of this amendment that there was no limitation on the amount that could be recovered from an assignee before the amendment was passed. The Bank maintains that this provision was just a clarification to remedy an ambiguity in the Code.

We do not agree with either interpretation of the action the Legislature took in 1990. Admittedly, neither W. Va. Code, 46A-2-102(5) [1974], nor any of its counterparts nor the definitions contained in W. Va. Code, 46A-1-102, provided any definition of the term fraud. However, W. Va. Code, 46A-2-121 [1974], expressly deals with conduct that is unconscionable which we have equated with fraudulent conduct. See, *e.g.*, *Orlando v. Finance One of W. Va.*, Inc., 179 W. Va. 447, 369 S.E.2d 882 (1988); *United States Life Credit Corp. v. Wilson*, 171 W. Va. 538, 301 S.E.2d 169 (1982).

This is reinforced by W. Va. Code, 46A-5-101 [1974], which outlines the types of additional damages that may be recovered for various violations of Chapter 46A, and specifies "illegal, fraudulent or unconscionable conduct (§46A-2-121)[.]" This section goes on to provide: "The consumer has a cause of action to recover actual damages and in addition a right in an action to recover from the person violating this chapter a penalty in an amount determined by the court not less than one hundred dollars nor more than one thousand dollars."

Thus, while W. Va. Code, 46A-2-102(5) [1974], allows the consumer to recover an amount not to "exceed the amount owing to the assignee at the time of such assignment," its exception for an additional amount because of fraud is controlled by W. Va. Code, 46A-5-101 [1974]. As we have seen under this latter section, the additional damages for fraud or unconscionable conduct are limited to actual damages and, if the court so determines, a penalty of not less than one hundred nor more than one thousand dollars. Consequently, punitive damages are not available under the fraud or unconscionable conduct provisions of W. Va. Code, 46A-2-121 [1974], and W. Va. Code, 46A-2-102(5) [1974].

With this understanding of the damages available under the 1974 provisions, it is apparent that the 1990 legislative revision holding fraud to "the total sought shall not exceed the amount of the original obligation" is designed further to limit recovery. This section now precludes the recovery of any actual damages and the penalty.

Therefore, the answer to the first certified question is that W.Va. Code 46A-2-102 does limit the amount of damages available to be recovered. This answer thereby renders the second certified question moot.

Accordingly, the certified question having been answered, this case is ordered dismissed from the docket of this Court.

Certified question answered.

DUBIN v. HUDSON COUNTY PROBATION DEPARTMENT
267 N.J. Super. 202, 630 A.2d 1207(1993)

Plaintiff, the owner and operator of a check cashing business, sued the Hudson County Probation Department. Plaintiff seeks payment for three checks, apparently issued by defendant, which plaintiff cashed, and which were subsequently returned unpaid by the bank. (Venue was transferred from Hudson County to Essex County.) The facts are undisputed.

Three individuals each presented to plaintiff's employee a check from the Hudson County Probation Department, dated 3/13/92, to cash them. Upon the individuals having presented identification, plaintiff cashed each check in the amounts of $334.50, $183.00, and $360.50. When plaintiff thereafter presented the checks to the drawer bank, the checks were returned to plaintiff with a stamp indicating the subject account had been closed. The bank charged a fee to the plaintiff of $10.00 per each returned check, and plaintiff includes this fee in the amount claimed here.

Prompted by the return of the checks, plaintiff contacted the County Police and an investigation ensued. The account had been closed and zeroed out on October 1, 1991. The boxes of unused, blank, unendorsed checks were locked in a storage room. Several months after the account had been closed, the Probation Department acquired a paper shredder, and an employee working as a mail clerk was instructed to shred the blank checks.

The shredding was done in the mail room, which was locked every day from 4:00 p.m. to 9:00 a.m., but unlocked from 9:00 a.m. to 4:00 p.m. while the mail clerk was working in the room. The mail clerk's duties required him to leave the mailroom to run errands and, apparently, the door to the mailroom was closed but unlocked during these periods. While there has yet to be a determination of exactly how or when the checks were stolen from the Probation Department, it is believed that the checks were stolen from the mail room at some time during the day while the room was unlocked and unattended.

Plaintiff alleges gross negligence by defendant in two regards. First, plaintiff states defendant was grossly negligent in causing a delay of several months in destroying the checks from the closed account. Secondly, plaintiff alleges that defendant was grossly negligent in leaving the room, where the blank checks were being shredded, unlocked and unattended.

Generally, defendants deny any negligence, but state that if there was negligence it was simple negligence and did not rise to the level of gross negligence. Additionally, defendants argue the comparative negligence of plaintiff in failing to verify the check before having cashed it. Finally, defendant states that they are immune from liability under the Tort Claims Act, N.J.S.A. 59:2-1 to 59:12-3.

The cause of action sounds in two forms: negligence and contract. The complaint alleges the gross negligence of the defendant, while the cause of action is based on commercial paper and purely statutory law of the Uniform Commercial Code. Analysis of the cause under both theories provides different results, because the theory of comparative negligence applies in cases of negligence but is not a defense in a contract action. Thus, if the cause of action is based on defendant's alleged negligence, any comparative negligence of plaintiff would diminish plaintiff's recovery or, if plaintiff's negligence was greater than defendant's negligence, would bar recovery by plaintiff. N.J.S.A. 2A:15-5.1. I find the case, while making allegations of negligence, addresses a strictly contractual issue, and is founded solely in statutory law and its interpretation. The underlying issue presented by the facts here, whether plaintiff/payor can recover from defendant the value of the cashed checks, stolen from defendant and drawn on a closed account, is based in the law of commercial paper. Allegations of negligence are relevant only as far as the Uniform Commercial Code addresses negligence in connection with stolen checks and forged or unauthorized signatures. Thus, any argument based on plaintiff's comparative negligence is irrelevant.

The Uniform Commercial Code protects the rights of a holder in due course. A holder in due course is one who takes an instrument for value, in good faith, and without notice that it is overdue or has been dishonored or of any defense against or claim to it on the part of any person. N.J.S.A. 12A:3-302. If an individual qualifies as a holder in due course, the instrument is taken free from all claims to it on the part of any person and all defenses of any party to the instrument with whom the holder has not dealt, with certain stated exceptions. N.J.S.A. 12A:3-305. The rule only accepts certain defenses, known as real defenses, as enforceable against a holder in due course in the absence of estoppel.

Plaintiff is a holder in due course in the case presented here. Plaintiff took the checks for value by paying out the full amount of each check to the named payees. What defendants chose to characterize as plaintiff's comparative negligence, may be considered, (under the terms of the UCC), as a lack of good faith, which would prevent plaintiff from qualifying as a holder in due course.

Defendant alleges that plaintiff did not apply the usual commercial standards in conducting his business, because he did not call the Hudson County Probation Department to verify the check prior to cashing it.

Good faith means honesty in fact in the conduct or transaction concerned. N.J.S.A. 12A:1-201(19). Plaintiff testified that his customary practice is not to call to verify each check because of the volume of checks cashed each month. Plaintiff maintains a listing of companies for whom he will cash checks, and verifies checks from unknown companies, usually by calling the payor/bank to verify that there are sufficient funds in the account. An additional criteria used by plaintiff, in determining whether to call the maker, is the size of the check, but plaintiff testified that the amounts here were not large enough to prompt him to call. I find that the customary practices of plaintiff constitute a showing of good faith.

"Good faith is determined by looking to the mind of the particular holder." *General Investment Corp. v. Angelini*, 58 N.J. 396, 403, 278 A.2d 193 (1971), citing New Jersey Study Comment 1B to N.J.S.A. 12A:3-302, at p. 134; *Breslin v. New Jersey Investors, Inc.*, 70 N.J. 466, 471, 361 A.2d 1 (1976). The study comment points out that most courts, including New Jersey's, have adopted the "white heart" test, where good faith is determined by looking to the state of mind of the particular holder who is claiming to be a holder in due course, not what the state of mind of a prudent man should have been. *Breslin, supra* at 471, 361 A.2d 1. "The test is neither freedom from negligence in entering into the transaction nor awareness of circumstances calculated to arouse suspicions either as to whether the instrument is subject to some defense not appearing on its face or whether the promise to pay is not as unconditional as it appears therein." *General Investment Corp., supra* 58 N.J. at 403, 278 A.2d 193, citing *Joseph v. Lesnevich*, 56 N.J.Super. 340, 348, 153 A.2d 349 (App. Div.1959). The test is a subjective standard, and given the above stated facts, there is no evidence presented which indicates that plaintiff was aware or even had any reason at all to suspect that a fraud was being perpetrated.

Defendant argues that the face of the checks themselves should have put plaintiff on notice that the checks were forgeries. As examples of the differences in the forged checks from real checks, defendant points to the signature stamp of an unknown person, that the check is completed by a typewriter and not the normal computer generated print, and that the signature is not printed in tricolor as with the authentic checks of the department. Defendant testified that because plaintiff had cashed Hudson County Probation Department checks in the past, these differences should have been noticed.

I find that plaintiff's having cashed Hudson County Probation Department checks in the past is evidence of plaintiff's good faith belief in the authenticity of these checks, rather than proof that plaintiff had constructive notice of the forgeries. The Uniform Commercial Code states that a purchaser is on notice of a claim or defense to the instrument if it is "so incomplete, bears such visible evidence of forgery or alteration, or is otherwise so irregular as to call into question its validity, terms or ownership." N.J.S.A. 12A:3-304. While I do not doubt that the differences cited by defendant in the forged checks were obvious and apparent to the payor, I find that they are not of such significance on the face of the checks as to alert one who sees thousands of different checks per month, in possibly equally as many different forms. It is unreasonable to hold plaintiff to remember the named signature on the check or the type or color of print. Given all of the above, I find that plaintiff is entitled to the rights of a holder in due course.

Accordingly, in finding that plaintiff has the status of a holder in due course, I find that under several provisions of the Uniform Commercial Code defendant is liable plaintiff. Generally stated, and most simply, if plaintiff is a holder in due course, the defense of theft must fail. N.J.S.A. 12A:3-305 and 3-306(d); *O.P. Ganjo, Inc. v. Tri-Urban Realty Co., Inc.*, 108 N.J.Super. 517, 522-23, 261 A.2d 722 (Law Div.1969).

N.J.S.A. 12A:3-115, addressing incomplete instruments states: "(2) If the completion is unauthorized, the rules as to material alteration apply (12A:3-407), even though the paper was not delivered by the maker or drawer."

N.J.S.A. 12A:3-407(1)(b) defines the unauthorized completion of an incomplete instrument as a material alteration. The rule further states: "(3) A subsequent holder in due course may in all cases enforce the instrument according to its original tenor, and when an incomplete instrument has been completed, he [sic] may enforce it as completed."

"A holder in due course sees and takes the same paper, whether it was complete when stolen or completed afterward by the thief, and in each case, he [*sic*] relies in good faith on the maker's signature. The loss should fall upon the party whose conduct in signing blank paper has made the fraud possible, rather than upon the innocent purchaser." Uniform Commercial Code Comment 5 to N.J.S.A. 12A: 3-115.

Additionally, the Code provides that [a]ny person who by his [*sic*] negligence substantially contributes to a material alteration of the instrument or to the making of an unauthorized signature is precluded from asserting the alteration or lack of authority against a holder in due course or against a drawee or other payor who pays the instrument in good faith and in accordance with the reasonable commercial standards of the drawee's or payor's business. [N.J.S.A. 12A:3-406.]

Defendant argues that plaintiff's actions did not constitute reasonable commercial standards, but as I found above, plaintiff's actions were reasonable and in good faith. I find that to require plaintiff to verify every check, by calling every maker prior to cashing every check, would be commercially unreasonable and unduly burdensome. Nothing about the subject checks alerted plaintiff otherwise.

Defendant argues that plaintiff has not proven gross negligence, and if defendant was negligent, it was only simple negligence. The language of N.J.S.A. 12A:3-406 does not support a distinction between gross and simple negligence. The phrase used in the statute, "substantially contributes," is plainly read to be a substantial contribution to the forgery rather than the negligence that must be substantial. *Gast v. American Casualty Company of Reading, Pennsylvania*, 99 N.J.Super. 538, 543, 240 A.2d 682 (App.Div.1968). "The phrase 'substantially contributes' indicates causal relationship and is the equivalent of the 'substantial factor' test applied in the law of negligence generally." *Id.* at 544, 240 A.2d 682. What constitutes negligence depends upon the facts of each particular case. "The most obvious case is that of the drawer who makes use of a signature stamp or other automatic signing device and is negligent in looking after it." Uniform Commercial Code Comment 7 to N.J.S.A. 12A: 3-406.

I find the facts presented here to be equally obvious in showing defendant's negligence, as it applies under N.J.S.A. 12A:3-406 to bar defendant's assertions of unauthorized signatures and alterations of the checks. Defendant's actions, in not shredding the checks for several months and leaving the blank checks in a place where they were accessible to the public, are dispositive of defendant's negligence in contributing to the theft. Defendant could have (and should have) easily locked the door to the mailroom when the room was unattended. Consequently, defendant's negligence substantially contributed to the theft, and thus, they are precluded from asserting the defense of forgery.

Defendant relies on the case of *Brogan Cadillac-Oldsmobile Corp. v. The Central Jersey Bank and Trust Company*, 183 N.J.Super. 333, 443 A.2d 1108 (Law Div.1981), aff'd 190 N.J.Super. 500, 464 A.2d 1141 (App.Div.1983). The Court held in *Brogan* that where checks were stolen from a bank vault and there was no evidence of negligence on the part of defendant/bank, the statute (N.J.S.A. 12A:3-406) did not apply. I find the present case factually distinguishable from *Brogan*.

In *Brogan*, the checks were stored in a bank vault, which was not located in an area open to the public and where only a limited number of people were authorized to enter. The checks were drawn on a different bank and were mainly used by defendant bank for the payment of certain obligations. Defendant bank learned that two checks had been cashed in another area of the state, and thereafter discovered that a total of 22 prenumbered checks were missing from the vault. Neither the bank nor the police were able to ascertain how the checks came to be missing. The Court based its holding on the belief that it would be unjust to require one to anticipate that a crime will be committed unless there has been a warning or previous criminal act on the premises. *Id.* at 336, 443 A.2d 1108. *Brogan* found that the conduct of defendant bank was outside the law's conception of fault. Since there was no clear evidence that the stolen check was ever in the hands of the bank officials, and it was just as likely that the checks were stolen prior to being delivered to the defendant bank, the facts did not support a conclusion of negligence and the statute did not apply. *Id.* at 338, 443 A.2d 1108.

Here, the conduct of defendant supports a conclusion of fault on the part of defendant. The facts show that the checks were in defendant's possession after the account had been closed and support a finding that they were stolen from defendant. The testimony was uncontested that the checks were stolen from the unlocked mailroom. All of the sections of the Uniform Commercial Code cited above support the conclusion that plaintiff, as a holder in due course, is entitled to payment.

Defendant also argues that it is not liable based on the principles of the New Jersey Tort Claims Act, N.J.S.A. 59:1-1 to 59:12-3, but I find that in this case the Tort Claims Act does not bar the action. "Nothing in this act shall affect liability based on contract . . . against the public entity or one of its employees." N.J.S.A. 59:1-4. As stated above, I find that this was an issue based on contract concepts and the Uniform Commercial Code.

Accordingly, I find judgment for the plaintiff for $908 plus interest and costs.

Glossary

Allonge - Separate document used for indorsements

Bearer - Anyone who has possession of a negotiable instrument

Collection guarantor - Person who guarantees payment on a negotiable instrument

Commercial paper - Negotiable instrument

Dishonor - To refuse to pay the face amount of a check or the amount due on a promissory note

Draft - Three-party negotiable instrument

Drawee - Person who promises to pay on a draft

Drawer - Person who creates a draft

Holder - Person with possession of a negotiable instrument

Holder in due course (HDC) - Holder who takes for value, in good faith, and without notice of any claim against the note

Indorse - Sign the instrument to transfer it

Indorser - Person who transfers by his or her signature a negotiable instrument

Maker - Creator of a note

Meddling stranger - Third person who interferes with a commercial paper

Negotiation - Give-and-take discussion or conference in an attempt to reach an agreement or settle a dispute

Negotiable instrument - Cash substitute

Note - Two-party instrument

Order to pay - Made payable to a specific person

Payee - One who receives the money under a negotiable instrument

Payment guarantor - Person who promises payment of a negotiable instrument if dishonored

Presentment - Making a demand for payment of a promissory note when it is due

Promise to pay - An unconditional obligation to perform

Shelter rule - Transferee takes the status of the transferor

Subject to - Referring to the acquisition of title to real property upon which there is an existing mortgage or deed of trust when the new owner agrees to take title with the responsibility to continue to make payments on the promissory note secured by the mortgage or deed of trust

Sum certain - A specific amount stated in a contract or negotiable instrument at the time the document is written

Unconditional - All of the terms of the payment must appear on the face of the instrument itself

Exercises

1. Discuss the importance of the use of negotiable instruments to commercial enterprises.

2. Give three examples of *value* that can be used by a person to become an HDC.

3. Indicate some problems that might be encountered with the use of bearer instruments.

4. Discuss why the drawee is not held primarily liable to the payee of a draft.

5. Discuss the difference between a transfer and a presentment.

Chapter Five

REAL PROPERTY

Introduction

Property law has often been called a bundle of rights. This bundle forms one of the three most fundamental components of the modern legal system. Along with contract and tort law, the doctrines under the heading of property form the basis of most other legal concepts. Consequently, an understanding of the principles of property law is necessary to gain an understanding of law as a whole.

Property law is divided into two distinct areas: **real property**, the rules of law concerned with land and anything that is permanently affixed to the land, and **personal property**, which is defined as all nonreal property, such as jewelry, furniture, clothes, equipment, tools, stocks and bonds, etc.

This chapter will examine those areas of real property law that directly apply to the creation and operation of commercial enterprises. To this end, emphasis will be placed on estates in land, fixtures, conveyancing, mortgages, landlord-tenant and third-party rights with respect to the use and possession of the land.

Estates in Land

The term **estate** refers to a possessory interest in a parcel of realty. There are two distinct categories of estates: freeholds and leaseholds. A **freehold** estate is one in which the titleholder holds the property for an indefinite period of time. A **leasehold** estate is one in which the person holds the property for a definite period of time as described in a contract called a **lease**. Leaseholds will be discussed later in the chapter.

Freehold estates are also divided into two broad categories: fees and life estates. A **fee**, or **fee simple absolute**, is the highest estate recognized by the law. A fee holder has the right to sell, divide, gift, or will his or her interest in the property, and the property is subject to the claims of the fee holder's creditors. Further, the estate is held for an indefinite period of time. A life estate, the second category of freehold, is an estate that is held only during the estate holder's life or the life of another person designated in the **title**. In addition, the estate holder's ability to alienate the estate is limited to the rights and interests that can be transferred during the tenant's life or the lifetime of the measuring life. Any person who holds an interest in property is referred to as a **tenant**, derived from the French term *tenir*, meaning "to hold," and the type of tenancy the person has is dependent upon the nature of the estate.

There are six types of fee simple estates:

1. **Tenancy in severalty**. This type of estate is a fee simple estate that is held by just one person. As stated above, it is the highest form of property ownership that exists under the law.

> *Example:* A land developer buys five acres of land on which the developer intends to build several homes. At the present time, the developer is the only owner, so the developer has the title as a tenancy in severalty.

2. **Tenancy in common.** This type of estate is a fee estate that is held by two or more persons collectively. Each tenant in common holds a divisible interest in the property, has the right to alienate his or her portion of the property, and shares the right of possession equally with the other co-tenants. Although the tenants have the equal right of possession, they do not necessarily own an equal share of the property; the co-tenants may own differing percentages of the fee. Further, a tenancy in common may be created over time—it does not need to be created at the same moment.

> *Example:* The developer from the previous example decides to sell interests in the property in order to raise cash to construct the homes. The developer sells one-quarter interests to two friends. The developer has now created a tenancy in common, the developer owning a 50% interest and each of the friends owning a 25% interest. Despite the different percentage interests in the property, each of the tenants has an equal right of possession to the entire property.

3. **Joint tenancy.** A joint tenancy is a fee estate that is held by two or more persons collectively, but unlike a tenancy in common, there are certain requirements necessary to create the estate. The requirements to create a joint tenancy are referred to as the **four unities** of time, title, interest, and possession. This means that all of the joint tenants must acquire equal rights to the property with the same title under the same instrument and have equal rights of possession. Unlike the tenancy in common, the joint tenant's interest is nondivisible, and there is a right of survivorship in the remaining joint tenants. A joint tenant may alienate his or her interest during his or her lifetime but cannot will his or her interest. At death, the joint tenant's interest passes automatically by operation of law to the surviving joint tenants (the right of survivorship), and this occurs until there is only one joint tenant left who holds the title as a tenancy in severalty. Any attempt to alienate a joint tenancy during the joint tenant's life destroys the joint tenancy with respect to the portion so alienated, and a tenancy in common is thereby created. If two or more persons acquire property together and do not specify a title, the law assumes a tenancy in common because it is more beneficial for the parties, permitting the free alienation of each divisible portion.

> *Example:* Two brothers decide to buy an apartment building as an investment. When they make the purchase, they indicate that they will hold title as joint tenants. Several years later they begin to disagree, and one of the brothers sells his interest to an outsider. This sale destroys the joint tenancy, and a tenancy in common is thereby created with the remaining brother and the outsider. However, if the dissatisfied brother had only started to negotiate with the outsider when he suddenly died, the remaining brother would automatically inherit the deceased brother's interest. The joint tenant may not will the interest away.

4. **Tenancy by the entirety.** In many jurisdictions that do not have **community property** (see below), this form of title exists for legally married couples. A tenancy by the entirety is similar to a joint tenancy with the addition of a fifth requirement of a valid marriage. Unlike a joint tenancy in which a joint tenant may alienate his or her interest during life, thereby extinguishing the joint tenancy, one spouse is incapable of alienating his or her interest without the other spouse's consent. Upon the death of the first spouse, the entire property passes to the survivor as a tenancy in severalty. In jurisdictions that permit this form of estate, if a married couple acquires property and fails to designate a title, the law will assume a tenancy by the entirety because it is more favorable to the parties.

> *Example:* *A husband and wife decide to purchase a candy store as a family business. When they buy the store they indicate that they are holding the property as a tenancy by the entirety. When they start to disagree about the business, neither one alone is able to sell off his or her interest; the couple must join in the sale.*

5. **Community property.** Nine jurisdictions in the United States, primarily in the West and Southwest, allow for community property, a title afforded to property acquired by a legally married couple during the marriage. Community property differs from a tenancy by the entirety in that with community property each spouse is deemed to own one-half of the property outright and there is no automatic right of survivorship in the surviving spouse. In the states that have community property, if no title is indicated by the couple, community property ownership is assumed.

> *Example:* *A married couple in New Mexico, a community property state, purchases an apartment building during their marriage as an investment. Each spouse is deemed the owner of one-half of the building. The wife decides to give up the investment and sells her share to her son. The father and son now own the property as tenants in common.*

6. **Tenancy in partnership.** This form of title was created exclusively for business partnerships (see Chapter Eight). If the business partners do not specify a different form of ownership, all business property acquired by the business is deemed to be held in tenancy in partnership, and as such has the following attributes:
   - No one partner may possess the business property for other than business purposes without the other partner's consent.
   - No one partner can sell the business property (a nonbusiness sale) without the other partner's consent.
   - The individual creditors of each partner may not attach such property to satisfy the personal obligations of the partner/debtor.
   - The property itself passes by operation of law to the surviving partners at a partner's death, but the surviving partners must pay the deceased partner's heirs the value of the deceased partner's interest in the property so acquired.

> **Example:** *A brother and sister, both attorneys, decide to form a law practice as partners. All of the property they acquire for the law firm is held as a tenancy in partnership, and when the brother dies, his interest in the property automatically passes to his sister.*

These last five types of fee estates are referred to as **concurrent estates** because more than one individual holds them. As stated above, the law automatically applies several forms of the concurrent titles if the parties themselves do not specify a different form of title. However, all persons are free to indicate the specific title they wish to attach to the realty, and that title will generally prevail.

If two or more persons acquire a concurrent title to property that they wish to change, they may do so by the legal convention of transferring the title to a third person, known as a **straw man**, who will then immediately convey the property back to the people under the title they wish to use. Note that many jurisdictions have, by statute, eliminated the need to use a straw man, and a titleholder may transfer his or her title to him or herself and another as a joint tenancy. If the co-tenants cannot agree on a different title and no longer wish to own the property together, they may petition the court to **partition**, or judicially divide, the property into tenancies in severalty for each of the tenants.

> **Example:** *Two cousins inherit a tract of land from their grandmother as joint tenants. One cousin wants to use the land as a private home, the other wants to use the property for commercial development. They cannot agree, and neither wants to buy the other out, so they petition the court to partition the property into two equal portions that they can now hold as individual owners. If they could have agreed by themselves, they could have used a straw man to effectuate this change.*

Life estates are also divided into two categories: regular **life estates**, in which the life tenant holds the property only during his or her life, and **life estate** *pur autre vie*, in which the tenant holds the title to the property only during the life of another person, referred to as the **measuring life**.

> **Example:** *A woman inherits a farm from her deceased husband for the remainder of her life, and then the farm goes to their children. The woman no longer wishes to farm the land and wants to travel the world. Her neighbor has always wanted to buy the farm to increase his acreage and is willing to buy the widow's interest in the property. The woman has inherited a regular life estate; when she sells her interest to the neighbor, the neighbor has acquired a life estate* pur autre vie—*he may use the property only during the widow's lifetime; at her death the title to the farm goes to the children.*

At the termination of the life estate, the property will either revert to the **grantor**, the person who transferred and created the life estate, known as a **reversion**, or will pass to a different individual who is considered to have a **remainder interest**. It is possible to have multiple successive life estates but eventually the title must pass to a fee interest.

> **Example:** In the previous example, the widow is the life tenant and the children have the remainder interest. In this instance, there can be no reversion, because the grantor is deceased.

A life estate is considered to be a freehold estate because it is of uncertain duration (life is uncertain), but the rights of the life tenant are more circumscribed than are those of a fee holder. A life tenant may make any ordinary use and profit from the land but is precluded from doing anything to the property that would destroy the interest of the remainderman. This potential injury to subsequent interest holders is known as **waste**. There are four types of waste recognized under the law.

1. **Voluntary waste** occurs when the life tenant actually engages in conduct that lessens the value of the property. Examples would be knocking down a building on the property so that the life tenant can have a better view. With respect to certain income-producing rights that attach to the land, such as mineral rights, oil, timber, etc. the life tenant may make any ordinary profit from the exploitation of these assets but may not totally strip the land of value to the detriment of the remainderman. An exception exists if the only use to which the land can be put is exploitation.

2. **Permissive waste** occurs when the life tenant simply permits the property to become run down by failing to preserve the property. No deliberate action on the part of the life tenant that diminishes the value of the property is permitted. Life tenants are also under a legal obligation to maintain the land and structures thereon in a reasonable state of repair and are required to pay ordinary taxes on the property, as well as all current mortgage payments (see below).

3. **Ameliorative waste** is any act that benefits the land but may be against the wishes of the remainderman. Examples of ameliorative waste would be the construction of additional buildings on the property or the expansion of existing roads. The courts rarely hold the life tenant financially liable for this type of waste unless the remainderman can demonstrate that the change may reduce the ultimate value of the property.

4. **Equitable waste** results from the life tenant failing to exercise good husbandry with respect to the property. Good husbandry refers to using the soil and natural resources in a manner that preserves its value. An example would be crop rotation to maintain the mineral content of the soil. This form of waste is rarely litigated and is usually encompassed in either voluntary or permissive waste.

The foregoing titles (legal interests) are usually specified with respect to realty; however, the businessperson must be alert to the fact that these titles, as well as the leaseholds apply to interests in personal property as well, with all of the indicated rights and obligations.

Fixtures

Real property law refers to land and anything permanently affixed to the land. The most common type of property that is permanently affixed to land is a building, which, under American law, is deemed to be part of the land itself. However, personal property, referred to as **chattels**, may be attached to buildings and, dependent upon how they are attached and the purpose for which they are attached, may have the effect of changing the property's attribute from that of personalty to a fixture. This concept becomes increasingly important when one realizes that if the item is a fixture, it follows the title of the land and may not be removed by the person who affixed it. When the item so attached is deemed to become integrated with the building, it is called a **fixture** and is treated like realty.

An item is considered to be a fixture if the intent of the party who attached the item is to incorporate the chattel into the realty. The determination is usually made by the nature of the chattel, the manner in which the item is attached, the amount of damage that would be caused by its removal, and the manner in which the item is adapted to the use of the realty.

> *Example:* *A land developer constructs a tract of suburban homes. The developer used plywood and then covered the floors with wall-to-wall carpeting. Because the carpeting, which is chattel, has been totally integrated into the structure, it is now deemed to be a fixture and cannot be removed by a purchaser of the home when that person subsequently resells the house.*

A special problem exists in this area with respect to commercial enterprises. Many businesses require special types of chattels to be installed in furtherance of their business objectives, items that are attached to the property for a commercial use rather than in furtherance of the building's value. These types of fixtures are referred to as **trade fixtures**, and the commercial tenant is permitted to remove such items at the termination of his or her interest in the property. However, if the commercial tenant fails to remove the trade fixture within a reasonable time after his or her interest has expired, that item becomes a regular fixture and is thereafter deemed to be part of the realty. Also, if the item could not be easily removed without damaging the building, it becomes a part of the realty.

> *Example:* *A woman purchases some property to open an art gallery. She installs track lighting to showcase the work she intends to sell. Several years later when she decides to relocate and sell the store, she takes the lighting with her. Because these lights were added for a commercial purpose, they are trade fixtures and may be removed.*

Conveyancing

Conveyancing is the legal term employed to denote the transfer of real property from the transferor (**grantor**) to the transferee (**grantee**). To effectuate a lawful conveyance of realty, certain requirements must be met. Although there may be slight variations in the requirements in particular jurisdictions (each jurisdiction's procedures must be individually scrutinized), the same general process is used throughout the country.

To convey an interest in real property, the conveyance must be in writing to be enforceable. As discussed in Chapter Three, an interest in realty is one of the items covered by the Statute of Frauds. In order to meet the requirements of the Statute of Frauds, thereby giving the parties enforceable rights, the conveyance must be in writing, signed by the party to be charged, and must contain certain enumerated items of the transfer: the parties, the price, and a description of the land. These items appear in the contract for the sale of the land.

In many jurisdictions, once the contract is signed the risk of the loss or destruction of the property passes to the grantee under a concept called the **doctrine of equitable conversion**. Pursuant to this doctrine, the grantee is considered to be the owner of the realty, and the grantor is now deemed to be the owner of the proceeds of the sale. If the property is destroyed, under this doctrine, the grantee is still obligated to complete the sale.

Some jurisdictions have adopted the **Uniform Vendors' and Purchasers' Risk Act**, which changes the common law doctrine of equitable conversion. Under this act, the risk of loss remains with the seller-grantor until the buyer-grantee pays for the property or acquires title to the property. The grantee's possession of the property alone is insufficient to transfer the risk of loss, although possession with something else, such as making improvements on the property or actually inhabiting it, may operate to transfer the risk.

The determination of who bears the risk of loss affects whether or not a party should obtain insurance on the property.

> *Example:* An alcohol manufacturer sells one of his factories to a competitor. The parties have contracted for the sale but have not yet closed (see below). Before the closing, there is an explosion in the factory and it is totally destroyed. Under the doctrine of equitable conversion, the buyer bears the risk of loss and must still pay for the factory. Under the Uniform Vendors' and Purchasers' Risk Act, the risk has not yet transferred, and the loss is on the original owner and the buyer can avoid the contract.

Closing refers to the moment when the sales contract provisions are fulfilled and the **deed**, the document indicating the title to real property, is transferred to the grantee. All contracts for the sale of land include a **warranty of marketability,** that the grantor has a title sufficient to provide a marketable title to the grantee at the closing. Marketable title demands that the grantor have a title to the property that is free from any present or foreseeable litigation. A title would be considered unmarketable if there is
- a defect in the chain of title (see below) indicating that the grantor may not be the titleholder
- a claim of **adverse possession** exists with respect to the property. Adverse possession refers to the situation in which a person other than the titleholder has **actual possession** of the property in a manner that is open, notorious, and against the interests of the true titleholder. Each jurisdiction has a statutorily determined period of years specified which, if met by the adverse possessor, operates to transfer title to the possessor away from the titleholder. The adverse possessor can solidify the title by initiating an action to **quiet title** with the court. The titleholder, if the statutory period has not expired, may oust the adverse possessor by initiating an action for **ejection**.
- an **encumbrance** on the property, such as a mortgage, liens, easements, or any other significant encroachments to the complete and unfettered use of the property
- a zoning violation on the property. Note that a zoning restriction (see below) does not affect marketability, only existing violations of such restrictions affect title.

The grantor must be able to provide a marketable title at the closing; if the grantor cannot present marketable title at the closing, the grantor will be deemed to be in breach of contract, entitling the injured grantee to contractual remedies (see Chapter Three).

At the closing, the grantor transfers the property's deed to the grantee. To have an effective transfer, the deed must be delivered by the grantor and accepted by the grantee. The grantor must indicate a present intent to deliver the deed, although actual physical transfer is not necessary. Once the deed is delivered, the grantor is precluded from revoking the transfer.

The deed is considered transferred when it is delivered to the grantee or to a third person that is the agent of the grantee. Note that delivery to an agent of the grantor with instructions to complete the delivery may not be considered a completed delivery. The acceptance on the part of the grantee usually determines when the delivery has been made.

Generally, there are three types of deeds in common use; however, it is always wise to check the jurisdiction for that jurisdiction's peculiarities with respect to deeds for property located within its borders. The laws of the states in which the property is situated always control real property transfers.

All modern deeds are considered to be **bargain and sale deeds**, even if the transfer is effectuated by a gift. There are three types of deeds in general use:

1. **General warranty deed**. This type of deed conveys the property with the following covenants, or guarantees:
    - **Covenant of seisin**. The grantee warrants that he or she has the type of title that he or she is purporting to transfer.
    - **Covenant of right to convey**. The grantor warrants that he or she has the legal ability to transfer the property.
    - **Covenant against encumbrances**. The grantor warrants that there are no encumbrances on the property.
    - **Covenant for quiet enjoyment**. The grantor warrants that the grantee's possession will not be disturbed by a lawful claim to the property by a third person.
    - **Covenant of warranty**. The grantor warrants that he or she will defend against the claims of third parties to the property.
    - **Covenant for further assurances**. The grantor promises to do whatever is necessary to protect the title being conveyed.

Collectively, these six warranties are known as the **usual covenants**. The first three are called the present covenants because they exist at the time the deed is transferred and, if they are not breached at that time, they are extinguished. The last three covenants are known as future covenants because they survive the transfer of the deed.

2. **Special warranty deed**. This type of deed, created by state law, has two limited warranties: the grantor has not conveyed the estate to anyone other than the grantee and the estate is free from any encumbrances arising out of, from, or through the grantor.

3. **Quitclaim deed**. This deed purports to transfer whatever interest the grantor has, but no warranties or covenants are made with respect to that interest. With a quitclaim deed, the grantee has no recourse against the grantor provided that the grantor did in fact convey whatever interest the grantor had.

Transfers of real property are recorded in the county recorder's office in the county in which the property is located. Under the common law, if a grantor conveyed the property multiple times,

the first grantee in time prevailed over the subsequent transferees and was considered to be the legitimate titleholder. Today, every jurisdiction has enacted recording statutes to specify which grantee would prevail in a case of multiple conveyances. The three types of recording statutes in use (each jurisdiction must be individually checked) are:
1. **notice statutes**. A later grantee may prevail over an earlier grantee if the later grantee gave consideration for the transfer and had no actual or constructive notice of a previous conveyance.
2. **race-notice statutes**. A subsequent purchaser for value prevails only if he or she had no notice of an earlier conveyance and was the first to record the deed at the recorder's office.
3. **race statutes**. The first to record prevails, regardless of notice. Only two states have race statutes.

In order to determine whether the grantor has a valid title to the property, the potential purchaser must perform a **title search** to check the chain of conveyances as they appear in the county recorder's office. There are two methods utilized for recording title to realty. The **block and lot**, or **tract index**, in which deeds and conveyances are recorded according to the description of the land, or the **grantor-grantee index**, in which deeds and conveyances are recorded according to the names of the transferring parties.

Every jurisdiction uses one of these methods of recordation. To protect oneself against problems with titles, most purchasers acquire **title insurance** that will compensate them for any damage suffered because of a faulty conveyance due to a title problem.

Mortgages

Few individuals or businesses purchase land on a completely cash basis, putting up the full purchase price from their own funds on the day of closing. Most persons acquire real property by financing the transaction—obtaining loans from banks and other financial institutions. For commercial enterprises, utilizing a loan to make such acquisitions is extremely beneficial, not only for the obvious reason of enabling the enterprise to purchase additional property, but also for the tax benefits that can accrue and the ability of the enterprise to maintain sufficient cash reserves on hand.

When a financial institution advances funds for the purchase of property, it usually requires some **security**, or **collateral**, that it can attach in case the debtor defaults on the loan. This security interest reduces the risk of default for the lender, and when encountered in a real estate transaction, it is usually referred to as a **mortgage**.

Generally defined, a mortgage is a security interest in property used to secure a loan for the purchase of realty. The borrower, the one who is purchasing the property, gives this security interest, or mortgage, to the lender. For the purposes of the mortgage, the debtor-borrower is called the **mortgagor**, and the creditor-lender is called the **mortgagee**. The mortgage is a separate document from the underlying loan, but the mortgage follows the loan, meaning that they are intertwined.

Both parties to the mortgage are permitted to alienate, or assign, their interests. If the mortgagee assigns the right to receive the interest and principle on the loan, the mortgage, or security interest, will automatically follow the note and become the right of the assignee (see Chapter Three). If the mortgagor transfers his or her interest, the grantee takes that interest **subject to the mortgage**—meaning that the original mortgagor remains principally liable on the note. Should the original mortgagor default, the mortgagee may attach the property to satisfy the debt. Conversely, if the grantee **assumes the mortgage**, the grantee becomes primarily liable on the note, and the original mortgagor becomes a surety on the obligation. When the mortgage is assumed, the grantee has less risk of having the property taken away through no fault of his or her own.

If the mortgagor defaults on the loan, the mortgagee is entitled to two types of relief. The mortgagee can sue the mortgagor in an action based on the default of the underlying note, or, if the mortgagor has insufficient funds to satisfy the debt, the mortgagee can foreclose on the property. To **foreclose** on the property means that it is sold at public auction to satisfy the loan obligation. If the proceeds of sale are insufficient to meet the outstanding loan obligation, the mortgagee may sue the mortgagor for the deficiency between the proceeds of the sale and the remaining debt (if the sale brings in more than the debt, the excess belongs to the mortgagor).

When the mortgagor defaults, the mortgagee must select one of the two foregoing procedures to satisfy the debt. The mortgagee may not institute an action for debt and an action to foreclose at the same time.

The mortgagor may forestall the public sale of the property any time up to the sale under the equitable right of **redemption**, *i.e.*, paying off the outstanding debt to the mortgagee. About half of the states also provide for a **statutory right of redemption,** which permits the mortgagor to redeem the property for a period of time after the public foreclosure sale; a statute sets the time period.

Be aware that a commercial enterprise may be either a mortgagor or a mortgagee in any given situation.

Landlord-Tenant Law

The second major category of estates in land is the leasehold. Under a leasehold, the tenant has a present possessory interest in the property and the landlord has a reversion in the possessory right. The title respecting the ownership of the property remains in the landlord.

Most leaseholds are created by means of a written contract called a **lease**, which is a regular contract in which the subject matter, or consideration, is the possessory interest in realty. The landlord is known as the **lessor**, and the tenant is known as the **lessee**. There are four main types of landlord-tenant relationships:

1. **Tenancy for years**. These tenancies are created by written leases that automatically terminate at the dates specified in the agreements. In these leases, the lessor retains the right of entry in the premises that permits the lessor to terminate the lease for breach of a covenant, such as failure to pay rent or not maintaining the premises as agreed to in the lease.
2. **Periodic tenancy**. These tenancies are for successive periods, such as month-to-month, or year-to-year, and may be created by an express agreement or by implication if the lessor rents the property for a rent of $500 payable monthly, or by operation of law if the tenant remains in possession after the lease terminates (see below).
3. **Tenancy at will**. These tenancies are created by express agreement and can be terminated at any time by either party.
4. **Tenancy at sufferance**. These tenancies arise when a lessee unlawfully remains in possession after the expiration of a lawful tenancy. The tenancy remains in effect until

the lessor attempts to evict the lessee. No notice of termination is required with this type of tenancy.

If a tenant remains in possession of the property after the termination of the lease, the lessor may either evict the tenant or bind the tenant to a new periodic tenancy that is determined by the terms of the expired tenancy. This right of the lessor is called the **holdover doctrine**. If the lessor notifies the holdover tenant that the tenant will be permitted to remain at an increased rent, the increased rent is binding even if the tenant objected, provided that the tenant remains in possession.

Once a valid landlord-tenant relationship has been formed, the tenant assumes the following duties:
- The tenant must maintain the premises in good repair and, similar to a life estate discussed above, may not commit waste on the property. If the tenant has specifically contracted to make repairs under the lease, the duty to repair is higher than the obligation of ordinary maintenance and may include the obligation to reconstruct the premises if they are destroyed. If the property is destroyed without fault of either party, absent an agreement or statute to the contrary, neither side has a duty to reconstruct, but the tenant remains obligated for the rent until the termination of the lease.

Example: *An office building in Florida is destroyed by a hurricane. The landlord has not agreed to reconstruct the building and, in fact, wishes to sell the property. The tenant must continue to pay rent until the lease terminates.*

- The tenant is precluded from using the premises for an illegal purpose.

Example: *A man rents an office and uses it to operate a gambling operation. The tenant is in violation of the lease and may be evicted.*

- The tenant is obligated to pay the agreed-upon rent. If the tenant fails to pay the rent, the landlord may elect to evict the tenant or may sue the tenant for the rent arrears.

Example: *A doctor has failed to pay the rent on her office for the past three months. The landlord may either evict her or sue her for the back rent.*

If the tenant unjustifiably abandons the property, the landlord is still entitled to rent from that tenant, although many jurisdictions now require the landlord to attempt to mitigate damages by finding a new lessee. If the tenant surrenders the leasehold to the lessor, the rent obligation remains intact until the surrender.

The landlord owes several duties to the lawful tenant. The landlord must deliver possession of the premises to the lessee; this must be actual possession, meaning that there can be no other party with a possessory interest or in possession at the start of the lease. The landlord impliedly contracts that the lessee will have quiet enjoyment of the premises. If the lessor excludes the lessee from the premises, it is deemed to be an **actual eviction**, and the lessee's rent obligation is thereby terminated. If the tenant is excluded from a portion of the leased premises, it is deemed to be a **partial eviction**, which also terminates the rent obligation even though the tenant retains possession of the residue of the premises. If the lessor does something that renders the premises uninhabitable, this is considered to be a **constructive eviction**, and the tenant may end the lease and sue for damages. Be aware that services that are the obligations of a landlord for residential leases differ from the obligations of a landlord for commercial leases. Many services are the obligations of the commercial tenant, and the landlord's failure to provide such services does not constitute a constructive eviction. The landlord is obligated under an **implied warranty of habitability** for residential leases, and the warranty is nonwaivable.

> *Example:* A designer has entered into a lease to rent a studio and showroom space for five years from a commercial landlord. On the day that the lease is to start, the designer discovers that the prior tenant is still in possession and has no immediate plans to vacate. Under these circumstances, the landlord is considered to have breached the lease agreement and may be deemed to have evicted the designer.

> *Example:* The designer is now in possession of the leased premises and, after several weeks, is served with a summons from the city for failing to provide for trash removal. The designer thought that the landlord is responsible for such services even though the lease was silent on this point; however, cartage (the term for such services) is the responsibility of the commercial tenant, and the designer is liable to the city.

Unless there is a special agreement to the contrary, both parties are free to assign their interests. Note that an assignment of a lease is a transfer of the entire term remaining on that lease, and the assignee becomes primarily liable for the rent. If the tenant retains any part of the remaining lease, the transfer is a **sublease**, and the tenant remains liable to the landlord for the rent; the sublessee is liable to make rent payments to the tenant.

> *Example:* A lawyer rents an office in a commercial building. When she has three years left on the lease, she is offered a one-year teaching position to teach American law at the University of Madrid, so she wishes to sublease her office space. She finds another tenant for the one year, but when the landlord finds out, the landlord insists that the lawyer arrange to have the rent paid to him from her own checking account and make her own arrangement with the sublessee. In this fashion, the landlord is protected, and the risk falls to the sublessor/tenant. However, the landlord could agree to accept rent from the subtenant and, if the subtenant defaults the landlord may still seek the rent from the lawyer, who remains primarily liable on the lease.

If the leased property is condemned, the lease is terminated, as is the rent obligation. However, if the property is taken by the government for a temporary period, the tenant is still liable for the rent but is entitled to a portion of any consideration that the landlord may receive for such use by the government.

> *Example:* The city government wishes to expand an existing road and provide additional electric, gas, and telephone service to the area. To accomplish this, the city must evacuate the buildings in a two-block area until the work is completed, which should take two months. The commercial tenants in one of the buildings cannot use the premises but still must pay rent while the city performs its work. If the city compensates the landlord for the temporary taking, the tenants are entitled to a pro-rata share of such consideration.

Under the common law, a lessor had no duty to make the premises safe. However, under modern statutes there are several exceptions:

- *Latent defects.* If the landlord knows of a defect in the structure that is not readily ascertainable by a reasonable inspection, the landlord must disclose such defect to the tenant when the lease is entered into. The landlord has no duty to repair the defect.
- *Public use.* The landlord is liable for injuries to the general public if at the time of the lease the landlord knew of a dangerous condition on the premises, knew the general public would be using the premises, and failed to repair the defect.
- *Repair.* If the landlord undertakes the repair of the premises after the tenant takes possession, the landlord is liable for any injuries that result from failing to make such repairs properly.
- *Short-term furnished residences.* In this instance, the landlord is responsible for any defect that causes injury.

> *Example:* An entrepreneur rents an abandoned warehouse with the intention of using the facility for public conventions. The landlord is aware of the intended use but fails to alert the entrepreneur to the fact that there is a major structural problem with the roof, which is not visible. When the convention center opens, the roof collapses, injuring several dozen people. In this instance, the landlord will be held responsible for the injuries.

> *Example:* An apartment house owner rents furnished apartments on a monthly basis. A student rents one of the units for a semester (four months). After the student has been in the apartment for three weeks, the radiator pipe bursts, severely burning the student. The landlord is responsible for these injuries.

A tenant (and all other possessors of land) is under a legal obligation of care for persons who enter the leased property. Under the common law such persons were classified into three groups:

1. **Trespassers.** Persons who had no legal right to enter the land. The possessor of the land only had a duty to warn such persons of dangerous unnatural conditions.

> *Example:* A hitchhiker wanders on to the woodland owned by a paper manufacturer. The hitchhiker, not knowing the land, stumbles over a fallen log and falls down a ravine. The paper manufacturer is not liable for the injuries because the hitchhiker was a trespasser, and the injury resulted from a natural condition on the land.

2. **Licensees**. Persons who are social guests on the property to whom the possessor owes the duty of ordinary care.

> *Example:* A couple invites their families to come to their leased apartment for Thanksgiving dinner. The couple knows that the hinge on the closet door is broken but have not yet had a chance to repair it. On Thanksgiving Day, one of their cousins goes to put her coat in the closet, and the door falls on her. The couple had a duty to warn her of the defect and will be liable, even though she was a guest in their home.

3. **Invitees**. Persons who enter the premises for the business interest of the possessor, such as customers and clients, to whom the possessor owes a higher degree of care and who must be warned of latent defects that might cause injury.

> *Example:* A customer in a bar needs to use the restroom, which is down a long flight of stairs. The boards on the last three steps are loose. The tavern owner knows about the problem but has failed to post a sign. When the boards come loose, the customer falls down the steps and breaks his leg. The tavern owner is liable for the injuries to his invitee.

Under modern trends, persons entering on the land are owed a duty of ordinary care by the possessor of the land, the specifics of which are determined by state statute.

Third-party Rights

In addition to the person who has a title to the property, either as a freehold or leasehold, there are other persons who may be entitled to certain rights with respect to the land.

Easements

An **easement** is the right of one person to use or enter another person's property. Easements are created in one of the following ways:

- *Express grant* or *agreement*. The property holder specifically agrees that someone else may have access to the property. Because an easement is an interest in land, the agreement must be in writing to satisfy the Statute of Frauds.

> *Example:* The owner of a lakefront hotel agrees in writing that a homeowner who lives across the road may use the hotel's path to get to the lake. This is an easement created by agreement.

- *Implication*. This easement comes about by operation of law and is implied from the reasonable and necessary use of the easement holder, such as access to a main road.

> **Example:** *A land developer is constructing a housing subdivision. Until all of the homes are built and the roads constructed, some of the original homebuyers must cross other lots to gain access to the road into the subdivision. The homeowners whose land the other residents must travel are required to permit the use for access to the road.*

- *Necessity.* An easement may be created if access over an adjoining property is necessary for access to a public road.
- *Prescription.* This easement comes about in a manner similar to adverse possession, the difference being that with adverse possession the possessor acquires title to the property, whereas with an easement by prescription the easement holder acquires the right to enter and use a portion of the property.

> **Example:** *For more than ten years, a property owner has been crossing the undeveloped land of his neighbor to go to a local shopping center. When the neighbor suddenly decides to build a house on the property that would effectively stop this use, the long use the neighbor has made of the property may have given him as easement by prescription, thereby forestalling the property owner from doing any construction that would interfere with this use of the property.*

Easements are categorized by the nature of the use. An **easement appurtenant** arises when the subject land, known as the **servient tenement**, adjoins the land of the easement holder, known as the **dominant tenement**. An **easement in gross** is the right to use the land without possessing an adjacent tract, such as the right of the government to run cables and pipes on a person's property.

The agreement of the parties, the abandonment of the right by the easement holder, or the merger of the rights can terminate an easement when the easement holder and the property owner become the same person. Unless the easement holder agrees, an easement cannot be terminated by the person over whose property the easement lies, and the easement holder may prevent the property owner from doing anything that would interfere with the right to the easement.

> **Example:** *In the previous example, instead of constructing a house, the property owner decides to sell the land, and the neighbor who has the easement purchases it. Because the easement holder now owns the property, the easement is extinguished.*

Licenses

A **license** is a privilege granted by the landowner permitting someone to enter the land. The license, unlike an easement, may be ended at the will of the landowner, and the licensee cannot transfer the license. Note that the easement is transferable to anyone who acquires the property that has the easement right.

Profits

A **profit** is the right of a person to enter on the land of another person to remove resources such as timber, crops, etc., that are on the land. Profits are similar to licenses and are granted in the same manner but exist exclusively for the purpose of removing resources.

Example: A farmer has sold his entire corn crop to a breakfast food manufacturer. As part of the agreement, the manufacturer may enter the farm to harvest the crops. Once the crops are harvested, the profit no longer exists, and the manufacturer may not reenter the property without the farmer's consent.

Covenants running with the land

A **covenant running with the land** is a written promise from the property owner to do or not do something with respect to the use of the land. These covenants, known as **real covenants**, run with the land, meaning that they are enforceable against all subsequent owners of that property (the promise attaches to the land, not just the promissor). A covenant will be considered a real covenant if it is intended to run with the land and subsequent title holders have notice of the covenant. A real covenant is enforceable against anyone who is in privity with the original covenantor. If the covenant is breached, the injured party may seek damages at law.

Generally associated with real covenants are **equitable servitudes**, which may arise by implication and will be enforceable against persons who have notice of its existence. The remedy for breach of an equitable servitude is an injunction. No privity is necessary to enforce an equitable servitude.

The major difference between a real covenant and an equitable servitude is the remedy being sought. If the injured party is seeking damages, it is usually referred to as a real covenant; if the injured party is seeking an injunction, it is referred to as an equitable servitude.

Example: A land developer constructs a housing subdivision and in the contract for the sale of the property specifies that no homeowner may construct a building on the land that exceeds two stories. This agreement in the contract is filed with county recorder's office as part of the subdivision's plan and becomes a real covenant, enforceable against all subsequent property owners of parcels of this subdivision. If a homeowner attempts to construct a third-story addition, the other homeowners may seek damages.

Governmental restrictions

The government may infringe on a person's right with respect to real property in two ways: eminent domain and zoning.

Eminent domain is the right of the government to take private property if it is needed for a public use such as the construction of a road, a public park, and so forth. Under the provisions of the U.S. Constitution, the government must pay the property owner reasonable compensation for the property. If the government exercises eminent domain, the property owner is defenseless and must relinquish the land.

> **Example:** The government has decided to construct a highway to ease traffic. In order to create the highway, it must acquire several commercial buildings. The owners may argue the value of the compensation the government is willing to pay, but they must eventually convey the property to the government for the public use.

Zoning refers to municipal and county regulations with respect to how geographic areas may be used, such as a residential use, commercial use, or mixed residential and commercial use. Once an area has been zoned, the property owner must comply with these requirements unless the property owner can convince the **zoning board**, the governmental body that oversees the zoning regulations, that he or she should be granted a **variance**, a permit by the board to use the property in a manner inconsistent with the zoning regulations.

Zoning affects not only the use of property in a given area, but also includes height and space restrictions and historical landmark designation. The zoning board can have direct impact on what a commercial enterprise may put on its property.

> **Example:** An area of the city was zoned many years ago for mixed commercial and residential use, and there are several stores in the area. Recently, because of increased development, the zoning board has changed the designation to residential use only. The existing storeowners may keep their stores because they were in existence before the regulation changed, but a new store may not be constructed in the area unless the owner receives a variance from the zoning board.

Chapter Summary

The law pertaining to real property is a conglomeration of rights and obligations rather than a set of organized rules and regulations. Unlike many other areas of law, because property law concerns very diverse aspects of the use and ownership of land (and chattels), the law is fairly complex and is dependent upon the exact right or obligation under examination.

Real property law concerns the land and anything that has been permanently affixed to the land. Its rules have developed from the common law dealing with the acquisition and transfer of estates in land. These estates in land are divided into freehold and leasehold estates. Freeholds include fee simples, both individually and concurrently owned, and life estates, in which the estate terminates with death. Leaseholds give possessory interests in real property rather than ownership.

Title under property law is also an abstract concept, which includes interests other than just ownership—it also encompasses the right of possession and use. Therefore, the impact of real property law concerns the use, ownership, and possession of realty, all of which are distinct. Under these concepts, the law will also include easements, profits, licenses, and covenants—all rights that affect the use of land without necessarily giving the holder any title to the property in question.

In addition to these general theories, a whole body of law exists concerning the lease of real property that incorporates overlapping concepts of property and contract law, not dealing with ownership titles to property. Because these laws only affect possessory interests, the holder of the right is not only subject to the lease, but also to the other underlying property rights and obligations that may attach to the land so rented.

Edited Judicial Decisions

TOWN OF STRATFORD v. MUDRE
1993 Conn. Super. LEXIS 2997

The plaintiff, Town of Stratford, filed a nine-count complaint dated January 28, 1991, against the defendants, Charles Mudre (Charles) and Mary Mudre (Mary); Benham Industries; United Illuminating; and Hi-Ho Petroleum. The plaintiff alleged that certain taxes were assessed against the defendant Charles' property and sought foreclosure of the property for nonpayment of those taxes. On January 27, 1992, the court granted the plaintiff's motion for judgment of foreclosure by sale. The foreclosure sale resulted in proceeds of $114,500. A surplus of $77,312.98 remains after all debts are paid.

Mary and Charles filed motions in the foreclosure action for determination of their interests in the proceeds. Mary received a life estate in the property by her mother's will in 1983. The will provided that upon Mary's death the property would be transferred to Charles. The defendants Mary and Charles have each filed supporting memoranda.

The defendant Charles argues in his memorandum that the defendant Mary committed waste when she failed to pay taxes and that the life estate was terminated by the foreclosure sale. The defendant Charles argues that the remaining proceeds, therefore, should be paid solely to him as the remainderman. The defendant Mary argues that forfeiture of her interests in the property is not a proper remedy under Connecticut law. Furthermore, the defendant Mary argues that she is entitled to the total net proceeds of the sale because the terms of her mother's will reveal the testator's intent to provide for Mary's support and welfare.

A life tenant has the duty to pay all property taxes during the life tenancy. *Hart v. Heffernan*, 35 Conn. Sup. 101, 103, 397 A.2d 910 (1978); General Statutes, §12-48. Although there is no Connecticut case law directly on point, the court may look to other jurisdictions that have held that failure of the life tenant to pay all property taxes constitutes waste; *Union Mortgage Co. v. Nelson*, 82 N.Y.S.2d 268, 269 (1949); even where the property is unproductive. *Thayer v. Shorey*, 287 Mass. 76, 191 N.E. 435, 437(1934). A life tenant who commits waste may be held liable to the remainderman for damages to the property. General Statutes, §52-563.

While it is the duty of the life tenant to pay the taxes, that is "a matter between him and the remaindermen, and it [is] incumbent upon them, if they [wish] to protect their expectant interest, to see to it that the life tenant [pays] them, or, failing that, to pay the taxes themselves, or in a proper case recover the property . . . ." *Schofield v. Green*, 115 Ind. App. 160, 56 N.E.2d 506 (1944). The remainderman does have options other than allowing foreclosure of the property. See, *e.g.*, *O'Toole v. O'Toole*, 39 A.D. 302, 56 N.Y.S. 963, (1899). The remainderman could pay the taxes to prevent the foreclosure sale of the property; see, *e.g.*, 126 A.L.R. 873; or could petition the court for a sale to reinvest the property prior to the foreclosure sale. See, *e.g.*, *O'Toole v. O'Toole, supra*.

In determining the proper distribution of proceeds from a foreclosure sale, courts either impose forfeitures of the life tenant's interest in the proceeds or they place the proceeds in a fund with the interest paid to the life tenant and the principal paid to the remainderman. In jurisdictions that destroy the life tenant's interests in the proceeds, the courts are acting under the authority of forefeiture statutes. In those jurisdictions, the courts hold that where the property is sold at a foreclosure sale because of the life tenant's failure to pay taxes, the life tenant loses all interests in both the land and the proceeds from the foreclosure sale. See, *e.g., Leatherman v. Maytham*, 66 Ohio App. 344, 33 N.E.2d 1022 (1940); *Meadows v. Meadows*, 216 N.C. 413, 5 S.E.2d 128 (1939). In other jurisdictions, the life tenant's failure to pay taxes is considered permissive waste and not "such waste as would constitute an absolute forfeiture of the estate . . . ." *St. Paul Trust Co. v. Mintzer*, 65 Minn. 124, 67 N.W. 657, 658 (1896); see also, 16 A.L.R. 3d 1349. The courts that do not impose forfeiture on the life estate hold that even though the life tenant has committed waste, the proceeds should be placed in a fund with interest paid to the life tenant and the principal paid to the remainderman. See *O'Toole v. O'Toole, supra*.

Forfeiture of a life estate for waste is not permitted in the absence of specific statutory authority; 16 A.L.R. 3d 1350; and General Statutes, §52-563, which states that the life tenant is liable for waste, does not specifically provide for the remedy of forfeiture. The jurisdictions that provide for forfeiture of estates upon the life tenant's waste are acting under specific statutory authority. *Leatherman v. Maytham, supra*; *Meadows v. Meadows, supra*. Furthermore, "forfeitures are not favored by the law." 16 A.L.R. 3d 1349.

Where the entire interest in the property is sold by court order, the rights of the parties in the land are transferred to the proceeds of the sale. *Beliveau v. Beliveau*, 217 Minn. 235, 14 N.W.2d 360, 366 (1944). In *Beliveau*, the court determined that the life tenant committed waste by not paying the property taxes or the interest on the mortgage. *Id.* The court appointed a trustee to manage the net proceeds from the judicial sale of the property and to administer the fund "as nearly as possible as the land would have been handled had there been no conversion." (Citation omitted.) *Id.*

The proceeds remaining from a judicial sale, after satisfaction of all debts, may be held in a fund in substitution for the land, and the life tenant may receive the income from the fund during her life with the principal going to the remainderman upon the death of the life tenant. See, *e.g., Id.*; *O'Toole v. O'Toole, supra*; 51 Am. Jur. 2d 335.

In a New York case, where the property was sold at a mortgage foreclosure sale because of the life tenant's default, the surplus cash from the sale was reinvested for the benefit of the life tenant with the remaining principal payable to the remaindermen. *Mosher v. Wright*, 200 Misc. 792, 111 N.Y.S.2d 669 (1951).

In the present case, nothing in the facts indicates that the defendant Charles attempted to pay the delinquent taxes to prevent the foreclosure or petitioned the court for a sale of the property prior to the foreclosure. Although the defendant Mary did commit permissive waste by failing to pay the property taxes, it was not sufficient waste as to result in the forfeiture of her interests in the property. Because there is no statutory authority to forfeit the life tenant's interests in the property, the net proceeds from the foreclosure sale are ordered placed in a FDIC insured interest earning fund with the interest distributed to the defendant Mary and the principal to go to the defendant Charles upon the life tenant's death.

MAISCH v. HUNT MIDWEST MINING, INC.
1997 U.S. Dist. LEXIS 2356

By this diversity action, plaintiffs, lessors under a mineral lease with defendant lessee, seek termination of the lease, damages for limestone mined by defendant since the termination, and statutory damages and fees. The matter is presently before the court on the parties' cross-motions for summary judgment (Docs. 24, 36) and defendant's motion to amend the pretrial order (Doc. 34). The parties' summary judgment motions are granted in part and denied in part. The court concludes that the lease automatically terminated on January 1, 1993, and therefore grants plaintiffs partial summary judgment on Count I. Plaintiffs are also entitled to statutory damages in the amount of $100, although statutory attorney fees will not be awarded at this time; thus, plaintiffs are granted partial summary judgment on Count V. The court further concludes that the lease was valid with an enforceable termination provision; the court therefore grants defendant summary judgment with respect to Count III (lease void for lack of term), Count IV (lease created periodic tenancy or tenancy-at-will), and Count VI (lease void for mutual mistake). Finally, the court denies defendant's motion to amend the pretrial order.

I. FACTS

The facts are generally undisputed.

On March 4, 1971, Killough-Clark, Inc., defendant's predecessor-in-interest, entered into a lease agreement with Oscar Bone and James Bone. The lease gave Killough-Clark the right to quarry and remove limestone from an 80-acre tract of land in Miami [*3] County, Kansas. As consideration for the lease, Killough-Clark agreed to pay the Bones a royalty of five cents for each ton of limestone removed. The lease contained the following termination provision:

It is mutually agreed that the lease rights herein granted shall expire only upon mutual agreement of the parties or upon the failure of [Killough-Clark] to pay to [the Bones] during any calendar year either by royalty . . ., or by supplemental cash payment, or by both, totaling $100, and upon the payment of the total of $100 by royalty, supplemental cash payment, or both during any one calendar year, this lease shall extend for the subsequent calendar year.

The lease was recorded with the Miami County Register of Deeds on March 8, 1971.

The 1971 lease was amended in 1984 and 1986 to raise the royalty payment, first to seven cents, then to ten cents per ton of limestone. In 1989, Killough-Clark paid the Bones only $6.30 under the lease. Killough-Clark paid the Bones $147.70 in 1990 and $2,419.20 in 1991.

On February 4, 1992, Killough-Clark and the Bones executed a document titled "Amended Lease Agreement," the terms of which were virtually identical to those of the 1971 lease. The 1992 lease called for royalty payments of 12 cents per ton of limestone. The lease contained the same termination provision:

It is mutually agreed that the lease rights herein granted shall expire only upon mutual agreement of the parties, or upon the failure of [Killough-Clark] to pay to [the Bones] during any calendar year either by royalty . . . or by supplemental cash payment or by both, totaling $100 and upon the payment of the total of $100 by royalty, supplemental cash payment, or both during any one calendar year, this lease shall extend for the subsequent calendar year.

The lease also contained the following paragraph:

This amended lease is being executed to place on record a lease agreement reached between the parties on the 4th day of March 1971, the original of which has been lost or destroyed without recording.

The 1992 lease was drafted by Killough-Clark's attorney, who is no longer living.

In 1992, Killough-Clark paid the Bones $8.64 in royalties under the lease. James Bone and Oscar Bone both died in 1992. Killough-Clark paid the Bones' estate a total of $134.44 during the calendar year 1993. In 1994, the estate was settled, leaving the Bones' property to Jay Rashell and Margaret Maisch. Mr. Rashell and Ms. Maisch subsequently divided the property, with Ms. Maisch assuming ownership of the 80-acre tract in Miami County. Ms. Maisch and her husband, plaintiffs in this action, moved into a house on the tract in 1995. Mr. Rashell and Ms. Maisch accepted payments under the lease totaling $2,092.59 in 1994 and $1,363.05 in 1995, although they did not know that Killough-Clark had failed to make the required $100 payment in 1992.

On August 24, 1995, the Maisches' attorney sent Killough-Clark a letter asserting that the 1992 lease was invalid and demanding a release from Killough-Clark. Killough-Clark disagreed by letter dated August 25, 1995. On August 31, 1995, Killough-Clark merged with defendant Hunt Midwest, and on January 30, 1996, Killough-Clark's interest in the lease was transferred to defendant. By letter dated January 25, 1996, the Maisches again asserted that the lease was invalid, and they demanded release of the lease pursuant to K.S.A. §55-201. On January 30, 1996, the Maisches sent another notice of termination of the lease to defendant. On February 19, 1996, defendant filed a notice of nonforfeiture in Miami County. The Maisches did not accept any payments under the lease after first challenging the validity of the lease.

On April 25, 1996, plaintiffs filed the instant action in state court; defendant removed the action to this court on May 16, 1996. In Count I, plaintiffs seek a declaratory judgment that the lease was terminated on January 1, 1993. Plaintiffs also seek damages to compensate for the limestone taken from the tract since that date. Plaintiffs asserted a fraud claim in Count II; that claim was dismissed on November 22, 1996. By Count III, plaintiffs allege, in the alternative, that the lease is void for lack of a definite term. By Count IV, plaintiffs allege, in the alternative, that the lease created a periodic tenancy or a tenancy-at-will. In Count V, plaintiffs seek damages and attorney fees pursuant to K.S.A. §55-202. In Count VI, plaintiffs seek rescission of the lease based on mutual mistake.

II. SUMMARY JUDGMENT STANDARD

Summary judgment is appropriate if "there is no genuine issue as to any material fact and ... the moving party is entitled to a judgment as a matter of law." Fed. R. Civ. P. 56(c); *Anthony v. United States*, 987 F.2d 670, 672 (10th Cir. 1993). The court views the evidence and draws any inferences in the light most favorable to the party opposing summary judgment, but that party must identify evidence sufficient to require submission of the case to a jury. *Anderson v. Liberty Lobby, Inc.*, 477 U.S. 242, 249-52, 106 S. Ct. 2505, 2510-12, 91 L. Ed. 2d 202 (1986); *Anthony*, 987 F.2d at 672.

III. DISCUSSION

A. Termination of the Lease

Plaintiffs seek a declaratory judgment that the mineral lease terminated on January 1, 1993, because of the lessee's failure to pay the required $100 during 1992. In construing and enforcing the lease, the court applies Kansas law. See *Reese Exploration, Inc. v. Williams Natural Gas Co.*, 983 F.2d 1514, 1519 (10th Cir. 1993) (when court sits in diversity jurisdiction, Kansas law governs construction of oil and gas leases located in Kansas). In Kansas, "the law applicable to oil and gas leases applies with equal force to mineral leases" that grant the right to quarry rock. *Smith v. Holmes*, 181 Kan. 438, 441, 312 P.2d 228 (1957).

The court agrees with plaintiffs that, by its terms, the lease here terminated on January 1, 1993. The lease unambiguously provided that the parties' rights under the lease "shall expire" upon the failure of the lessee to pay the lessors at least $100 under the lease during any one calendar year. It is uncontroverted that the lessee failed to pay that amount in the calendar year 1992. Accordingly, the lease expired by its terms at the end of that year, on January 1, 1993.

Defendant argues that the lease should not be declared terminated, trotting out the old maxim that the law abhors forfeiture. The rule may still hold in general terms, but throughout this century, Kansas courts have ignored that maxim when an oil and gas lease or a mineral lease has expired under its own terms. For instance, in *Gasaway v. Teichgraeber*, 107 Kan. 340, 191 P. 282 (1920), the Kansas Supreme Court affirmed the cancellation of an oil and gas lease where the lessee failed to drill or pay a delay rental by the required date and the lease provided that it would become void in such event. *Id.* The court stated: "While forfeitures are abhorred by the law, this is not strictly a forfeiture, but a mere holding of a party to the contract it has made." *Id.* at 340.

This language from *Gasaway* was quoted in *Hinshaw v. Smith*, 131 Kan. 351, 291 P. 774 (1930), in which the Kansas Supreme Court affirmed the cancellation of a mining lease. *Id.* at 356. The court also stated:

In the same connection we are reminded by appellant that forfeitures are abhorred by the law, but that does not apply when parties deliberately bind themselves by the terms of a contract capable of being fulfilled . . .

. . . The law does not abhor the fulfilling of contracts where parties have bound themselves to certain definite requirements or the loss of the lease in unambiguous terms. *Id.* at 356-57.

The court relied on *Gasaway* again in *Morton v. Sutcliffe*, 175 Kan. 699, 266 P.2d 734 (1954), in which the court, in cancelling an oil and gas lease, stated that it was "merely holding defendants to the contract they made." *Id.* at 703. Morton involved a lease similar to the one at issue here—it provided that in any year when the lessees failed to pay a minimum of $160, in the form of royalties or an additional rent payment, the lease would "thereupon cease to be of any force or effect between the parties." *Id.* at 700.

Finally, in 1988, the Kansas Court of Appeals quoted *Gasaway* in holding that an oil and gas lease had expired by its own terms when the lessee failed to pay the delay rental when due. *Rice v. Hillenburg*, 13 Kan. App. 2d 155, 161-62, 766 P.2d 182 (1988), review denied (Kan. Mar. 14, 1989); see also *M&C Oil, Inc. v. Geffert*, 21 Kan. App. 2d 267, 274, 897 P.2d 191 (1995) (although the law abhors a forfeiture, Kansas Supreme Court has declared a forfeiture if the express language of the lease requires it), review denied (Kan. Aug. 29, 1995).

Thus, it is clear that Kansas courts will not hesitate to cancel a lease if, as here, the lease has expired in accordance with its own express, unambiguous terms. Nor, therefore, does this court hesitate in enforcing the 1992 limestone lease as written.

B. Waiver or Estoppel

Defendant also argues that plaintiffs waived any right to terminate the lease by accepting royalty payments in 1993, 1994, and 1995. The court concludes, however, that, under Kansas law, the lease expired automatically, and plaintiff therefore could not waive the effect of the lease's termination provision.

The opinion by the Kansas Court of Appeals in *Rice* controls this issue. In *Rice*, the parties had entered into an "unless" oil and gas lease, which provided that if drilling operations had not commenced by a certain date, the lease would terminate, unless the lessee paid $100 as a delay rental by that date. *Rice*, 13 Kan. App. 2d at 156. The lessee did not drill or pay the rental by the due date, however, because the lessee had been sued by another company, who claimed the exclusive right to lease all of the minerals under the property. *Id.* at 157. The lessors were aware of the litigation over the validity of the oil and gas lease. *Id.* The litigation ended in favor of the lessee, but at approximately the same time, the lessors began to seek termination of the lease. *Id.* at 157-58. After the lessors brought suit to cancel the lease, the trial court granted the lessee summary judgment, pointing to the lessee's expenditure of over $6,000 in defending the lease in the prior litigation, the lessor's awareness of that litigation, and equitable considerations. *Id.* at 158.

The Court of Appeals began by noting that "courts have been substantially unanimous in holding that if a lessee fails to pay or tender the rental on or before the due date under an 'unless' oil and gas lease, the lease terminates automatically." *Id.* at 159. The court then quoted two treatises, which concluded that, although the rule may be harsh, it was correct because the "unless" type clause is one "of limitation, not one of covenant or condition." *Id.* (quoting 3 Williams, Oil and Gas Law §606.2 (1986) and 1 David E. Pierce, Kansas Oil and Gas Handbook §9.35 (1986)). The court noted that Kansas courts had normally required strict compliance with such clauses, but had excused the failure to pay in two situations: "where the lessee attempted to make payment, but the payment failed for some reason;" and "where the lessor attacked the lessee's title before the payment became due, and the attack had not been resolved at the time payment should have been made." *Id.* at 159-60. The court concluded that, because the case before it involved neither situation, the existing authority compelled "a holding of leasehold forfeiture." *Id.* at 161 (citing *Doornbos v. Warwick,* 104 Kan. 102, 177 P. 527 (1919) and *Gasaway,* 107 Kan. 340, 191 P. 282).

The court then considered the lessee's argument that the lessor had waived the lease's termination. The court defined waiver as follows:

A waiver is an intentional renunciation of a claim or right and exists only where there has been some absolute action or inaction inconsistent with that claim or right.

Id. (quoting *Proctor Trust Co. v. Neihart,* 130 Kan. 698, 705, 288 P. 574 (1930)). The court held that the termination of the lease had not been waived:

The problem with a finding of waiver in this case is that such theory assumes a party with the right to terminate must take some affirmative action to invoke the right. The major characteristic which distinguishes an "or" oil and gas lease from an "unless" oil and gas lease is the lessee's nonpayment of a delay rental under an "or" lease violates a covenant and allows lessor to cancel the lease while nonpayment under an "unless" lease automatically terminates the lease. The Rice family was not obligated to take any action to enforce the termination of the lease and it could not have waived such termination by failing to act. The doctrine of waiver does not apply. *Id.* at 162 (citation omitted).

The court in Rice also rejected an argument based on the doctrine of equitable estoppel.

The elements of equitable estoppel have been enumerated by our Kansas Court as follows: (1) There must have been a false representation or concealment of material facts; (2) it must have been made with knowledge, actual or constructive, of the facts; (3) the party to whom it was made must have been without knowledge or the means of knowing the real facts; (4) it must have been made with the intention that it should be acted upon; and (5) the party to whom it was made must have relied on or acted upon it to his prejudice.

Id. (citing *Place v. Place,* 207 Kan. 734, 739, 486 P.2d 1354 (1971)). The court held that equitable estoppel did not apply in that case because the lessors had not made any false representations or concealed any material facts. *Id.*

The court concludes that the Kansas Supreme Court would in this case follow the well-reasoned analysis in *Rice*, which compels the conclusion that the doctrine of waiver does not prevent termination of the lease here. The 1992 lease's termination provision was comparable to the standard "unless" clause in *Rice* because under either provision the lease expired if a certain payment was not made. Restated, the provision at issue here required termination unless a minimum of $100 was paid during the calendar year. Thus, the lease provided for an automatic, self-executing termination in the event of nonpayment, and, under *Rice*, waiver is therefore inapplicable.

Defendant attempts to distinguish *Rice*, arguing that the court in that case considered only the lessors' failure to take any action to terminate the lease. Defendant concedes that plaintiffs were not required to act affirmatively to terminate the lease here; defendant argues, however, that plaintiffs' affirmative acts of accepting royalty payments were inconsistent with their right of termination and so constituted a waiver. This argument must fail. In *Rice*, the court did not base its decision on any scrutiny of the lessors' action or inaction. Rather, the court relied on the nature of the payment provision, with its automatic termination, in holding that the doctrine of waiver did not apply. See *Id.*

Defendant also cites dictum from *Hinshaw* in support of its position. In *Hinshaw*, the Kansas Supreme Court held that the lessors, by accepting future royalty payments, did not waive their right to terminate an oil and gas lease for failure by the lessee to drill continuously. 131 Kan. at 355. Defendant points to the following language:

But the question is, does the acceptance of such deposits by the [lessors'] bank waive the right of the [lessors] to insist upon a forfeiture for the failure of the [lessee] to meet the requirements of the lease as to continuous drilling and prospecting? It is further conceded that if the failure complained of were in connection with the payment of rents or royalties, the payment to the agent would be a waiver. But here the failure relied upon by the landowners for the forfeiture is a continuing one, viz., the failure of continuously drilling and prospecting. The payment of the royalty did not relieve that situation. *Id.*

The court concludes that this dictum, which is from a case decided 66 years ago, does not control the present case. First, the lease in *Hinshaw* contained the following termination provision:

Any failure to comply with and perform any of the terms and requirements of this lease in good faith at any time shall end and determine (terminate) the same, and the party of the first part may declare an ouster and reenter upon and hold said demised premises without notice.

Id. at 353 (emphasis added). This provision, by virtue of the highlighted language, could reasonably be interpreted to require action by the lessee to effect termination. Thus, unlike the lease in the present case, the *Hinshaw* lease does not unambiguously provide for automatic termination, and it is that quality on which the *Rice* decision turns. Second, the dictum from *Hinshaw* may refer to a situation in which the lessor later accepts the very payment missed. Such situation is inapposite to the present case, which does not involve any explicit attempt by defendant to make up the missed payment.

In *Rice*, the court reviewed the existing precedent and concluded that the failure to pay under an "unless" lease had been excused in only two types of cases. Because neither exception applies here, the court concludes that plaintiffs cannot have waived the termination of the lease. Moreover, equitable estoppel does not apply here because, like the lessors in *Rice*, plaintiffs did not make any false representations or conceal any material facts. Accordingly, the lease expired by its terms on January 1, 1993, and plaintiffs are entitled to partial summary judgment with respect to this issue.

C. Other Challenges to the Lease

In Count III and Count IV, plaintiffs allege, in the alternative to Count I, that the lease is void for lack of a definite term or that it created a periodic tenancy or a tenancy-at-will. The court's conclusion that the lease contained a valid, enforceable termination provision disposes of these claims, and the court grants defendant summary judgment on Count III and Count IV.

Plaintiffs also assert, in Count VI, that the lease should be rescinded for mutual mistake. Plaintiffs rely on the fact that, although the 1992 lease states that it was executed because the original lease was lost and not recorded, the 1971 lease had in fact been recorded.

Defendant is entitled to summary judgment on this claim. As defendant points out, the people who executed the 1992 lease are deceased, and plaintiff has presented no other evidence concerning the circumstances surrounding the execution of the second lease. The language in the lease, by itself, is not enough. Thus, plaintiffs have not met their burden of providing sufficient evidence that the mistake had "a material effect on the agreed exchange of performances." Restatement (Second) of Contracts §152(1)(1981); see *Potucek v. Cordeleria Lourdes*, 310 F.2d 527, 532 (10th Cir. 1962) (mistake justifies relief when the mistake is material and goes to the basis for the transaction); *Albers v. Nelson*, 248 Kan. 575, 580, 809 P.2d 1194 (1991) (mistake must go to essential terms of the contract); see also *Baker v. Penn Mut. Life Ins. Co.*, 788 F.2d 650, 661-62 (10th Cir. 1986) (applying Restatement in consideration of a claim of mutual mistake under Kansas law).

D. Statutory Damages and Fees

Plaintiffs have also brought a claim for statutory damages and attorney fees. K.S.A. §55-201 requires a lessee, within 60 days or upon later demand by the lessor, to surrender "any oil, gas or other mineral lease" that has become forfeited. Under K.S.A. §55-202, if the lessee fails to execute such a release, the lessor may recover, in an action to obtain such release, the sum of $100 as damages, and all costs, together with a reasonable attorney's fee for preparing and prosecuting the suit, and he or she may also recover any additional damages that the evidence in the case will warrant.

"The awarding of damages, costs, attorney fees and additional damages under K.S.A. 55-202 is discretionary with the trial court." *Adolph v. Stearns*, 235 Kan. 622, 631, 684 P.2d 372 (1984).

The court concludes that, because defendant refused to release the 1992 lease, which had expired by its terms, plaintiffs are entitled to collect $100 from defendant in statutory damages. Accordingly, the court grants plaintiffs partial summary judgment with respect to such claim.

Defendant, relying on *Berryman v. Sinclair Prairie Oil Co.*, 164 F.2d 734 (10th Cir. 1947), argues that plaintiffs cannot recover under this statute because they have not alleged any "special damages." Defendant misapprehends *Berryman*, however. There the Tenth Circuit stated: "Both Oklahoma and Kansas have held that plaintiffs must prove the loss of an opportunity to release the premises in order to support a judgment for special damages on account of the failure of one to release the lease of record." *Id.* at 737 (citing *Mollohan v. Patton*, 110 Kan. 663, 202 P. 616 (1921)). Plaintiffs are not seeking special damages under the statute; they seek only the $100 statutory damages, costs, and attorney fees. Their claim for damages under Count I, which might also be construed to be under section 55-202, represents actual loss; it is not a claim for general damages suffered as a result of a cloud remaining on the lease. See *Id.* Therefore, plaintiffs were not required to plead the loss of an opportunity to enter into a lease with someone else in order to recover under the statute.

The court also rejects defendant's argument that its refusal to surrender the lease was in good faith. See *Mollohan*, 110 Kan. at 669 (opinion denying rehearing) (mere attempt to justify refusal was not enough in itself to show good faith as a defense under the statute). Defendant states that plaintiff did not assert the failure to make the minimum payment as a basis for cancellation until after this action had commenced. Defendant and its predecessor, however, are charged with knowledge of the terms of the lease and its own payments under the lease, and therefore defendant cannot be heard to argue that it was operating under the mistaken belief that the lease was still effective.

The court, in its discretion, denies both parties' motions for summary judgment with respect to plaintiffs' claim for statutory attorney fees. Because this order does not dispose of the entire case, the court believes that consideration of a claim for attorney fees would be premature at this time.

...IT IS THEREFORE ORDERED BY THE COURT THAT plaintiffs are granted partial summary judgment on Count I, and the lease between the parties is declared to have terminated on January 1, 1993. Defendant's motion for summary judgment is denied with respect to that count.

IT IS FURTHER ORDERED THAT plaintiffs are granted partial summary judgment on Count V, and plaintiffs are awarded statutory damages in the amount of $100. Plaintiffs' motion for summary judgment with respect to their claim for statutory attorney fees is denied at this time without prejudice to plaintiffs pursuing the issue at the conclusion of the case. Defendant's motion for summary judgment with respect to Count V is denied.

IT IS FURTHER ORDERED THAT defendant's motion for summary judgment is granted with respect to Count III, Count IV, and Count VI, and those claims are hereby dismissed. Plaintiffs' motion for summary judgment with respect to those claims is denied.

Glossary

Actual eviction - A landlord preventing a tenant from possession of the rented premises

Actual possession - The physical possession of the property

Adverse possession - A means to acquire title to land through obvious occupancy of the land, while claiming ownership for the period of years set by the law of the state where the property exists

Ameliorative waste - Waste that actually improves the value of the property

Assume the mortgage - The assignee becomes personally liable for the underlying mortgage debt

Bargain and sale deed - Term for all modern deeds for realty

Block and lot index - Method of recording land descriptions

Chattel - Personal property

Closing - The final step in the sale and purchase of real estate in which a deed of title, financing documents, title insurance policies, and remaining funds due are exchanged

Community property - Title ownership in nine jurisdictions for legally married couples in which each spouse owns one-half of the property

Concurrent estates - Fee title held by two or more persons collectively

Constructive eviction - Action by a landlord that has the effect of preventing the tenant from enjoying the property

Covenant running with the land - Enforceable promise on landowner with respect to the use of the property

Conveyance - Transfer of title to land

Deed - Writing used to convey title to realty

Deficiency - Amount still owed on a loan after a sale of the property

Doctrine of equitable conversion - Risk passes to the buyer after the contract for the sale of land is signed

Dominant tenament - Easement holder

Easement - Right of use or access over someone else's land

Easement appurtenant - Easement for adjoining properties

Easement in gross - Easement held by nonadjoining property owner

Ejection - A lawsuit brought to remove a party who is occupying real property

Eminent domain - Right of the government to take private property, for compensation, for a public use

Encumbrance - Anything that affects marketability of title

Equitable servitude - Restriction on the use of land enforceable by an injunction

Equitable waste - Waste occasioned by poor husbandry

Estate - Interest in land

Fee (fee simple absolute) - The highest form of ownership

Fixture - Chattel that is permanently affixed to the land, thereby being treated as realty

Foreclosure - The right of a mortgagee to sell the mortgaged property at public auction in case of default

Four units - Time, title, interest and possession

Freehold - Estate in land for an indefinite period

General warranty deed - Deed with the usual covenants and warranties

Grantee - Transferee of title to land

Grantor - Transferor of title to land

Grantor-grantee index - Method of recording title to realty by the names of the transferring parties

Holdover tenant - Tenant who remains in possession after the termination of the lease

Lessee - Tenant

Lease - Contract for the right of possession of property

Leasehold - Estate created for a specific time evidenced by a contract

Lessor - Landlord

License - Privilege to enter onto another's land

Life estate - Estate held for the tenant's lifetime

Life estate *pur autre vie* - Life estate held for the life of a person who is not the tenant

Mortgage - Security used to acquire a loan for the purchase of land

Mortgagee - Lender who takes a security interest in the property acquired by the loan

Mortgagor - Borrower who gives a security interest in the property that was purchased with the loan

Partial eviction - Landlord does something that prevents the tenant from complete possession of the property

Partition - Action to divide concurrent title into separate units

Permissive waste - Waste caused by letting the property dissipate in value

Personal property - Nonreal property

Profit - Right to enter land to remove resources

Quiet title - Action to determine title to property

Quitclaim deed - Transfer in which the transferor makes no warranties with respect to its title

Real covenants - A promise is attached to the land, not just the promissor

Real property - Land and anything permanently affixed thereto

Redemption - Right of a defaulting mortgagor to reclaim property that has been foreclosed

Remainder interest - Holder of future title

Reversion - Title going back to the transferor

Security (collateral) - Property pledged to secure a loan or debt, usually funds or personal property as distinguished from real property

Servient tenement - Property subject to an easement

Special warranty deed - Deed in which grantor only warrants against claims caused by or through him

Statutory right of redemption - Right to reclaim foreclosed property after it has been sold at foreclosure

Straw man - Method of changing title to property by transferring it to a third-party who conveys the title according to the parties wishes

Subject to the mortgage - Grantee of the mortgagor does not assume personal liability on the mortgage debt

Sublease - Transfer of a portion of a leasehold

Tenancy at sufferance - Landlord permitting a tenant to stay after the lease has expired; can be terminated at the will of the lessor

Tenancy at will - Leasehold that can be terminated by either party without cause

Tenancy by the entirety - Joint tenancy for legally married couples; neither spouse may alienate his or her share without the other's consent

Tenancy in common - Concurrent ownership with no right of survivorship; each tenant owns a divisible portion of the whole

Tenancy in partnership - Concurrent ownership for property owned by business partners

Tenancy in severalty - Fee estate in just one person

Tenancy for years - Leasehold for a specified number of years

Title - Legal interest in property

Title insurance - Insurance to prevent injury due to a defective title to realty

Title search - A list of conveyances as they appear in the county recorder's office; it is used to determine whether the grantor has a valid title to the property

Tract index - Method of recording title to land by geographic areas

Trade fixture - A piece of equipment on or attached to the real estate which is used in a trade or business

Uniform Vendors' and Purchasers' Risk Act - Statute that changes the doctrine of equitable conversion

Variance - An exemption from the zoning laws

Voluntary waste - Action that causes waste to the land

Warranty of marketability - A condition in sale of land contracts that the grantor has a marketable title to the grantee at closing

Waste - Anything that diminishes the value of realty

Zoning - Government rules for the use of geographic areas

Zoning board - Governmental unit that oversees zoning regulations

Exercises

1. Why is it important to do a title search before purchasing a parcel of real estate? Go to the county recorder's office in your county and locate the title for your residence.

2. Differentiate between the five types of concurrent titles to property. Why are these differences important? Discuss.

3. Discuss the rights and obligations of a landlord and a tenant. Obtain a copy of a lease and analyze its provisions for these rights and duties.

4. Under what circumstances may a person legally enter onto another's property? Discuss according to the provisions of your own state's law.

5. Discuss the rights of a mortgagee if the mortgagor defaults. Obtain a copy of a mortgage agreement from your local bank or financial institution.

Chapter Six

PERSONAL PROPERTY

Introduction

Personal property, or **personalty**, is defined as all nonreal property. If the property in question is land, or anything permanently affixed to the land (fixtures), the property is considered realty (Chapter Five). If the property does not fall into this grouping, it is personalty.

Personal property itself is divided into two broad categories. **Tangibles** refer to all personal property that can be touched or moved and whose value is intrinsic to the object itself, such as a computer or a painting. **Intangibles** are all other items of personalty whose value is not intrinsic to the object but whose true value is represented by the object. One of the most common examples of an intangible is a bank check (Chapter Four) because the value of the paper itself is negligible, but it represents the right to receive the amount indicated on its face that may be quite substantial. In this respect, intangible property may be considered rights that are valuable, the right itself being represented by a tangible item that itself, intrinsically, has negligible value.

As discussed in Chapter Four, most commercial enterprises operate with intangible property, notably commercial paper that is used as a medium of exchange. Most commercial enterprises realize funds by means of issuing intangible property, such as stocks, bonds, and loans. The focus of this chapter will be with items of personalty that do not easily fall into one of the general chapter headings of this text: intellectual property, bailments, accession, confusion, and the rights and obligations of innkeepers and common carriers with respect to personal property.

Intellectual Property

One of the most important types of intangible property is **intellectual property**, those intangibles that come about by a person's creative process. With intellectual property, the created object itself is tangible property, but the right granted by the government for the exclusive use of the object is the intangible because it is a protected property right evidenced by a government paper that itself, as a piece of paper, has little value. There are basically three types of intellectual property: copyrights, patents, and marks.

A **copyright** is the grant of exclusive use given to an author or the creator of a work of art by the government. This right permits the holder to limit the use of such items for the creator's life plus 70 years. During this period the item may only be used or reproduced with the holder's permission. To generate income, the creator will grant such permission by means of a license, a contract in which the creator is given a fee, called a **royalty**, for every use the license holder makes of the copyrighted item.

> **Example:** *An author copyrights a play that she writes. A production company wants to produce the play, and the author agrees, providing that the producer gives her a royalty for every production. When the author dies, she can will her copyright to friends or relatives because the right will continue to exist for 70 years after her death.*

A **patent** is a government grant of exclusive use given to the inventor of a scientific invention that exists only for one 20-year period. Just as with a copyright, the holder generates income from the invention by licensing its use.

> **Example:** *A man invents a better mousetrap and obtains a patent on the device. He then licenses it to a manufacturer who will produce the mousetrap and pay the inventor a royalty for each trap sold.*

A **mark** is a word or symbol that identifies a particular product or service (**trademark** and **service mark**). The government grants the person who registers a unique mark the right to that mark for a period of ten years. Unlike copyrights and patents, the mark can be renewed indefinitely. The mark holder generates income by licensing the use of the mark.

> **Example:** *Walt Disney marked the image of Snow White. Every time anyone uses that image, in costumes, lunch boxes, notebooks, etc. that person can only do so with a license from Walt Disney, which receives a royalty for such use.*

Bailments

A **bailment** is the transfer of possession of personal property from one person, the **bailor**, to another person, the **bailee**. A bailment does not transfer title to the object, simply the right of the bailee to possess, and sometimes use, the object until the object must be returned. A bailment may be created by an express agreement, but a writing is not necessary. A bailment may also be created orally.

No bailment exists until the object is physically transferred. If the bailment was created by contract, the bailor's failure to transfer possession to the bailee may constitute a breach of contract. In addition, many states specify that possession alone may not be sufficient to create a bailment—a bailment cannot be thrust upon a person. To be a bailee, the person must have the ability to exercise control over the object.

Note that some jurisdictions will imply a bailment if mere possession exists, but in those states, the possession, while creating a bailment, does not impose duties on the bailee, duties that do attach once control is demonstrated (see below). Further, a person may become a bailee even if he or she does not know of the precise value of the object but has in fact demonstrated the intent to exercise control over the object. This situation is referred to as a **constructive bailment**.

> *Example:* *The owner of a parking lot accepts possession of a customer's car. The owner is deemed to have constructive knowledge that the car may contain items that are usually stored in an automobile, such as a spare tire or an emergency flare, even though the owner has not specifically seen or been told of such items. However, if the trunk of the car contains a computer the car owner was transporting, no bailment would arise with respect to that computer unless the parking lot owner was informed of the fact, because such items would not reasonably be in the car. The lot owner is not responsible for such hidden objects.*

Several problematic situations have arisen over the years with respect to bailments:

- *Parking lots.* Merely leaving a car in a parking lot does not in and of itself create a bailment, because no actual transfer of possession has taken place. However, if the car owner leaves the keys to the car with the parking lot attendant, a bailment has been created because the attendant now has possessory control of the car.
- *Safe deposit boxes.* Because both the bank and the bank customer have keys to the box, the law has determined that a bailor-bailee relationship exists, holding the bank liable as a bailee (see below).
- *Cloakrooms.* A patron leaving a coat with a cloakroom attendant creates a bailment situation; however, the liability of the owner of the cloakroom may be limited by specific state statute.
- *Bathhouses and retail stores.* The owner of a bathhouse is a bailee for the patron's clothing left in a locker while the facility is being used, even if the patron retains the locker key. A retailer is a bailee for items set aside while the customer shops, such as putting down a coat to try on some clothes.
- *Pledges.* A **pledge** is a form of a bailment in which the possession of personal property is transferred to secure a debt, similar to collateral for a loan. The bailee, in this instance the creditor, has possession of the object until the debt is repaid. If the debtor defaults, the bailee may acquire title to the property. A pawnbroker typifies this type of relationship. In the normal bailment situation, the eventual transfer of title is not an element.

Note that a bailment only transfers the right to the possession and sometimes use of the property. It does not transfer title, as would be the case with a sale or a gift.

As a general rule, the bailee is entitled to absolute possession of the object and, during the period of the bailment, may maintain legal actions against anyone who attempts to interfere with this possessory right. Further, a bailee may have certain rights with respect to the use of the property.

- *Express use.* The parties to the bailment may contract, or agree, that the bailee may use the property during the term of the bailment.

> *Example:* *A manufacturer is in need of additional transport and hires some trucks from a neighboring business. The terms of the contract specify that the manufacturer may use the trucks to transport merchandise for the period of the lease.*

> **Example:** *To impress a potential client, a lawyer borrows her friend's pearl necklace. The friend has agreed that the lawyer can wear the necklace at the upcoming business meeting.*

- *Implied use.* Certain types of personal property by their nature indicate that the bailee may use the property.

> **Example:** *A horse breeder must stable his horses at a commercial stable while his own stable is being refurbished and he is away on business. In order to maintain the horses' health, the commercial stable owner can exercise them.*

- *Incidental use.* To effectuate the bailment, certain necessary use by the bailee may be expected and permitted.

> **Example:** *A woman stores her car in a commercial garage. The garage attendant has the right to move the car to provide access for other cars in the lot.*

If a bailee uses a bailed item for any use not expressly agreed to (or implied), the bailee will be held liable to the bailor for any damages that result from such unauthorized use of the item.

The modern trend of most jurisdictions is to hold the bailee liable for ordinary negligence that causes damage to the bailed items (Chapter Two). However, the bailee may be held to a standard of absolute liability if the bailee departs from the terms of the bailment or misdelivers the bailed item to someone other than the bailor.

> **Example:** *A woman leaves her very expensive foreign sports car with a garage. The parking attendant has always admired that make of car and decides to take the car out for a test run on the highway. The lot owner is absolutely liable for any damage that results, because such use of the car is beyond the scope of the terms of the bailment.*

> **Example:** *The bailee, when returning a car to the bailor, inadvertently parks it in the bailor's neighbor's garage. That night the neighbor's garage is burglarized, and the car is stolen. The bailee is held absolutely liable because of the misdelivery.*

The parties may agree to a limitation of liability clause in their contract (Chapter Three), but an unfettered waiver of liability is generally disfavored. The bailor may maintain an action against the bailee for breach of contract, for tort, or for conversion of the property if the bailee wrongfully retains possession of or destroys the item.

Accession

Accession occurs when one person's labor or material added to another's property increases the value of that property. If this additional value can be severed from the original item, the court will order such removal. If removal is impossible, the original party may sue for damages; if the change is so significant that the object is completely altered and its value is greatly increased, the title to the property will pass to the person whose labor or property created the change.

Example: *A person takes lumber from a lumberyard and makes storage crates with the wood. The owner of the lumberyard is entitled to the value of the lumber taken, but the trespasser who made the crates may keep the boxes because the nature of the lumber has now been completely changed. This result is true if the trespasser took the lumber unintentionally, believing that he had purchased it. However, if the trespasser willfully took the lumber knowing that he had no right to it, the crates will belong to the owner of the lumberyard. The law does not benefit an intentional wrongdoer.*

Confusion

Confusion is somewhat similar to accession. **Confusion** occurs when the personal property of two individuals are mixed together. If the goods are of the same kind and quality, the mixture is considered to be owned by both parties as tenants-in-common. If the confusion was caused by the willful action of one of the parties, the wrongdoer is required to identify his or her portion. If identification is impossible, the entire mixture belongs to the innocent party. If the property can be separated, no confusion exists, and the court will order separation.

Example: *Two farmers send their grain to the same mill to have it ground into flour. The mill owner fails to realize that two different farmers have brought the grain because they both use the same carrier. He innocently mills all of the grain together, and it cannot be determined how much each farmer owns. In this situation, both farmers as tenants-in-common will own all the flour.*

Common Carriers and Innkeepers

A **common carrier** is a commercial enterprise that transports goods and persons for consideration. The definition does not encompass state agencies that might perform the same services. A common carrier is held to the responsibility of an insurer for all goods it transports, meaning that the common carrier is held to be liable for the value of the goods if they are damaged or destroyed, even if the injury is caused by an act of God. However, unless there is an agreement to the contrary, the carrier will not be liable if goods are not delivered according to its printed timetable or its estimated time of delivery.

An **innkeeper** is a commercial enterprise that rents temporary accommodations to members of the public. As such, the innkeeper is deemed to be an insurer of the guests' property. However, despite this insurer liability, the innkeeper will not be liable if damage or loss to the property is caused by the guests' own neglect or fault, an act of God, or a fire not caused by the innkeeper's negligence. The innkeeper is liable for any loss due to burglary, theft or negligence, and the burden is on the innkeeper to demonstrate that it was not negligent. The innkeeper may limit its liability for loss if it conspicuously posts a notice of such limitation of liability.

Both common carriers and innkeepers have insurer liability with respect to goods left in their possession. Both types of entrepreneurs are entitled to a lien on the property in their possession. A **lien** is a right (therefore intangible personal property) held by a person who has improved property to retain possession of that property until the improvement has been paid for. To create a lien, there is a debt caused by the lienor having performed a service on the item; title to the property is in the debtor, and possession of the property is in the lienor.

A common carrier has a lien on all items it has agreed to transport for the item's owner; however, no lien attaches if the property is received from persons other than the owner. Innkeepers have liens on all property a guest brings into the inn, even if the property does not belong to the guest. The lienor has the right to retain possession of the items until the debt is discharged. If the debt is not discharged, title will vest in the lienor.

> **Example:** *A couple flies on a commercial airline between Seattle and Washington, D.C. At D.C.'s Reagan National airport, someone steals their luggage. The thief checks into a hotel in downtown Washington with the luggage. The thief stays for two days and then leaves without paying. The commercial airline is liable to the couple for the value of their luggage (although it may have limited its liability). The hotel may retain the luggage left by the thieving guest, even though the luggage did not belong to the thief.*

Chapter Summary

Personal property is defined as all nonreal property. One type of intangible property in which a commercial enterprise may become involved is intellectual property. Intellectual property consists of copyrights, patents, and marks, items that evolve from a person's creative process and for which the government grants the holder the right of exclusive use for a period of time. The holder of this right can generate income by licensing its use.

Bailments are transfers of the possession of personal property with no transfer of the title. Under modern trends, the bailee, the person who acquires possession, is held to the ordinary standard of care for the items while they are in his or her possession. The bailee has the right of possession against the entire world, even the bailor, until the bailment is terminated.

Accession occurs when one person improves the value of the property of another in circumstances in which the improvement is not intended as consideration for a contract or as a gift. In this situation, the improvement belongs to the person who made the improvement unless the action was wrongfully done, in which case the property belongs to the original owner and the wrongdoer receives nothing.

Similar to accession, confusion results when two persons' property is commingled so that they cannot be separated. The law specifies that the two property owners hold title of this mixture as a tenancy-in-common.

Commercial enterprises that operate their business as common carriers or innkeepers are held to the standard of insurers for the property they accept on behalf of their customers. The law does permit these businesses to limit this liability, but only if notice of such limitation of liability appears in a conspicuous writing and the customers knew, actually or constructively, of the limitation.

Edited Judicial Decisions

THE JEFFERSON AIRPLANE & AFTERTHOUGHT PRODUCTIONS, INC. v. BERKELEY SYSTEMS, INC.
886 F. Supp. 713 (N.D. Cal. 1994)

I. ISSUES.

The issue raised by this motion is whether, under the 1971 Sound Recording Amendment to the Copyright Act of 1909, the registration of a copyright over a sound recording encompasses the artwork on the album cover.

II. BACKGROUND.

The Jefferson Airplane is a world-famous musical group that was at the center of the rock music scene of the late sixties and early seventies. In 1973, The Jefferson Airplane released a record album entitled *Thirty Seconds Over Winterland* (*Thirty Seconds*). The album cover features an illustration depicting a group of two-slice, fifties-style, rounded toasters with white wings and clocks flying in squadron formation across the sky. In 1989, the album was re-released on compact disc with the same cover art. To date, about 500,000 copies of the record and compact disc have been sold worldwide.

Afterthought Productions, Inc. is a California corporation responsible for managing most of the business affairs of The Jefferson Airplane. It is owned by The Jefferson Airplane, Bill Thompson (The Jefferson Airplane's long-time manager) and China Kantner (the daughter of two of the band's members). Afterthought Productions, Inc. owns and operates a record label called Grunt Records. Afterthought Productions, Inc., dba Grunt Records, produced or held titular ownership in certain sound recordings created by The Jefferson Airplane and other groups. Grunt Records produced and owns the copyright to *Thirty Seconds*.

Defendant Berkeley Systems (Berkeley) creates and sells software for personal computers. In 1989, it introduced a screen saver computer product entitled After Dark. A screen saver prevents burn-in damage to the user's monitor by displaying moving images during periods of inactivity. After Dark comes with a number of different display choices, called modules. One such module, called Flying Toasters, shows a squadron of two-slice, fifties-style, rounded toasters with wings flying across the computer screen. The Flying Toasters module was introduced in 1990 and has become very popular in the computer industry.

Sound recordings were not copyrightable by law until February 15, 1972. On April 19, 1973, the sound recording *Thirty Seconds* was registered with the Copyright Office of the United States, on the newly available Form N, which was established specifically for registering a claim of copyright in a published sound recording. The Form N filed for *Thirty Seconds* listed plaintiff Grunt Records as the author of the sound recording. On the published album, the circle P (phonorecording copyright notice) appears on the label in the center of the LP and the circle c (copyright notice) appears on the backside of the album cover.

Berkeley has obtained a United States copyright registration and trademark registration for the Flying Toasters module. In 1993, Berkeley brought a copyright and trademark infringement lawsuit in the Northern District of California against the Delrina Corporation, a software manufacturer and competitor of Berkeley. Delrina had begun to market a competitive screen saver program that incorporated the Flying Toaster design protected by Berkeley. On

October 8, 1993, this court (Lynch, J.) found that Berkeley made a *prima facie* showing of copyright infringement and granted Berkeley's Motion for a Preliminary Injunction against Delrina.

On June 14, 1994, plaintiffs filed this action, claiming that Berkeley's After Dark Flying Toaster module infringes their copyrights to the *Thirty Seconds* album. Defendants filed this Motion to Dismiss for Lack of Subject Matter Jurisdiction and for Failure to State a Claim under Fed. R. Civ. P. 12(b)(6).

III. DISCUSSION

A. Legal Standard

A plaintiff may not bring an action for copyright infringement unless the copyright claim is registered with the Copyright Office of the United States. 17 U.S.C. §411(a) (West 1994). Such registration is a jurisdictional prerequisite to a suit for infringement. *Hung Tang v. Ho Yong Hwang*, 799 F. Supp. 499, 503 (E.D.Pa 1992). For plaintiffs to state a claim for which relief can be granted, and for the Court to assert jurisdiction over this case, the Court must find that the registered copyright claim to *Thirty Seconds* includes the disputed artwork that appears on the cover of the published record album and compact disc.

B. Governing Law

The Copyright Act of 1976 substantially revised copyright law in the United States. The 1976 Act superseded, to a large extent, the previously governing Copyright Act of 1909. In determining the corpus of law that governs a particular situation, the governing law is the law in effect when the infringement or other activity upon which a suit is based arises. D. Nimmer & M. Nimmer, 5 Nimmer on Copyright Overview at OV-9 (1993) (Nimmer). The 1976 Act generally governs any infringement or undertaking allegedly occurring after January 1, 1978, the date the 1976 act took effect. The 1909 Act continues to govern any infringement or undertaking allegedly occurring before January 1, 1978. *Id.*; See *e.g.*, *Lone Ranger Television, Inc. v. Program Radio Corp.*, 740 F.2d 718 (9th Cir. 1984) (applying the Copyright Act of 1909 to interpret scope of a copyright registered in 1954 and allegedly infringed in 1979).

1. 1973 Law Controls in Determining Scope of Copyright

The *Thirty Seconds* copyright was registered prior to January 1, 1978. The Transitional and Supplementary Provisions of the 1976 Copyright Act provide that the Copyright Act of 1909 governs the scope of a copyright registration for phonorecords first published before January 1, 1978, as it existed on December 31, 1977. Copyright Act of 1976, Transitional and Supplementary Provisions §109 & 110 (1976) reprinted in 5 Nimmer app. at 2-148. Further, the adequacy of the notice requirements for any phonorecord publicly distributed before January 1, 1978 is governed by the Copyright Act of 1909. The Copyright Act of 1976 governs the notice requirements for any phonorecord publicly distributed on or after January 1, 1978. Copyright Act of 1976, Transitional and Supplementary Provisions §108 (1976) reprinted in 5 Nimmer app. at 2-147.

2. Current Law Controls in Determining Whether The Jefferson Airplane Has Standing to Sue

The alleged copyright infringement at the core of this suit occurred no earlier than 1989. Current copyright law therefore governs whether or not The Jefferson Airplane has standing to sue.

C. Plaintiffs' Registration of Copyright for Sound Recording Did Not Include the Cover Artwork

The 1909 Copyright Act provided that the "application for registration shall specify to which of the following classes the work in which copyright is claimed belongs." Copyright Act of 1909, 17 U.S.C. §5 (1977). In 1977, Section 5 of title 17 provided fourteen classes (class A through class N) of works in which copyright may be claimed. For example, class A protected books, class D protected dramatic compositions, class E protected musical compositions, etc. Class N was added to section 5 by a Congressional amendment on October 15, 1971. 17 U.S.C.A. §5 (West 1972). Effective February 15, 1972, class N provided copyright protection in sound recordings for the first time. *Id.* Congress created class N in order to deal with the pirating of sound recordings, a problem exacerbated by the increasing popularity of phonographs and cassette tape recorders. House Report on the Sound Recording Amendment of 1971, H.R. Rep. No. 92-487, 92nd Cong., 1st Sess. (1971), reprinted in 6 Nimmer app. at 18-1.

Copyright Office rules expressly stated that sound recordings had to be registered in Class N. Circular #56, "Copyright for Sound Recordings", Copyright Office of the United States, p.6 (1976) ("Circular #56"). The nature of the works to be registered in Class N was defined in the Code of Federal Regulations:

> Sound recordings (Class N): (a) This class includes published sound recordings, *i.e.* works that result from the fixation of a series of musical, spoken, or other sounds. Common examples include recordings of music, drama, [etc.] . . . as published in the form of phonorecords such as discs, tapes, cartridges [etc.] . . . 37 C.F.R. §202.15a(a) (1973).

Defendant argues that the scope of plaintiff's class N copyright registration No. N6051 includes the musical recording only, not the art on the cover of *Thirty Seconds*, which should have been registered separately in class K, labeled "Prints and pictorial illustrations including prints or labels used for articles of merchandise." Because the class N registration is plaintiff's only copyright registration relating to *Thirty Seconds*, defendant claims the disputed artwork is unregistered; therefore, this action must be dismissed for failure to state a claim and for lack of subject matter jurisdiction.

While a colorable argument can be made that cover art is included in a registration of a sound recording under Class N, the language defining class N and subsequent pronouncements and practices of the Copyright Office make clear that separate registrations are required.

The Ninth Circuit rule is that "the Register has the authority to interpret the copyright laws and that its interpretations are entitled to judicial deference if reasonable." *Marascalco v. Fantasy, Inc.*, 953 F.2d 469, 473 (9th Cir. 1991), cert. denied, 504 U.S. 931, 112 S. Ct. 1997, 118 L. Ed. 2d 592 (1992). If controlling, these Practices establish the plaintiffs' proffered copyright registration covers the facially claimed sound recording work only.

Defendant has provided the Court with a certified copy of a portion of the Copyright Office Examination Practices to support its interpretation of the scope of plaintiffs' sound recording registration. The Practices state:

Sound recording distinct from other copyrightable component parts. Registration in Class N cannot extend protection to copyrightable matter appearing on a jacket, liner notes, or container, etc., even though such items form a part of the deposit for registration in Class N. One basis of this rule is the divergent statutory requirements regarding the correct form of notice applies to all works except sound recordings, which works demand a special form of notice.

"Practices of the Examining Division in the Registration of Sound Recordings (Class N)," dated June 22, 1972. Defendants also provide a Declaration from the current Register of Copyrights, Marybeth Peters, who was an Examiner in the Music Section of the Examining Division of the Copyright Office from 1966 to 1975. Ms. Peters declares:

> As a matter of practice, the Examining Division would not, and to the best of my knowledge, did not, issue a single registration to cover both a sound recording in Class N and other copyrightable material. Pursuant to the Practices . . . Class N registrations were limited in scope to the sound recording itself. Liner notes, lyrics, illustrations, booklets, and another material accompanying the sound recording were required to be registered separately in either Class A or Class K. Peters Decl., P 4.

Further support for defendant's position is provided by the Copyright Office publication, Circular #56, one portion of which is entitled "Copyright for Sound Recordings". It states, "in many cases sound recordings are first published with other copyrightable material as a unit. Examples are: discs published in jackets which contain substantial original textual or pictorial matter and which bear a copyright notice appropriate for that material..." Circular #56, p. 6. Circular #56 then provides that "with the exception of the sound recording," these other materials "may qualify for registration as a 'book' on Form A" if appropriate notice is given, *e.g.*, a circled "C". *Id.* (emphasis added). Critically, it continues:

> While registrants have the option of registering one claim in class A for a published combination of various material, separate registrations may be made of the different parts, provided that they bore their own copyright notices from the time of first publication. Separate registration in Class N must be made in every case for the sound recording.

Id. (emphasis added). The reasonable conclusion drawn from Circular #56 is that separate registration was required for the sound recording and the album cover art.
Plaintiffs contend that, even if the registration was faulty, it was merely an error in classification that cannot affect the copyright protection afforded the artwork. Indeed, Section 5, after listing each of the classes in which copyright registration may be made, provides that "the above specifications shall not be held to limit the subject matter of copyright . . . nor shall any error in classification invalidate or impair the copyright protection secured under this title." Title 17 U.S.C. §5; see also, *Hearst Corp. v. Stark*, 639 F. Supp. 970, 974 (N.D.Cal. 1986) ("errors in copyright registration . . . do not invalidate the copyright or render the registration certificate incapable of supporting an infringement action"). Registration in separate classes was intended to enhance the efficiency of the Copyright Office, and not to legally limit the scope of copyrighted material. House Report on the Copyright Act of 1909, H.R. Rep. No. 2222, 60th Cong., 2nd Sess. (1909) ("Section 5 refers solely to a classification made for the convenience of the Copyright Office and those applying for copyrights") reprinted in 6 Nimmer app. at 13-15.

Even if plaintiffs' failure to separately register the cover artwork could be interpreted as a mere error in classification, a conclusion the Court does not reach, there is no mistaking the fact that the registration application unambiguously claims a copyright in music alone. Complaint, Exh. B. There is no explanation for plaintiffs' failure to expressly describe in the application for registration all materials in which copyright is allegedly claimed. It is well settled that merely depositing the album cover with the Library of Congress cannot expand the scope of the copyright claimed in the registration. *National Conference of Bar Examiners v. Multistate Legal Studies, Inc.*, 692 F.2d 478, 487 (7th Cir. 1982), cert. denied sub nom, *Multistate Legal Studies, Inc. v. Ladd*, 464 U.S. 814, 78 L. Ed. 2d 83, 104 S. Ct. 69 (1983); see also 2 M. Nimmer & D. Nimmer, Nimmer on Copyright, §7.17[A] at 7-178.5 (1993). No matter what is deposited with the Copyright Office, a work must be claimed before it can be considered registered.

IV. CONCLUSION.

For the foregoing reasons, plaintiffs' copyright claim is DISMISSED. The Court declines to exercise pendant jurisdiction over the remaining state law claims; they are also DISMISSED. 28 U.S.C. §1367(c)(3) The Clerk of the Court shall close the file.

TWIN BOOKS CORPORATION v. THE WALT DISNEY COMPANY
877 F. Supp. 496 (N.D. Cal. 1995)

Plaintiff, a former nonexclusive licensee of Disney products, brings this suit for infringement of derivative copyrights in the book *Bambi*. Plaintiff alleges that last year it acquired certain rights in *Bambi* and seeks profits from the *Bambi* motion picture and an injunction prohibiting further exhibitions of the film.

The parties' cross-motions for summary judgment came on regularly for hearing before the Court on September 9, 1994. The Court thereafter directed the parties to submit supplemental briefing. Having considered oral argument of counsel and all the papers submitted, the Court hereby GRANTS defendant's motion and DENIES plaintiff's motion, as follows.

STANDARD FOR GRANTING SUMMARY JUDGMENT (deleted)

I. BACKGROUND.

Bambi was written by Felix Salten, an Austrian citizen. The book was first published in the German language in Berlin, Germany, in 1923, without a copyright notice. A second German language edition was published in Germany in 1926, with a copyright notice.

At the time of both publications, the 1909 Copyright Act governed copyright law in the United States. Under the 1909 Act, the maximum 56-year term of copyright was divided into periods: the initial period of 28-years, and a second 28-year period upon renewal in the year. A claim to copyright the 1926 edition of *Bambi* was registered in the United States Copyright Office in 1927.

On December 3, 1936, Salten and his publisher assigned rights in the *Bambi* book to Sidney Franklin (the Salten assignment). On April 6, 1937, Franklin assigned all his rights under the Salten assignment to Walt Disney Productions (the Franklin assignment). Defendant The Walt Disney Company is the successor in interest to Walt Disney Productions. Both of these assignments were recorded in the Copyright Office in 1939. These assignments transferred all copyrights except literary rights to publish the original *Bambi* text and translations thereof.

Disney first released the *Bambi* motion picture in 1942, under its rights from the Franklin assignment. The picture has been re-released several times, and Disney has marketed many other products based on it.

Salten died in 1945. The copyright in the *Bambi* book was renewed in 1954 by Salten's daughter, Anna Salten Wyler. The renewal certificate shows that it was for a work registered as published, and 1926 was listed as the original publication date.

In 1958, following extensive negotiations, Anna Wyler executed three agreements with Disney concerning rights to the *Bambi* book (the Anna Wyler agreements).

Anna Wyler died in 1977, leaving her husband, Veit Wyler, as her sole heir and successor to her rights in the literary properties of Salten. In 1993, Veit Wyler and his two children assigned all their rights in the *Bambi* book to plaintiff (the Viet Wyler assignment).

II. DISCUSSION.

Defendants originally moved for summary judgment on three theories: (1) no infringement because the *Bambi* book is in the public domain; (2) no infringement because the 1958 Anna Wyler agreements granted Disney renewal copyrights in its *Bambi* motion picture throughout the second copyright term; and (3) the Viet Wyler assignment made plaintiff a nonexclusive licensee only; thus plaintiff does not have standing to bring this suit.

Plaintiff cross-moved for summary judgment that Disney is liable for copyright infringement, and that some of Disney's affirmative defenses fail. In response to plaintiff's papers, defendants concede that plaintiff has raised triable issues of fact concerning the interpretation and effect of the Anna Wyler agreements. Because the meaning of the 1993 Viet Wyler assignment depends on the effect of the Anna Wyler agreements, defendants' motion for summary judgment now rests solely on its argument that the *Bambi* book is in the public domain.

A. Public domain

Defendants argue in the alternative that *Bambi* fell into the public domain

(1) In 1923 upon publication without copyright notice (2) in 1926 upon publication with a 1926 copyright notice, or (3) in 1951 when Anna Wyler failed timely to renew the copyright. The Court is persuaded by defendant's third argument and thus does not rule on the first two.

Even if *Bambi* did not fall into the public domain in 1923 or 1926, it is clear that under the 1909 Act, the *Bambi* book fell into the public domain at the end of its first 28-year period unless Anna Wyler promptly renewed the copyright. 1909 Copyright Act, 17 U.S.C. §24 (superseded 1976); 2 Nimmer §9.05[B] at 9-68. It is also clear that, under the 1909 Act, the term of copyright protection commences when the work is first published, with or without a copyright notice. 17 U.S.C. §§24, 26 (1909 Act); see, *e.g.*, *Basevi v. Edward O'Toole Co.*, 26 F. Supp. 41, 47 (S.D.N.Y. 1939); *American Code Co. v. Bensinger*, 282 F. 829, 836 (2d Cir. 1922). Relying on *Heim v. Universal Pictures Co.*, 154 F.2d 480 (2d Cir. 1946), plaintiff argues that the copyright term for *Bambi* began on the date of publication with notice in 1926. This argument is totally without merit. In *Heim*, the court held that, unlike publication in the United States without the appropriate copyright notice, publication abroad without notice of United States copyright would not necessarily preclude the owner from subsequently obtaining a valid United States copyright. *Id.* at 480.

The court in *Heim* never mentioned the effect of its ruling on the term of a copyright. There is no basis for plaintiff's leap from the *Heim* ruling to the conclusion that the term of copyright protection does not start in such cases until the work is published with notice.

Accordingly, the *Bambi* copyright, assuming its validity, expired in 1951. Anna Wyler's failure to renew timely in 1951 resulted in *Bambi's* release into the public domain. However, in 1960 President Eisenhower issued a proclamation, as follows:

That with respect to . . . (1) works of citizens of Austria subject to renewal of copyright under the laws of the United States of America on or after March 13, 1938, and prior to July 27, 1956, there has existed during several years of the aforementioned period such disruption or suspension of facilities essential to compliance with the conditions and formalities prescribed with respect to such works by copyright laws of the United States of America as to bring such works within the terms of the [1909, Act], and that accordingly the time within which compliance with such conditions and formalities may take place is hereby extended with respect to such works for one year after the date of this proclamation.

There are no cases or other authorities interpreting or applying this proclamation. Thus, the Court must determine its applicability to the case at bar as an issue of first impression. Plaintiff argues that this proclamation operates retroactively to render Anna Wyler's 1954 renewal timely and valid. Defendants argue that the proclamation should be interpreted to allow a copyright owner whose copyright had expired to file for renewal in the one year period after the proclamation. The language of the proclamation is susceptible to either interpretation.

Defendants argue that no intent for retroactive application appears on the face of the proclamation or in Section 9(b). Section 9(b) provides that no liability shall attach for lawful uses of copyrights prior to the effect of a proclamation. Thus, if the proclamation applied to Wyler's 1954 renewal, it would restore copyright protection for *Bambi* as of 1960, and not retroactively to 1954. However, this does not resolve the question of whether, to take advantage of the proclamation, Wyler must have filed for a renewal of copyright after the proclamation was issued in 1960.

The Court finds some guidance in an analogy to the North American Free Trade Agreement. (NAFTA), which provides for a one-year cure period for restoring copyright protection for certain motion pictures which had fallen into the public domain because of failure to comply with notice formalities. Under NAFTA, copyright owners must file a statement of intent with the Copyright Office regarding films for which they wish to restore protection. See NAFTA Implementation Act, Pub. L. 103-182 §334, 17 U.S.C. §104A (1993). It is true that Congress imposed different and more stringent requirements in NAFTA than those in Section 9(b). On the other hand, NAFTA was enacted after the passage of the Copyright Act of 1976, which relaxed the stringent formalities imposed by the 1909 Act. It follows that the 1960 proclamation, in the context of the more stringent 1909 Act, should not be construed more liberally to provide automatic retroactive validation of copyrights that would otherwise have expired. Rather, the proclamation must be interpreted to require copyright owners who had previously made a defective renewal to file a corrective renewal within a year after the proclamation.

On a policy level, this interpretation would put copyright owners who had failed to renew effectively on equal footing with those who had been unable to renew at all, and who thus had only one year after the proclamation to do so. If, on the contrary, copyright owners could take advantage of the proclamation without filing any corrective documents, the Copyright Office and the public would not know which works were still protected despite defective renewals, and when such copyright protection would expire.

The facts at bar illustrate the necessity of the requirement that corrective documents be filed. Wyler's 1954 renewal recited 1926 as the first date of publication. Thus, one cannot discern from the face of Wyler's 1954 renewal that it was a defective filing cured by the 1960 proclamation. Nor could one discern that the copyright would expire three years earlier than the renewal indicates.

Accordingly, the Court holds that Anna Wyler's copyright is not saved by the 1960 Presidential Proclamation because Wyler failed to file a corrective document to cure her inaccurate and late renewal within a year after the proclamation. Therefore, the copyright in *Bambi* expired, and fell into the public domain, in 1951.

B. Licensee estoppel

Plaintiff raises licensee estoppel as a defense to defendants' claim that the copyright is in the public domain, asserting that as a licensee of the copyright, Disney is estopped from challenging its validity. Once again, this is an issue of first impression. Although the Supreme Court has held that licensee estoppel is inapplicable to patent licensees, see *Lear v. Adkins*, 395 U.S. 653, 23 L. Ed. 2d 610, 89 S. Ct. 1902 (1969), no court has decided whether copyright licensees are estopped. However, the Ninth Circuit holds that "where precedent in copyright cases is lacking, it is appropriate to look for guidance to patent law, 'because of the historic kinship between patent law and copyright law.'" *Harris v. Emus Records Corp.*, 734 F.2d 1329, 1333 (1984) (quoting *Sony Corp. of America v. Universal City Studios*, 464 U.S. 417, 104 S. Ct. 774, 787, 78 L. Ed. 2d 574 (1984)). See also 3 Nimmer §10.15[B] at 10-125 ("On the basis of *Lear*, which has been applied outside the patent realm to copyright cases as well, plaintiffs may no longer argue licensee estoppel.")

Plaintiff's reliance on *Saturday Evening Post Co. v. Rumbleseat Press, Inc.*, 816 F.2d 1191 (7th Cir. 1987), is unpersuasive. First, as defendant note, in that case the court upheld an explicit no-contest clause in the copyright, license, and limited its holding to that situation: "Our case involves a negotiated clause rather than a doctrine that in effect reads a no-contest clause into every licensing agreement." *Id.* at 1200. In the dictum cited by plaintiff, the court opined that the economic argument made by the Supreme Court in *Lear* does not apply to copyright licensees, because the "economic power conferred is much smaller." *Id.* Plaintiff's attempt to rest on this argument, given the $490 million in economic power wielded by Disney by virtue of its *Bambi* license, is singularly unpersuasive.

Accordingly, the Court holds that licensee estoppel does not apply in this case.

III. CONCLUSION.

1. Defendants' motion for summary judgment is GRANTED on grounds that the copyright in *Bambi* expired, and *Bambi* fell into the public domain, at the latest in 1951, when Anna Wyler failed timely to renew the copyright; and licensee estoppel does not apply to bar defendant from raising the public domain issue as a defense.

2. Plaintiff's cross-motion for summary judgment is DENIED in its entirety as moot.

3. The Clerk shall enter judgment in favor of defendant, and defendant shall recover its costs from plaintiff.

IT IS SO ORDERED.

Glossary

Accession - Increase in the value of property caused by someone other than the owner without consideration or intended as a gift

Bailee - Person who is given possession of personalty

Bailment - Relationship created by the transfer of possession of personal property

Bailor - Person who transfers possession of personal property

Common carrier - Commercial enterprise that transports goods and people for consideration

Confusion - Situation in which property of two or more persons is co-mingled and cannot be separated

Constructive bailment - Information that one should be aware of because it is reasonably accessible

Copyright - Governmental grant of exclusive use given to an author or an artist

Innkeeper - Enterprise that rents temporary accommodations to the public

Intangible - Personal property that is only representative of something of value

Intellectual property - Copyrights, patents, and marks

Lien - Right to retain property by a creditor until the debt is paid

Mark - Word or symbol that distinguishes a product or service

Patent - Governmental grant of exclusive use given to the inventor of a scientific invention

Personal property (personalty) - All nonreal property

Pledge - Bailment used as collateral for a loan

Royalty - Consideration given for the use of intellectual property

Service mark - Mark for services

Tangibles - Personal property that can be touched or moved whose value is intrinsic to the object

Trademark - Mark for goods and products

Exercises

1. Distinguish between and give examples of confusion and accession.

2. Discuss the impact of the concept of bailments to commercial enterprises.

3. Discuss the difference between a lien and a pledge. Obtain a receipt from a pawnbroker to ascertain the rights the pledgee gives up.

4. Give three examples of bailments from your day-to-day life. Draft a document that would protect your property interest in an item you lend to a friend.

5. The United States government provides free packets with information and forms for acquiring intellectual property rights. Obtain such packets either by mail or by the Internet and analyze the information requested.

Chapter Seven

LAW OF AGENCY

Introduction

Almost every commercial enterprise involves a team effort of persons who may be owners of the enterprise, employees of the enterprise, or independent individuals hired by the enterprise to perform one particular and limited function. Because businesses often have one or more employees, business owners may be held legally responsible for the employees' actions. This liability arising from actions of one person causing another person to be held liable is referred to as vicarious liability—one person, or entity, being held legally responsible for injuries to a third person caused by the actions of someone acting on behalf of the person held liable.

For commercial law purposes, this concept of vicarious liability is generally labeled as the law of agency, which encompasses three separate types of relationships:

1. *Master-servant relationship*. An employer is liable for its employees' tortious actions that injure third persons.
2. *Principal-agent relationship*. A person is liable for the contracts entered into on his or her behalf by someone he or she has authorized.
3. *Independent contractor*. A person is generally not liable for the acts of the person he or she hired to perform a specific task.

In order to understand the various types of business organizations that will be discussed in the following chapter, it is important to understand how these relationships affect the business enterprises.

The Master-Servant Relationship

The **master-servant relationship** exists when one person, referred to as the servant, is employed to render services of any type, otherwise than in the pursuit of an independent calling, and who remains under the control of another, the master, in rendering such services. The master-servant relationship is typified by the ordinary employment relationship in which the employer controls the nature and extent of the employee's workload. One of the essential features of this type of legal relationship is that the master, or employer, controls the servant's, or employee's, action, and the employee has no discretion with respect to the work that must be performed.

Example: *A manufacturer hires a woman as a forklift operator at the company's loading dock. The employee's hours are set by the manufacturer, as is the location of her workstation. The forklift operator cannot, on her own initiative, decide that on a given day she will work on the assembly line rather than operate the lift at the loading dock. The manufacturer controls the operator's actions.*

The concept of the master-servant relationship is one of the fundamental relationships under tort law. Take note that federal and state statutes, and some common law contract principles govern most other aspects of the employment relationship.

The liability of a master with respect to the actions of his or her servant lies in tort. The basic doctrine, known as *respondeat superior* ("let the master answer," Chapter Two) states that a master is liable for the tortious actions of his or her servant that injures a third party if such action occurs while the servant is furthering the master's interests. The primary burden is on the injured party to prove that the injury occurred while the servant was furthering the master's interests and not on a frolic of his own, unconnected to the master's business.

> *Example:* *A wholesaler employs a salesperson to travel to specific geographic areas to sell the wholesaler's goods to retailers. To accomplish this purpose, the wholesaler provides the sales personnel with company cars. One day one of the sales people, to make an appointment with a large retailer, exceeds the speed limit to avoid being late. While speeding, the sales person hits a pedestrian. Because the salesperson was negligent (Chapter Two) while furthering the master's business (going to a sales meeting), the wholesaler may be held liable for the pedestrian's injuries.*

> *Example:* *Another salesperson for the same wholesaler has completed all of her rounds for the day and makes an appointment with a friend to play tennis. To get to the court on time, the salesperson exceeds the speed limit and injures a pedestrian. In this instance, even though the salesperson was using the company car, she was negligent in order to further her own interest (the tennis game with a friend), not the wholesaler's interests, so she may be held personally liable for the injury while she was on a frolic of her own.*

In addition to the concept of a frolic of his own, the law recognizes three exceptions to the doctrine of *respondeat superior*:

1. **Fellow servant exception**. This rule states that a master will not be liable for the negligent actions of one of his or her servants that injure another of his or her servants. This exception was formulated to encourage employers to hire people without having to continually worry about liability. Note that if a servant is injured on the job, the servant may seek redress under workers' compensation laws.
2. **Negligent hiring**. This rule holds a master personally liable in his or her own right and not vicariously if he or she hired a servant who is incompetent and that incompetence is the cause of the injury to the third person.

> *Example:* *A nursery school hires a janitor without checking his background. The janitor molests several children. It is then discovered that the janitor has several convictions for child molestation and sexual assault, which would have been disclosed had the school performed any reasonable background check. In this instance, the school may be held directly liable for negligent hiring.*

3. **Intentional torts**. A master is not liable for intentional torts committed by his servant unless that tort was committed while furthering the master's business and could be foreseeable as a consequence of the nature of the job. For example, a bouncer in a nightclub may intentionally injure a patron in his or her overzealous attempt to fulfill the function of a bouncer. The injured third person may sue the servant instead of the master but usually will seek redress from the business owner who is presumed to have "deeper pockets." The third person cannot recover from both unless they are jointly liable (Chapter Two), but if the master is sued and found liable, he or she may seek **indemnification** from the servant, thereby having the servant reimburse the master for the award the master had to pay because of the servant's actions. Note that the law on this point may vary from state to state.

The master-servant relationship exists until the employment relationship is terminated.

The Principal-Agent Relationship

The **principal-agent relationship** occurs when one person, called the **agent**, acts on behalf of another, called the **principal**, in order to enter into contractual relationships with third persons on the principal's behalf. In this fashion, the agent is acting as the principal's representative.

Unlike an employee in a master-servant relationship, an agent is expected to exercise independent discretion in order to perform the task for the principal, and the agent has the legal ability to bind the principal contractually to third persons. When the agent acts, the agent is acting as the principal's representative only and may only enter into contracts that the principal could legally enter into. Note that because the agent is acting as the principal's representative, only the principal needs contractual capacity—the agent's capacity is derived from the principal.

Example: A manufacturer asks his purchasing agent to acquire a specific number of lead pipes. The agent may use his discretion to locate the best deal by seeking bids from several suppliers, and the contract he enters into is a contract between the supplier and the manufacturer. The purchasing agent is not an actual party to the agreement; he is merely acting as the manufacturer's representative.

Example: A 12-year-old child is very interested in the stock market and follows several companies on a daily basis on the Internet. Eventually, she decides that she would like to spend her Christmas money on some shares in a company she has been tracking, but she is not old enough to make the purchase herself. She asks her mother to buy the stock for her. If the mother makes this purchase, the child is not bound, because a 12-year-old child lacks the capacity to enter into this relationship (Chapter Three).

The principal-agent relationship can be created by one of the following methods:

- *By agreement.* An agency relationship can be formed simply by the agreement of the parties, and may, but does not have to, be supported by consideration (a contract, Chapter Three).

- *By ratification.* An agency relationship can be created retroactively if the principal accepts the contract that was entered into on his or her behalf by someone who was not authorized to act when the contract was formed.

> *Example: A secretary overhears his boss say that she wants to purchase land to construct a new facility for the business. The secretary has a friend who has been trying to sell some undeveloped land in the geographic area in which the boss had indicated interest. The secretary represents himself as being able to sell the land on behalf of his friend, and the boss agrees to the purchase. When the friend is told about the contract, if the friend agrees, the agency will be deemed to have been created retroactively because the friend is accepting the benefits of the contract.*

- *By estoppel.* This agency relationship arises when a person intentionally or negligently causes a third person to believe that another is his agent, and the third person relies on such appearance in dealing with the supposed agent. In this situation, the presumed principal will be estopped, or barred, from denying the agency.

> *Example: A retail store indicates on its store directory that it has a repair department, and a customer brings a bracelet there for repairs. The repairman destroys the bracelet. The customer then discovers that the repairman is an independent contractor who just rents space from the store. Because the store let the customer believe that the repairman was part of its business, the store may be estopped from denying liability for the damage to the bracelet.*

Once it is determined that the agency relationship exists, it is then necessary to ascertain the nature of the agent's authority, or legal ability, to act on the principal's behalf. There are three types of authority that an agent may have:

1. **Actual authority.** The principal manifests his or her authority directly to the agent. This type of authority includes both **express authority**, which results from the specific words used by the principal, and **implied authority**, which arises from the custom, usage, and past dealings of the parties without specific words being used. Actual authority is determined by the actions of the principal viewed objectively and, if such authority is found, the principal is liable for the full contract price for all contracts the agent enters on the principal's behalf within the bounds of this authority.

> *Example: A book publisher employs a production manager to hire outside printers for the publisher's manuscripts. The production manager has the express authority to contract with printers and implicitly, because of the custom of the business, knows that the contract must specify that no payment will be made to the printer until the book has been delivered and accepted by the publisher.*

2. **Apparent authority.** Sometimes referred to as **ostensible authority**, this authority results from the manifestation that the principal makes, not to the agent directly, but to third persons who deal with the agent. This authority will be found if the third person

could reasonably believe what the principal has stated. If the agent is determined to have apparent authority, the principal will be bound to the full contract price.

> **Example:** *A business owner is constantly being annoyed by an aggressive salesman. In order to get rid of the salesman, the owner says that his secretary is the one who makes such purchases for the company. If the salesman then convinces the secretary to enter into a sales agreement for the company, the owner will be bound because of his representations to the salesman.*

3. **Authority by estoppel.** This arises when the principal intentionally or negligently allows a third person to believe that his or her agent is authorized to do something that the agent is not authorized to do, and the third person detrimentally relies on the representations to such an extent that it would be inequitable to permit the principal to deny the authority. In order for authority by estoppel to apply, the third person must have detrimentally relied on the representation (usually meaning lost money) and, if so, the recovery is limited to the actual financial loss, not the full contract price.

> **Example:** *A bookstore owner has a dental appointment but has no one employed to assist him. To keep the store open while he goes to the dentist, he asks his cousin to look after the store for him and to deal with the customers. The owner gives the cousin a jacket with the word "Manager" printed on the lapel. While the owner is gone, a publisher's representative enters the store, sees the "Manager," and convinces the cousin to purchase several titles. In this instance, the storeowner let the third person believe that the cousin had the authority, as a manager, to make such purchases, and the owner will be liable for any actual loss the publisher suffers if the contract is voided. Note that, because of the nature of this contract, there may in fact be no actual out-of-pocket losses, except perhaps shipping costs.*

An agent is deemed to be a fiduciary to the principal, a person having a position of trust, who is held to a standard of care higher than ordinary care. As a fiduciary, the agent owes the principal the following obligations:

- The agent must act personally and is prohibited from delegating any of the responsibilities except those that are mechanical, ministerial, usually delegated, or an act that the agent cannot lawfully perform him or herself, such as representing the principal in court if the court requires such representative to be an attorney.
- The agent must actually perform all acts he or she has agreed to perform.
- The agent must notify and inform the principal of all acts that are being performed on the principal's behalf.
- The agent must be loyal to the principal and may not **self-deal**—profit personally from a contract that should go to the benefit of the principal, excluding any agreed-upon compensation.

Conversely, the principal is not a fiduciary to the agent but owes the agent the following obligations:

- The principal must exercise the ordinary standard of care in providing space and materials to, and dealing with, the agent.

- The principal must compensate and reimburse the agent, if this has been agreed upon.
- The principal must cooperate with the agent so that the agent may fulfill his or her duties.

The purpose of the agency relationship, as indicated by its definition, is to enable the agent to enter into contracts with third persons on behalf of the principal. Therefore, the liability of the principal lies only in contract, not in tort, as with the master-servant relationship. However, be alert to the fact that the same two people may be involved in both types of relationships, and the liability will depend upon which relationship is being brought into question by the third party.

The principal-agent relationship may terminate at the date or event agreed to when the agency was created, by the loss or destruction of the subject matter of the agency, by the death or insanity of the parties, or by act of the parties. The principal can terminate the relationship by **revocation**, and the agent may terminate by **renunciation**. However, if the relationship was created by a contract, the terms of the contract will determine the parties' ability to terminate (Chapter Three).

Independent Contractor

An independent contractor is a person who is hired solely to accomplish results. The independent contractor is not under the control of the other party, and has total discretion with respect to the performance of the task.

The other contracting party is generally not liable for the contracts entered into by the independent contractor, nor is he or she liable for the contractor's tortious actions, absent an agreement to the contrary. However, there are three situations in which the other contracting party will be held legally responsible for the actions of the independent contractor:

1. The task for which the independent contractor is hired is inherently dangerous, such as demolition or using explosives.
2. The independent contractor has agreed to be controlled by the other contracting party.
3. The contracting party provides the tools that the independent contractor is to use, and those tools are the cause of the injury to the third party.

Generally, independent contractors can be considered as experts hired for a short time to accomplish a task for which their experience is needed, such as an accountant, a lawyer, or any other expert. For the most part, because the relationship is formed by contract, the terms of the contract determine the rights and liabilities of the parties (Chapter Three).

Chapter Summary

To be alert to potential liability, all persons who own, operate, or work for a commercial enterprise must be conversant with the concept of vicarious liability. For commercial enterprises, vicarious liability typically falls under the theories of the law of agency.

Three types of relationships are classified under the heading of the law of agency:

1. The master-servant relationship, in which the master's liability exists in tort for the negligent actions of the servant performed while furthering the master's business that injures third persons.
2. The principal-agent relationship, in which the liability is in contract for any contracts the agent enters with a third person on the principal's behalf, provided that the agent's ability

to act is authorized, ratified, or occurs under circumstances in which the court's equitable jurisdiction will demand the principal take responsibility.
3. The independent contractor whose actions, absent an agreement to the contrary, generally do not give rise to liability for the other contracting party unless the independent contractor is performing highly dangerous work, has agreed to be controlled by the other party, or is using tools the other party furnished the independent contractor that caused the injury to the third person.

It is important to remember that the same two individuals may be in several types of relationships simultaneously; therefore, an injured party must learn what the relationships between the individuals are to successfully pursue a claim based on vicarious liability. Further, in most instances, the actor may be liable (except perhaps for agents), but the injured third person is seeking redress from someone with more financial resources. If the third person sues and recovers from the actor, he or she cannot then maintain a suit based on vicarious liability. If a person is sued under a theory of vicarious liability, he of she may seek indemnification from the wrongdoer.

These relationships have a direct impact on the operation of all business organizations that will be discussed in the chapter that follows.

Edited Judicial Decisions

ZIMMER v. CARLTON COUNTY CO-OP POWER ASSOCIATION
483 N.W.2d 511 (Minn. App. 1992)

Paul W. Zimmer appeals from the trial court's grant of summary judgment in favor of respondent Carlton County Co-op Power Association.

Appellant was injured while working for an independent contractor hired by respondent. Appellant brought a negligence action against respondent, alleging that its failure to supervise the job site, its failure to require adequate safety precautions, and its failure to make sure that its independent contractor was qualified to do the work caused his injuries. The trial court granted summary judgment in favor of respondent. We affirm.

I. FACTS.

On June 17, 1985, appellant suffered electrical burns while he was performing maintenance on respondent's power lines. At the time of the accident, appellant was working as an employee of Northern Equipment Company, an independent contractor hired by respondent to service the oil circuit reclosures (OCRs) on its power lines. Northern Equipment is not a party to this action.

According to the depositions and answers to interrogatories, on the day the accident occurred, appellant was working with his supervisor, Garald Johnson. Appellant climbed a utility pole to disconnect the OCRs from the pole. Appellant began to disconnect the OCRs and, as he did so, fell onto the energized lightning arrester or an energized line and sustained electrical burns. Johnson did not see the accident occur because he was in the van preparing his equipment.

Prior to hiring Northern Equipment to service its OCRs, respondent had its own line crews remove and ship the OCRs to a Wisconsin company for servicing. Respondent's line workers were required to pass a state examination and complete a self-study program prior to performing their job duties. Respondent also required its employees to be familiar with its procedure and safety manuals and to attend regular safety meetings. Respondent's safety director regularly performed field checks on respondent's employees for safety violations. Respondent did not require Northern Equipment or its employees to be qualified in any way or to follow any of its safety procedures. At the time appellant was injured, he was not following the safety procedures that respondent required of its own workers.

When respondent entered into a contract with Northern Equipment, it checked Johnson's references but never checked appellant's credentials or his experience. Under the contract, Johnson was required to follow a regular schedule, to report his progress to respondent, and to report his location and substation area to respondent. A representative of respondent would periodically check Northern Equipment's progress.

II. ISSUES.

1. Does a power company owe a duty to an employee of its independent contractor to ensure that the independent contractor is qualified to do the work, hires employees that are qualified, and follows safe procedures?

2. Should power companies be prohibited from hiring independent contractors to service their power lines?

III. ANALYSIS.

On appeal from a grant of summary judgment, the role of this court is to review whether genuine issues of material fact exist and whether the trial court erred in its application of the law. *Hunt v. IBM Mid Am. Employees Fed. Credit Union*, 384 N.W.2d 853, 855 (Minn. 1986). Appellant argues that summary judgment was not appropriate because fact issues existed as to whether respondent was negligent or not.

Before someone can be found negligent, it must be established that that person owed a duty to the injured person. *Rasmussen v. Prudential Ins. Co.*, 277 Minn. 266, 269, 152 N.W.2d 359, 362 (1967). Whether one owes a legal duty to another is a question of law to be determined by the court. *Keeton, Prosser and Keeton on Torts* 5th ed. §37 p. 236. It was therefore appropriate for the trial court to decide the issue of whether a duty existed, and this court must only determine whether the trial court was correct in concluding that respondent did not owe a duty to appellant.

A. The issue of whether respondent owed appellant a duty is related to the extent to which a power company is responsible for accidents that occur on the job site of its independent contractor. It is well settled that an employer is liable for harm caused to third parties because of the negligence of its independent contractor. *Conover v. Northern State Power, Co.*, 313 N.W.2d 397, 404 (Minn. 1981). This vicarious liability does not apply, however, when the injured party is an employee of the independent contractor. *Id.*

Acknowledging that respondent cannot be held vicariously liable, appellant contends that respondent should be held personally liable for his injuries. He argues that a power company should be held personally liable for injuries incurred by an employee of its independent contractor as a result of the independent contractor's incompetence or its failure to use safe procedures.

The *Conover* court delineated two situations in Minnesota case law in which an employer has been held personally negligent and therefore liable for the injuries of its independent contractor's employees:

This personal negligence * * * may consist of a breach of a duty to exercise reasonably careful supervision of a jobsite where employees of the independent contractor are working when the employer retains control or some measure of control over the project. * * * Even where the employer retains no control, he may still owe a duty of care, as a possessor of land, to persons coming on the premises, including the employees of an independent contractor. Ordinarily this duty would be to inspect and warn before turning over the jobsite. *Conover*, 313 N.W.2d at 401 (citations omitted).

Neither of these types of personal negligence applies to this case. In order to be held personally liable because of retained control, the employer must retain "the general control and supervision of the work." *Thill v. Modern Erecting Co.*, 272 Minn. 217, 226, 136 N.W.2d 677, 684 (1965). The facts indicate that respondent did not retain general control over or supervise the OCR repair project. It only made periodic investigations into Northern Equipment's progress. Appellant conceded at the summary judgment hearing that respondent did not retain control. In fact, it is essentially appellant's argument that respondent was negligent in not retaining control over the project.

The duty imposed on an employer as a possessor of land is to inspect the premises for latent or hidden dangers and then to warn on comers of those dangers. See *Whirlpool Corp. v. Morse*, 222 F. Supp. 645, 652-53 (1963), aff'd 332 F.2d 901 (8th Cir. 1964). For example, in *Conover* the power company was liable for an injury that resulted from a severely rotted utility pole. *Conover*, 313 N.W.2d at 402. The court determined that the power company knew or should have known about the dangerous condition of the pole and should have warned the independent contractor's employees about it. *Id.* In contrast, in this case, the injury was not caused by a latent or hidden defect in the property but by an inherent and known danger of the property. Respondent had no duty to warn appellant of the dangers involved with power line work.

Because appellant's claim does not correspond to any previously established duty, he is asking this court to expand the law to hold an employer personally liable for injuries caused by its independent contractor's incompetence or failure to follow safe procedures. The only Minnesota case which has addressed this type of claim is *Schip v. Pabst Brewing Co.*, 64 Minn. 22, 66 N.W. 3 (1896). In *Schip*, the owner of a building hired an independent contractor to tear it down. The owner knew that the work was dangerous and required special skill and that the contractor did not possess the necessary skill. In reviewing a claim against the owner by the contractor's employee, the *Schip* court said:

> There are many cases which hold that the owner of premises cannot, by employing a contractor, relieve himself from the continuing duty which he owes to the public, ...but we can find no case which holds that the owner owes any such duty to the servant of the independent contractor. *Id.* at 24, 66 N.W. at 5.

The *Schip* court held that the owner was not liable for the injuries of the independent contractor's employee.

Appellant contends that because of the hazardous nature of power line work, the type of duty, which the Supreme Court refused to impose on the employer in *Schip*, should be imposed on power companies. We decline to impose such a duty. An independent contractor of a power company has its own nondelegable duty to its employees to use safe procedures. See *Baumgartner v. Holslin*, 236 Minn. 325, 327, 52 N.W.2d 763, 765 (1952). If we were to impose a duty on a company to make sure that its independent contractor uses safe procedures, then we would, in effect, impose a duty on the company to make sure that its independent contractor does not negligently injure its employees. Imposing such a duty would be the same as holding the company vicariously liable for its independent contractor's negligence. This is the kind of liability that the Supreme Court has specifically refused to impose on power companies. See *Conover*, 313 N.W.2d 397, 403-4 (Minn. 1981).

We also decline to expand the law to impose a duty owed to a power company's independent contractor's employees to ensure that its independent contractor is competent and qualified.

As the law exists, power companies do owe this duty to third parties. See *Conover*, 313 N.W.2d at 404. We see no need to expand it to employees of independent contractors. An employee has control over where and for whom he chooses to work, and if he chooses to work for an independent contractor that is incompetent and unqualified, he, rather than the employer of the independent contractor, should have to bear the burden of that decision. Third parties who are injured by the negligence of an independent contractor do not have such control and are entitled to compensation from the entity that hired the incompetent or unqualified contractor.

B. Appellant argues that, for policy reasons, power companies should be prohibited from hiring independent contractors to service power lines. The judiciary, if desirable, cannot institute such a rule. The place for appellant to pursue this request is with the legislature or the agency governing power companies.

IV. DECISION.

Summary judgment was appropriate because respondent owed no duty to appellant to use due care in hiring and supervising its independent contractor.

Affirmed.

LENSA CORPORATION v. POINCIANA GARDENS ASSOCIATION, INC.
765 So. 2d 296 (Fla. App. 2000)

We affirm a final judgment entered upon an order granting Poinciana Gardens Association, Inc.'s (Association) motion for directed verdict and motion for judgment notwithstanding the verdict following a jury verdict in favor of Lensa Corporation (Lensa). In entering its order in favor of Association, the trial court recognized that its president did not have actual or apparent authority to bind the non-profit homeowner's association to a sale of all or substantially all of its assets. We agree and affirm the decision of the trial court.

Association's president, Dr. Goodman, negotiated and agreed to the sale of all or substantially all of its assets, consisting of land, to BBG Appraiser Co. (BBG), a company owned by Mrs. Sandel, upon an understanding that it would assign its contract rights to Lensa, which would develop the property. The parties executed a written contract with Dr. Goodman signing on behalf of Association. Following the execution of the written agreement, counsel for Lensa discovered that Mr. Sandel (the owner of Lensa) had witnessed Dr. Goodman's signature. In order to avoid any problems with the contract, Mr. Sandel arranged to have a second contract executed. Before a second contract was executed, however, Mr. Sandel had a discussion with Ms. Stolle, Association's secretary. According to Mr. Sandel, Ms. Stolle told him that she was not aware that a sales contract existed on the land. Upon hearing this information, Mr. Sandel contacted Dr. Goodman and voiced his concerns. Dr. Goodman assured Mr. Sandel that he would call a board meeting and straighten out "whatever doubts [the members of the board of directors] had on the situation."

A meeting was held, attended by Association's officers, one general member, and two Association directors. It is undisputed that the persons in attendance did not constitute a quorum of the full board, the makeup of which was a matter of some confusion. At the meeting, those in attendance agreed that Dr. Goodman was authorized to sign the legal documents necessary for the sale to Lensa for the sum of $50,000. Unsigned minutes of the meeting were subsequently faxed to Mr. Sandel. Several days later, the parties executed a second contract, the terms of which mirrored those of the first contract.

Subsequently, Mr. Sterling, Association's new president, informed Mr. Sandel that Association would not honor the contract because Dr. Goodman was not authorized to sign the contract and the selling price was too low. Lensa then filed a breach of contract action against Association.

At jury trial, Lensa conceded that Dr. Goodman did not have actual authority to sell the property and that the board of directors did not meet and approve the sale of the property. The jury entered a verdict totaling $18,000. In reaching this decision, the jury found that Dr. Goodman had apparent authority to sign the agreement. The trial court granted Association's motion for directed verdict and judgment notwithstanding the verdict, finding that Dr. Goodman had no actual authority because the true board of directors did not vote on the sale of property; there was also no apparent authority because Dr. Goodman failed to obtain the approval of the directors (as required under the association's bylaws, as well as section 617.1202, Florida Statutes), and at no time did either the board or the membership confer such authority upon him.

The sale of all or substantially all of a non-profit corporation's assets is strictly controlled by section 617.1202, which provides, in pertinent part:

A sale, lease, exchange, or other disposition of all or substantially all of the property and assets of a corporation...must be authorized in the following manner:

> (1) If the corporation has members entitled to vote on the sale, lease, exchange, or other disposition of corporate property, the board of directors must adopt a resolution approving such sale, lease, exchange, or other disposition, and directing that it be submitted to a vote at a meeting of members entitled to vote thereon, which may be either an annual or special meeting....

> (2) If the corporation has no members or if its members are not entitled to vote thereon, a sale, lease, exchange, or other disposition of all or substantially all the property and assets of a corporation may be authorized by a majority vote of the directors then in office. Sec, 617.1202, Fla. Stat. (1995).

Association's bylaws do not require membership approval; therefore, the directors had the authority to sell the property and assets of the corporation. See §617.1202(2), Fla. Stat. Here, a majority vote of the directors was necessary in order to authorize the sale. There is nothing in the record to indicate that Association complied with section 617.1202 or the bylaws before executing the agreement. At no time was there a majority vote by the directors. Thus, it is clear that Dr. Goodman did not have actual authority to sell the land. Any liability of Association, therefore, must be based upon Dr. Goodman's apparent authority.

Three elements are needed to establish an apparent agency: (1) a representation by the purported principal; (2) reliance on that representation by a third party; and (3) a change in position by the third party in reliance upon such representation. See *Ideal Foods, Inc. v. Action Leasing Corp.*, 413 So. 2d 416, 418 (Fla. 5th DCA 1982). The reliance of a third party on the apparent authority of a principal's agent must be reasonable and rest in the actions of or appearances created by the principal, see *Rushing v. Garrett*, 375 So. 2d 903, 906 (Fla. 1st DCA 1979), and "not by agents who often ingeniously create an appearance of authority by their own acts." *Taco Bell of California v. Zappone*, 324 So. 2d 121, 124 (Fla. 2d DCA 1975). As to acts in the ordinary course of business, courts have consistently recognized that a presumption of authority exists in the case of acts made or done by presidents. See *Pan-American Constr. Co. v. Searcy*, 84 So. 2d 540 (Fla. 1955); *Miami Jockey Club v. Lillias Piper, Inc.*, 115 Fla. 612, 155 So. 806 (1934).

This sale was not made in the course of the corporation's ordinary business, and there is no basis for concluding that the sale of all or substantially all of Association's assets could be presumed to be within Dr. Goodman's authority. For an agent to act with apparent authority requires, as previously noted, that the principal create the appearance of the agent's apparent authority. Here, reliance on the signature of the president and on the minutes was insufficient to create apparent authority. The statute mandates that only the board has the power to authorize a sale. Here, the board did not make any representations or take any actions signifying either its consent or the president's authority to act.

Therefore, although the record may support the second and third elements of apparent authority, there is no record support for the first. Further, to hold otherwise would defeat the very charge of the statute that the board or membership must authorize the sale of all or substantially all of a non-profit corporation's assets. Therefore, the judgment is affirmed.

Glossary

Agent - A person or entity authorized to act on behalf of and under the control of another in dealing with third parties

Apparent authority (ostensible authority) - Authority that the principal manifests to a third person that the agent has

Express authority - Authority that is created by the actual words of the principal to the agent

Implied authority - Subset of actual authority that arises by usage, custom, and past dealings of the parties

Indemnification - Ability of a person held vicariously liable to recover from the actual wrongdoer

Master-servant relationship - A servant is one who is employed to render services of any type, otherwise than in the pursuit of an independent calling, who remain under the control of the master

Principal - One from whom an agent derives authority to act

Principal-agent relationship - Relationship in which one person is authorized to enter into contracts on behalf of another

Renunciation - The principal terminates the contractual relationship

Respondeat superior - Let the master answer

Revocation - The terminates the contractual relationship

Vicarious liability - One person being held legally responsible for another's actions

Workers compensation - State statute that provides for relief by workers injured on the job by fellow workers

Exercises

1. Give two examples of situations in which the same two people act as principal-agent, master-servant, and independent contractor simultaneously. How would you prove the role that this person was performing when the third party was injured?

2. Discuss the difference between the various types of authority an agent may possess. Draft an agreement indicating express authority.

3. What is your opinion of the concept of negligent hiring? Discuss.

4. Discuss the factors that would have to be established to determine whether the doctrine of respondeat superior would apply in a given situation.

5. Indicate three examples of independent contractors not mentioned in the chapter. Draft a contract for each type of independent contractor.

Chapter Eight

BUSINESS ORGANIZATIONS

Introduction

The first question every business must answer is: under what form will it operate? Although the legalities with respect to the operation of a business are fairly uniform regardless of the legal nature of the business' structure, a commercial venture must decide the nature of its organization and then, to be lawfully organized, follow the legal requirements for its establishment pursuant to state law.

In determining the requirements to create a business organization, the enterprise must look to the specifics of the particular state in question; there is no universal federal law dealing with the creation of a business enterprise. However, even though there is some slight variation among the states, for the most part the basic requirements are identical regardless of the particular jurisdiction. It must be stressed that when forming a commercial enterprise, the business person must look to state law where the business will operate.

This chapter will focus on the elements necessary to create a commercial enterprise. Attention will be placed on the most common and important of the legal formats a business may chose: a sole proprietorship, a general or limited partnership, a corporation, and a limited liability company. However, the entrepreneur must be alert to the fact that there are other formats that are available and may be appropriate to a given enterprise; these five are merely the most frequently encountered.

Sole Proprietorships

A **sole proprietorship** is defined as a business enterprise in which only one individual owns and operates the business for his or her own benefit. The operative factor with respect to this business format is the exclusive ownership in just one person. However, simply because only one person owns the enterprise does not mean that it is operated by that person alone. A sole proprietor may, and usually does, employ agents, servants, and independent contractors to assist in the day-to-day operations of the business. The sole proprietor's rights and obligations are those of a principal, a master, or a contacting party (see Chapter Seven). The exclusivity of the sole proprietorship rests with the ownership aspect, which engenders the greatest detriment associated with this business format. As sole owner, the sole proprietor is individually liable for all of the obligations of the business, and his or her personal assets may be reached to satisfy claims against the enterprise. With a sole proprietorship, there is no legal distinction between the business and the owner—they are considered one unit, and the owner's liability is unlimited.

> *Example:* An accountant operates an accounting business as a sole proprietorship. After several years, one of her clients sues her after that client trips over some books that were left on the floor. The accident permanently disabled the client. If successful in court, the client may reach not only the assets of the office but all of the accountant's personal assets as well.

Because the owner and the business are considered one entity, it is often difficult to fund a sole proprietorship. If the proprietor attempts to add another owner to raise capital, the business loses its identity as a sole proprietorship. Further, any loans the sole proprietor acquires for the business are dependent upon the owner's credit worthiness, and the owner remains personally liable on the note. Therefore, a sole proprietorship can only be funded with the assets of the owner.

> *Example:* A man wishes to operate a hardware store as a sole proprietorship. In order to rent space and acquire inventory, the owner must use his own funds and take out a loan for which he will be personally liable. The sole proprietorship never acquires its own separate credit rating.

The sole proprietorship, as the extension of the owner, is not responsible for income taxes—all of the income generated by the business is attributed to the owner as ordinary income and is reported by the owner on his or her own income tax return. The sole proprietor is permitted to take business deductions to offset the total income derived by the business, and only the profit is taxed. In order to indicate the income and expenses, the sole proprietor completes a **Schedule C**, an attachment to the individual tax return that is designed specifically for sole proprietorships.

> *Example:* In August, a sole proprietor's total sales from the business is $8,000. However, she has had expenses including rent, utilities, cartage, advertising, etc., totaling $6,000. As a result, the amount on which her income taxes will be levied is $2,000: $8,000 less $6,000.

Because of the various detriments of operating a sole proprietorship, it might seem that no one would wish to operate a business under this format. However, there are certain advantages associated with this type of business organization.

A sole proprietorship is easy to form. Most jurisdictions have no filing or regulatory requirements for forming a sole proprietorship. Therefore, simply stating it may create the business. However, if the owner wishes to operate the business under an assumed name, many jurisdictions, at the county level, require the owner to file a document called an **assumed name form** to alert the members of the public who may be injured by the business who owns it.

> *Example:* The owner of the hardware store from the previous example wishes to operate the business under the name of "Household Helper Hardware." To do so, the owner must file an assumed name form with the county clerk's office. This form is also referred to as a **dba form** because it states that the owner is "doing business as" Household Helper Hardware.

Also, because there is only one owner, the sole proprietor may freely make management decisions, such as deciding to change or expand the product line, without consulting with or gaining the approval of anyone else. For many individuals, this element of total control is one of the most attractive aspects of this type of business format.

> *Example:* *A woman operates a dress shop as a sole proprietorship. One day she decides to expand into men's wear as well. As the sole owner, she may make that decision immediately and then act on it.*

Because of the ease of formation and few, if any, regulatory filing requirements, sole proprietorships are one of the most common business formats utilized today.

General Partnerships

A **general partnership** is defined as an association of two or more persons engaged in business for profit as co-owners. All businesses are deemed, by law, to be operated for profit unless they are established exclusively as a charitable organization. A general partnership is immediately distinguishable from a sole proprietorship in that there is more than one owner.

Every jurisdiction has adopted a version of the **Uniform Partnership Act (UPA)**, which operates as a regulatory statute for creating and operating general partnerships. Broadly, the UPA provides that, unless the partners have an agreement to the contrary, all partners are deemed to be equal partners and share equally in the business profits and obligations. In other words, if the owners themselves have entered into a **partnership agreement**, the terms of that agreement, which is a contract (Chapter Three), will prevail over any contrary provision of the UPA. Conversely, if the agreement is silent on a given point, or no agreement exists, the UPA governs.

There is no specific requirement with respect to the methods in which the general partnership may be formed, except, of course, that the partners must agree to operate a business. However, an oral agreement to operate a partnership may be subject to the Statute of Frauds (Chapter Three), and partners should be aware of the potential unenforceability of an oral partnership agreement. Also, some jurisdictions require that before a general partnership may operate, as distinct from forming, it must file certain forms with the state or county government. Each jurisdiction's laws must be analyzed.

Once the general partnership has been formed, the partners are entitled to the **partnership rights** or **interests**, which are
- *the right to the physical assets of the business.* Partnership assets, unless specified to the contrary, are deemed to be held in a tenancy in partnership and subject to the specific rights and obligations discussed in Chapter Five.
- *the right to manage and control the business.* Unless the partners have an agreement to the contrary, each partner is entitled to equal management and control of the business. Partners are deemed to be agents for the partnership (Chapter Seven), and each partner has the ability to bind the other partners to contracts entered into on behalf of the business. However, the UPA specifies five types of agreements that require the assent of all of the partners in order for them to be bound:

1. Putting up partnership property as collateral for a loan
2. Selling the **goodwill** of the business—using the partnership reputation as the guarantor or surety for someone else's loans, etc.
3. Submitting a partnership claim to arbitration, because such submission denies the partner the right to have a day in court, a fundamental right that cannot be denied
4. Confession of judgment, in which one partner agrees to liability on behalf of the partnership in a lawsuit without actually trying or defending the case
5. Anything that would make it impossible to carry on the business, such acts to be determined on a case-by-case basis.

- *the right to the income, profit, and losses of the business.*

The first two partnership rights are personal to the partners and may not be assigned or transferred. The third right, the right to the income and profits of the business, may be assigned, but the assignee does not thereby become a partner. To be a partner, a person must be entitled to all of the partnership rights.

Example: *In order to produce theatrical shows, Mickey and Judy decide to form a partnership. The business is successful. Mickey, delighted with the partnership's success, goes on a spending spree, buying several houses, cars, and expensive electronic equipment. When he cannot meet his financial obligations, his creditors sue him and are successful. The creditors cannot attach the partnership property (Chapter Five) but can garnish one-quarter of Mickey's income from the partnership, with the court's approval. The creditors acquire a portion of Mickey's income but are not entitled to the other partnership rights. Note, however, if the purchases were made for the business, the creditors could attach the partnership property and attach Mickey and Judy's assets as well.*

In certain respects, a general partnership resembles a sole proprietorship in that each owner retains unlimited personal liability for the business obligations, and each partner is individually liable for the taxes on the income generated by the partnership attributable to his or her share of the business (see below).

Although each partner retains unlimited individual liability for the partnership obligations, the partner may seek **contribution** from the other partners for his or her portion of the obligation that the one partner was required to pay. The partners' liability is deemed to be **joint** in contract, **joint and several** in tort, meaning that if the basis of the lawsuit against the business is a breach of contract, all partners must be joined as defendants; whereas, if the suit is based in tort, the injured party may sue any one partner for the entire amount.

Example: *A partnership fails to pay one of its suppliers. If the suppliers sue the business, the suppliers must join all of the partners in the action because the lawsuit is based on contract.*

Due to the partnership's negligence, a customer breaks her leg on the partnership premises. The customer may sue one partner or all of them together, at the customer's option. If only one partner is sued, and loses, he or she may seek to receive a share of the judgment paid from the other partners according to the partners' shares of the business.

A partnership files an informational income tax return, simply indicating its income, expenses, profits or losses, and the names of the partners according to those partners' shares of the business. Each partner attaches a copy of this return to his or her income tax return and is liable for the tax on the portion of the profit that attaches to his or her ownership percentage. If there is a loss, the partners may use this loss to offset other income he or she may have to report.

Pursuant to section 62 of the UPA, a general partnership may terminate by agreement of the partners, by operation of law if the business activities violate the partnership agreement or general law, by the death or personal bankruptcy of one of the partners, or by court order under the court's equitable jurisdiction if it determines that it is in the best interests of the partners to terminate the business.

General partnerships are funded by the contribution each partner makes to acquire a partnership share or by loans to the business, which are personally guaranteed by the partners, similar to the methods of funding a sole proprietorship.

Limited Partnerships

Unlike sole proprietorships and general partnerships, to create a limited partnership, certain basic statutory requirements must be met. A **limited partnership** is defined as an association of two or more persons engaged in business as co-owners for profit, with one or more general partners and one or more limited partners. The general partner in a limited partnership retains unlimited personal liability because the general partner has the ability to manage and control the business. The **limited partners** are considered only to be investors, merely entitled to the profits or losses from the business with no management control; therefore, they are only liable to the extent of their contributions to the limited partnership, which was used to acquire their limited partnership shares.

For many decades, limited partnerships were governed by the **Uniform Limited Partnership Act (ULPA)**, a version of which was adopted by every jurisdiction. Beginning in the 1980s, many states began revising their statutes, and more than two-thirds of the jurisdictions have enacted significant revisions. Each state's laws must be analyzed to determine the rights and obligations of limited partnerships operating within its jurisdiction.

To create a limited partnership, the partners must enter into a **limited partnership agreement**, and many states require that the agreement, or a **certificate of limited partnership**, be filed with the state either at the county or state level to protect the interests of those persons who deal with the limited partnership.

Because the limited partners are considered to be investors in the business, limited partnerships may be regulated by various state **(blue sky)** or federal **securities laws**. The specifics of such regulation are beyond the scope of this text, but persons involved with limited partnerships must make sure that any required securities filings are made.

Limited partnerships generally operate in a manner similar to general partnerships, in that the general partners control the business, but a portion of the profits or losses are attributed to the investor limited partners. Also, because of this investment aspect, a limited partnership may increase its funding simply by selling additional limited partnership shares.

Management of the limited partnership lies with its general partner(s); however, the general partners are required to have the consent of the limited partners in the following situations:

- any act that would be beyond the scope of the limited partnership agreement
- confession of judgment
- possession of partnership property for other than partnership purposes
- any act that would interfere with the operation of the business
- The addition of a new general partner, because general partners can bind the business.

Limited partnerships provide certain benefits over sole proprietorships and general partnerships in that persons may become owners of the business without engendering unlimited personal liability by relinquishing management and control. Limited partnerships are a common business format used for theatrical and sports enterprises, as well as certain risky types of businesses such as oil exploration.

Corporations

The **corporation** is a very common business format for large businesses or businesses in which the owners could face a high degree of risk of personal liability. Corporations are artificial entities, created by state statutes, which may be best understood by reference to the following statements:

- A corporation is a legal entity, separate and distinct from its shareholders.
- Management of a corporation rests with its board of directors.
- Ownership of a corporation vests in its shareholders.

In order to form a corporation, the **incorporator**, the person wishing to form the business, must first file a document called a **certificate of incorporation** with the appropriate agency in the state in which the corporation wishes to operate. Once the certificate of incorporation is filed, the corporation comes into existence. A corporation is deemed to be a **domestic corporation** of the state in which it is incorporated. A corporation formed in one state is considered to be a **foreign corporation** in every other state. A corporation formed in another country is an **alien corporation** in the United States.

The certificate of incorporation serves the following functions:

- It indicates the name of the corporation; every jurisdiction requires that a corporation formed within its borders have a name unique to corporations in that state. The state may require that the name must include the word "corporation," "incorporated," or "limited," or the abbreviation of one of those terms, so the public will know it is dealing with a corporate entity.
- It indicates the corporation's registered office, the place where service of process may be sent if the corporation is sued.
- It authorizes the secretary of state to act as the corporation's agent for service of process so that a third person may satisfy procedural requirements by serving the secretary of state when suing the corporation.
- It indicates the total number of shares that the corporation may potentially sell in order to acquire shareholders (see below).
- It specifies the purpose for which the corporation is organized.
- It indicates the duration of the corporation. (Most states permit corporations to exist in perpetuity.)

Because certificates of incorporation are filed with the state, they are public documents. In addition to this certificate, all states require corporations to adopt **bylaws**, general rules that govern the corporation's day-to-day activities, including such matters as the titles and duties of officers, notice requirements for meetings, number of directors, methods for removal or replacement of directors, the date on which the corporation's tax year ends, etc. Bylaws are often published by corporate services and are general in their approach, but they are internal documents of the corporation and are not publicly available.

Once the corporation comes into existence, it is may adopt a **seal**, an imprint that is used to indicate authorized corporate acts.

The **board of directors** is composed of natural persons who act collectively as the agent for the corporation (the principal). The shareholders elect the members of the board, generally on an annual basis, to serve one-year terms. Many states permit directors to serve longer than one-year terms and may permit the directors to be elected not by all the shareholders but by class (see below). If the state statute permits, and the corporation wants such a variance, these variations must appear in the certificate of incorporation or the bylaws.

The directors, as agents, are deemed to be fiduciaries for the corporation and its shareholders. As such, the directors are held to a higher standard of care than ordinary care. This fiduciary standard for directors is called the **business judgment rule**, which states that directors must use the prudence and discretion of the ordinary business person in making decisions for the corporation. If the director does not meet this standard, the director will be held personally liable for any injury the corporation suffers. Further, the directors are prohibited from **self-dealing**, making a personal profit on a business transaction that should have gone to the corporation, and are expected to be loyal to the interests of the business.

Each state statute provides the minimum number of directors that a domestic corporation must have, but generally there is no maximum number. The directors, acting as the board, are the managers of the business and make all business decisions for the corporation.

The shareholders are the owners of the corporation whose ownership interests are represented by **shares of stock**. A share of stock is an example of intangible personal property because it represents the right to something of value (Chapter Six). The shareholder of a corporation has limited personal liability and may only lose his or her investment—the amount he or she paid to acquire the shares.

Every statute requires that domestic corporations have at least one share of stock that has **common stock rights**:

- the right to vote for directors and extraordinary corporate matters
- the right to receive dividends declared by the board (**dividends** represent the profit of the corporation as distributed to the shareholders)
- the right to the assets of the corporation when the corporation terminates.

If a corporation has shares that have any rights that are different from these common stock rights, those shares are deemed to be **preferred stock**, and the rights and obligations incident to these securities must be specified both in the certificate of incorporation and on the face of the share of stock itself. Having shares of stock with different rights create **classes**.

The number of shares appearing in the certificate of incorporation is referred to as the **authorized shares**, the total number of shares that the corporation may sell. When the directors decide to attempt to sell some shares, the number that is approved for sale is referred to as the **issued shares**. When the issued shares are actually sold and are held by a shareholder, they are deemed to be **outstanding**. Only outstanding shares are entitled to exercise the right to vote, receive dividends, and share in the distribution of assets upon dissolution.

As stated above, a shareholder is shielded from personal liability, provided that the shareholder maintains the corporation as a separate legal entity. If, however, the shareholder treats the corporation as an extension of himself or herself, the court may **pierce the corporate veil** that protects the shareholder's personal assets so that these assets may be used to satisfy creditors who have been injured by the corporation.

> *Example:* *A man is the sole shareholder of a corporation. He uses the corporation's assets—checkbook, supplies, and equipment—as his own property. When the corporation is unable to meet its obligations, the court may permit its creditors to pierce the corporate veil to attach the shareholder's assets because he has not maintained the corporation as a separate legal entity but has treated it as though it were his own property.*

Corporations are treated as separate entities and are responsible for reporting and paying income taxes on any profits they realize. Dividends may be paid to shareholders only after corporate income taxes have been paid. Also, because the corporation is deemed to be a separate entity, a corporation may borrow funds to finance its operation based on its own credit worthiness, and the shareholders do not become liable on these obligations. This affords the corporation another method for funding its own business.

Similar to limited partnerships, corporations are subject to securities regulation because all of the owners are investors in the enterprise.

Because a corporation can be formed only by filing documents with the state, for its existence to terminate, the corporation must file a **certificate of dissolution** with the state. It cannot simply stop operating and thereby consider itself terminated. A corporation may dissolve by a vote of its shareholders or by the date or circumstances indicated in its certificate of incorporation if it did not elect perpetual life. Its existence may be terminated by action initiated by the state Attorney General if the corporation engages in unlawful activities.

Limited Liability Companies

At the time of this writing, all of the states have adopted statutes that create a form of business enterprise known as a **limited liability company** or **LLC**. LLCs are designed with many features that are similar to sole proprietorships, limited partnerships, and corporations, and they are considered to be a potentially beneficial form for operating a business enterprise. However, each state's statute with respect to these organizations differs, and the peculiarities of each statute must be individually analyzed. Some states permit the creation of limited liability partnerships and limited liability professional companies as well.

Generally, in order to create an LLC, the entity must file a **certificate of registration** with the appropriate state agency. As part of this certificate, the LLC must attach its **articles of organization**, similar to a limited partnership agreement, which includes

- the name of the company, including the words "Limited Liability Company" or the initials "LLC"
- the location of its registered office
- the designation of the secretary of state as agent for service of process
- a statement regarding the liability of its members and a statement indicating whether it will be managed by members or hired managers
- the duration of the LLC.

The purpose behind the LLC is to provide its owners, known as **members**, with limited personal liability. Some jurisdictions permit LLCs to be formed by just one person, thereby avoiding individual personal liability associated with operating a sole proprietorship, but many states require at least two members. Unlike limited partnerships, its members may manage the LLC, or the members may select managers who will manage the business in the same fashion as a corporation's board of directors. LLCs are taxed in the same manner as a general partnership.

The appropriateness of the LLC format for a given commercial enterprise must be determined on a case-by-case basis by the businessperson involved.

Chapter Summary

An important initial decision for a commercial enterprise is what form it will take. If the businessperson simply starts to operate, he or she will automatically be considered a sole proprietorship (or a general partnership if done by two or more persons), thereby immediately engendering personal liability. Because of this potential liability, the decision with respect to the appropriate business format to use is an important one.

The most common legal formats currently in use are the following:

- The sole proprietorship, which has no formalities necessary to create it and provides the owner with total management control but engenders unlimited personal liability and difficulty in financing.
- A general partnership, in which unlimited liability is retained but is shared with other partners, whose expertise may create a better business but whose ability to act on behalf of the partnership may engender additional liability.
- The limited partnership, which has formalities to create it but permits a person to have an ownership interest without suffering unlimited personal liability, provided that the owner is willing to relinquish management control. This format may require security regulation filings.
- The corporation, one of the most common business formats, which is an artificial entity that is owned by its shareholders, who have limited liability, but is managed by a board of directors who are fiduciaries to the corporation and its owners.
- The limited liability company, the most recent type of business organization, which incorporates elements of the sole proprietorship, limited partnership, and corporation. It has formalities needed to create it but may be managed by its owner who can still retain limited personal liability.

Be aware that this list is not complete. There are several other types of business organizations that may be used to operate a commercial enterprise, but the preceding five are the most commonly encountered. The others have a more limited application for specific types of businesses. That state's statutes govern the type of business format permitted in a particular state, and all business organizations, with respect to their lawful formation, are creatures of state statute.

Edited Judicial Decisions

STATE OF ALASKA v. ABC TOWING
954 P.2d 575 (Alas. App. 1998)

This case involves the law of vicarious responsibility—the law defining when one person can be held criminally responsible for the conduct of another. More specifically, this case presents the question of whether a business run by a sole proprietor is an organization under AS 1.16.130(a), a statute which declares that organizations are criminally responsible for certain acts of their agents. We hold that a sole proprietorship is not an organization for purposes of AS 11.16.130(a).

Rodney E. Lewis does business as ABC Towing. When one of Lewis's employees discharged gasoline on the ground, the State brought criminal charges against both the employee and ABC Towing; both defendants were charged with violating an anti-pollution statute, AS 46.03.710.

Under Alaska law, organizations face broader vicarious criminal responsibility than do individuals. Generally speaking, an individual can be held criminally responsible for the conduct of another only if the individual asks or encourages the other person to commit the offense or if the individual helps to plan or commit the offense. See AS 11.16.110(2). The State presented no evidence that Lewis asked his employee to discharge the gasoline or that Lewis aided or abetted the employee's act. However, an organization can be held accountable for criminal conduct that its owners, members, officers, or directors did not know about until afterwards. Under AS 11.16.130(a)(1), an organization is criminally responsible for an offense committed by one of its agents if the agent was acting in behalf of the organization and within the scope of the agent's employment or if the organization subsequently ratified or adopted the agent's conduct. The State charged ABC Towing with the pollution violation, alleging that Lewis's employee had been acting within the scope of his employment, and in behalf of ABC Towing, when he discharged the gasoline on the ground.

The case against ABC Towing was tried to District Court Judge Natalie K. Finn on stipulated facts. The parties agreed that ABC Towing's employee had violated the anti-pollution statute and that the employee had been acting within the scope of his employment and in behalf of ABC Towing when he committed this violation. There was only one disputed issue, and that was an issue of law: was ABC Towing an organization for purposes of AS 11.16.130(a) so that it could be held liable for its employee's discharge of gasoline?

AS 11.81.900(b)(39) defines the term organization for purposes of Title 11. Under that definition, organization means, "a legal entity, including a corporation, company, association, firm, partnership, joint stock company, foundation, institution, government, society, union, club, church, or any other group of persons organized for any purpose."

Lewis's attorney contended that ABC Towing was not an organization because it was a sole proprietorship—an unincorporated business owned solely by Lewis. In a well-reasoned opinion, Judge Finn concluded that this contention was correct—that sole proprietorships are not organizations under the statutory definition. Judge Finn wrote:

> [A] sole proprietorship is not a legal entity. [It] has no legal significance apart from its sole proprietor. It cannot incur debts, conduct business, sue or be sued, or incur or pay taxes apart from its sole proprietor. Legally, it makes no difference whether the business is named ABC Towing or Rodney E. Lewis. The accountability of ABC Towing is therefore no different from that of an individual. ... This court finds that ABC Towing, a sole proprietorship, is not an organization within the meaning of AS 11.81.-900(b)(39) and is therefore not legally accountable [for acts of its agents under] AS 11.16.130.

Judge Finn therefore dismissed the complaint against ABC Towing, and the State now appeals Judge Finn's decision.

Under AS 11.81.900(b)(39), organization (for purposes of Title 11) means a legal entity. The statute does not define legal entity except by example, and the term, legal entity, is not further defined in Title 11 or, indeed, anywhere else in the Alaska statutes. However, the term, legal entity, does have a common-law meaning, and that meaning presumptively governs our interpretation of AS 11.81.900(b) (39). See AS 1.10.010 (the common law remains the rule of decision in this state unless it is inconsistent with the laws passed by the Alaska legislature or inconsistent with the federal or Alaska constitutions).

The concept of legal entity is a useful fiction employed by the law to distinguish an ongoing human endeavor from the people who presently own or control that endeavor. As Judge Finn correctly pointed out in her decision, the defining characteristic of a legal entity is its separate legal existence apart from its owners, officers, and directors.

At common law, sole proprietorships are not legal entities, neither are partnerships (for most purposes: compare *Pratt v. Kirkpatrick*, 718 P.2d 962, 967-68 (Alaska 1986)). Rather, sole proprietorships and partnerships are deemed to be the alter egos of the proprietor or the partners (as individuals). In a sole proprietorship, all of the proprietor's assets are completely at risk, and the sole proprietorship ceases to exist upon the proprietor's death. Harry J. Haynsworth, *Selecting the Form of a Small Business Entity* (1985), §1.02, pp. 2-3; see also Harry G. Hehn and John R. Alexander, *Laws of Corporations and Other Business Entities* (3rd ed. 1985), §18, p. 58. Similarly, a partnership is not a separate legal entity (for most purposes). Haynsworth, §1.03 pp. 4, 7; Hehn & Alexander, §19, pp. 63-64.

The common law adopted a strict view [of partnership] and accorded no recognition to the partnership as an entity for the purposes of ownership of real property, contract, suit, etc[,] although many of these disabilities have been abolished or altered by statute. Hehn & Alexander, §19, p. 64.

Alaska law recognizes the common-law rule. See *Williams v. Mammoth of Alaska, Inc.*, 890 P.2d 581, 584 (Alaska 1995) ("The nearly universal rule is that if the employer is a partnership, then each partner is an employer of the partnership's employees. This is because a partnership is not a legal entity separate from its partners."); *Berger v. Ohlson*, 120 F.2d 56, 10 Alaska 84, 93 (9th Cir. 1941) ("The Alaska Railroad is not a corporate or any other legal entity. It is a name only. The sole owner of the railroad and its terminals ... is the United States.")

With regard to a sole proprietorship, Alaska law deems the company to be simply an alter ego of the proprietor, who is engaged in commerce under a nom d'affaires—an assumed name adopted for business purposes. See *Roeckl v. Federal Deposit Insurance Corp.*, 885 P.2d 1067 (Alaska 1994), which contains a lengthy discussion of an individual's legal ability to conduct business or business transactions under an assumed name. *Roeckl* notes that, unless a person uses a fictitious business name in order to facilitate a fraud, it has always been legal for a person to transact business in the name of a fictitious entity that has no legal existence apart from the individuals running the business. *Roeckl*, 885 P.2d at 1073 (citations omitted). This practice is, in fact, normal for sole proprietorships and partnerships. *Roeckl*, 885 P.2d at 1074, quoting *United States v. Dunn*, 564 F.2d 348, 354 n.12 (9th Cir. 1977). *Roeckl* answers the State's contention that ABC Towing should be considered a separate legal entity because a business license has been issued in the name of ABC Towing.

With this background, we return to our definitional statute, AS 11.81.900(b)(39), and we find that it contains troublesome ambiguities. The statute declares that the term organization means a legal entity. If the legislature had stopped there, then neither a sole proprietorship nor a partnership would be considered an organization, because neither form of business is a legal entity. However, the statute then adds that the term legal entity includes partnerships as well as associations, societies, clubs, and any other group of persons organized for any purpose. This is a marked expansion of what the common law would recognize as a legal entity for other purposes (suing or being sued, holding title to property, employing workers, etc.).

The legislature undoubtedly has the authority to enlarge the definition of legal entity beyond its common-law boundaries. See *State v. Erickson*, 574 P.2d 1, 15 (Alaska 1978) (in statutes regulating drugs, the legislature can define narcotic differently from its normal pharmacological meaning). It appears that AS 11.81.900(b) (39) was intended to modify the common-law definition of legal entity by broadening it to include partnerships, informal associations and clubs, and (in general) "any other group of persons organized for any purpose." However, the statutory roster of legal entities does not specifically include sole proprietorships.

The State argues that a sole proprietorship becomes a firm, an association, or a group under AS 11.81.900(b) (39) whenever the sole proprietor hires other people to assist in the conduct of the business. We think that this is a strained interpretation of the statute.

Under the State's reading of the statute, an ice cream vendor or a house painter that employed a part-time helper during the summer would suddenly become a firm, an association, or a group. In fact, under the State's wide-ranging construction of the phrase "group of persons organized for any purpose," homeowners would seemingly become organizations whenever they hired someone to clean their house or maintain their lawn. Such a construction of the statute conflicts with the fact that employees generally do not direct the conduct of a business. Their contract of employment does not make them partners of the persons or entities who hire them, and they do not have the same legal rights and responsibilities as their employers. Based on the wording of AS 11.81.900(b) (39) and its legislative history, we doubt that the legislature intended the results advocated by the State.

Moreover, two rules of statutory construction counsel us to uphold the trial court's decision in this case. The first rule is that statutes in derogation of the common law should be construed strictly. That is, when courts are presented with a question involving the proper construction of a statute that modifies the common law, the normal rule of interpretation is that such statutes are construed so as to preserve the pre-existing common law unless the legislature has clearly indicated its purpose to change that law. See *Roeckl*, 885 P.2d at 1074; *University of Alaska v. Shanti*, 835 P.2d 1225, 1228 n.5 (Alaska 1992). The second rule is that statutes imposing criminal liability should be construed narrowly. When the scope of a criminal statute is unclear, courts should normally construe the statute against the government—that is, construe it so as to limit the scope of criminal liability. See *Magnuson v. State*, 843 P.2d 1251, 1253 (Alaska App. 1992).

The question in this appeal is whether sole proprietorships are to be treated as legal entities apart from their proprietors, so the government can prosecute sole proprietorships for the acts of their agents under the theory of vicarious responsibility codified in AS 11.16.130(a). Under the common law, sole proprietorships are not legal entities. The expanded definition of legal entities in AS 11.81.900(b) (39) does not include a specific reference to sole proprietorships. The State has presented some inventive arguments as to why sole proprietorships should be viewed as associations or firms for purposes of Title 11, but in the end, those arguments are only colorable, not convincing. On this point, the statute remains, at best, ambiguous.

This being so, we construe AS 11.81.900(b) (39) to preserve the pre-existing common law rule that sole proprietorships are not legal entities and to narrowly construe the scope of vicarious criminal responsibility imposed by AS 11.16.130(a). We conclude that sole proprietorships are not organizations for purposes of AS 11.16.130(a). The district court therefore correctly granted the defendant's motion to dismiss.

The judgment of the district court is AFFIRMED.

DEVEREAUX'S CARPENTRY SERVICES, LLC v. ERICSON
1999 Conn. Super. LEXIS 2709

The defendants, Charles and Jane Ericson, have moved this court for summary judgment as to count three of the plaintiff's Amended Complaint and the third count of their counterclaim. See Motion for Summary Judgment, August 4, 1999. In support of their motion they rely on the amended complaint, responses to requests to admit, an affidavit with attached exhibits and their memorandum of law. The plaintiff has filed a memorandum in opposition to the defendants' motion accompanied by the plaintiff's affidavit.

The following facts are not in dispute. The defendants are the real estate owners located at 14 Watrous Road, Bolton, Connecticut. This is also their primary residence. On September 14, 1995, the defendants entered into a written agreement with the plaintiff, Stephen Devereaux, doing business as Devereaux's Carpentry Service (DCS), for the construction of an addition to their residence. On December 1, 1995, Stephen Devereaux created a limited liability company known as Devereaux's Carpentry Services, LLC (LLC) and, as of that date, ceased doing business under DCS. The contract of construction for the addition to the defendants' home constitutes a home improvement contract as defined in General Statutes 20-419.

The work was completed on February 19, 1996. On March 26, 1996, the LLC filed a mechanic's lien on the premises of the defendants to secure the sum of $25,517.55. The LLC caused a copy of the lien to be served on the defendants as prescribed by statute.

The defendants have raised by way of special defense the claim that "the defendants had no agreement or contract with the plaintiff Devereaux Carpentry Service, LLC." The defendants seek summary judgment on count three of the plaintiff's amended complaint and summary judgment on the third count of their counterclaim.

The thrust of the defendants' motion for summary judgment is twofold. The basis of the first claim is that the plaintiff LLC has no written home improvement contract with the defendants and therefore pursuant to Connecticut General Statutes 20-429 there is no enforceable claim. They do not dispute that there is a written agreement with DCS. The additional claim is made that since the LLC did not furnish the services to the defendants it has no right to place a mechanic's lien on the defendants' property citing *Anthony Julian R.R. Const. Co., Inc. v. Mary Ellen Drive Associates*, 39 Conn. App. 544, 549, 664 A.2d 1177, cert. denied, 235 Conn. 930, 667 A.2d 800 (1995).

With respect to motions for summary judgment the movant must demonstrate that there exists no genuine issue as to any material fact, and the movant is entitled to judgment as a matter of law. *Daily v. New Britain Machine Co.*, 200 Conn. 562, 568, 512 A.2d 893 (1986). The burden is on the movant to demonstrate that no material issue of fact is in dispute and on the opponent to demonstrate that no material issue exists. *Strada v. Connecticut Newspapers, Inc.*, 193 Conn. 313, 317, 477 A.2d 1005 (1984).

In *C&J Builders & Remodelers, LLC. v. Geisenheimer*, 249 Conn. 415, 733 A.2d 193 (1999), the Supreme Court first had occasion to review the question of the legal effect of converting a sole proprietorship to a limited liability company. The Court noted the following facts:

On March 14, 1996, the defendants entered into a construction contract with Charles Pageau, doing business as C&J Builders (sole proprietorship), for the renovation of the defendants' summer residence located in Madison. The parties initially set the contract price at $ 267,000 and subsequently agreed on further renovations. The contract included a provision that required the parties initially to refer any disputes arising out of the contract to Duo Dickinson, an architect who had been involved in the renovations. In the event that either party was dissatisfied with Dickinson's decision, that party then could submit a written demand to compel a formal arbitration proceeding.

On October 24, 1996, Pageau, pursuant to General Statutes 34-120 and General Statutes (Rev. to 1997) 34-121, filed an operating agreement establishing the plaintiff, C&J Builders and Remodelers, LLC. Pageau then ceased doing business as the sole proprietorship and began conducting his construction operations as the plaintiff, a limited liability company. The plaintiff assumed virtually the same name as Pageau's sole proprietorship; it operated at the same business address; and it carried on the business operations of the sole proprietorship. Specifically, the plaintiff continued the renovations to the defendants' summer residence pursuant to the contract that the defendants had entered into with the sole proprietorship. Moreover, the plaintiff's operating agreement states that it is the "successor to Charles Pageau [doing business as] C&J Builders and Remodelers." The operating agreement further provides that Pageau maintains a 99 percent ownership interest in the plaintiff, and he exercises virtually absolute control over the plaintiff's business operations.

In June 1997, a dispute arose regarding $87,667.12 that the plaintiff claimed was owed on the contract. Thereafter, the plaintiff referred the dispute to Dickinson and forwarded documentation supporting its claim. Dickinson agreed to render a decision after the defendants had submitted documentation contesting the plaintiff's claim. The defendants, however, did not submit any documentation to Dickinson, and consequently, he refused to render a decision in the matter. The plaintiff then submitted to the defendants a written demand for formal arbitration. The defendants, however, did not comply with that demand.

Thereafter, the plaintiff, pursuant to 52-410, filed an application in the trial court seeking an order directing the defendants to submit to arbitration. The defendants, however, filed a special defense, claiming that the plaintiff was not a party to their contract with the sole proprietorship; therefore, the plaintiff was not entitled to compel the defendants to arbitrate the dispute. The trial court, however, concluded that the plaintiff was entitled to enforce the contract and ordered the defendants to submit to arbitration. The defendants subsequently appealed from the trial court's judgment to the appellate court. We transferred the appeal to this court pursuant to Practice Book 65-1 and General Statutes 51-199(c).

On appeal, the defendants claim that the trial court improperly concluded that the plaintiff is entitled to compel arbitration pursuant to 52-410. The plaintiff, however, contends that it is the "successor in interest" to the sole proprietorship and, as such, has assumed the rights and obligations of its predecessor by operation of law. Consequently, the plaintiff maintains that it is entitled to compel arbitration. We agree with the plaintiff.

The court began its analysis by first noting that the "term successor in interest ordinarily refers to a corporation that by a process of amalgamation, consolidation, or duly authorized legal succession, has become invested with the rights and has assumed the burdens of another [corporation] . . ." (Citation omitted; internal quotation marks omitted.) *C&J Builders & Remodelers, LLC v. Geisenheimer*, supra 249 Conn. 419. The court further noted that the issue of whether the transformation of a sole proprietorship into a limited liability company creates in the new business entity rights and obligations previously held by the sole proprietorship had not been previously considered by the court. After a rigorous statutory analysis of General Statutes 34-100 through 34-242, the court answered the question affirmatively concluding "where a sole proprietorship converts to a limited liability company, all the interests and obligations incurred by, or chargeable against, the sole proprietorship or its assets are transferred to the limited liability company by operation of law. Moreover, like the general partners in a converting general or limited partnership, the sole proprietor retains personal liability for all reconversion debts and obligations incurred by the sole proprietorship." *Id.* 22. Thus, the court permitted the limited liability company to enforce the arbitration provision in the contract between the defendant and the predecessor sole proprietorship. "Because the plaintiff constitutes a continuation of the sole proprietorship in limited liability form, the plaintiff assumed, by operation of law, all of the rights and obligations of the sole proprietorship." *Id.*

The fact that the present case involves a contract that falls within the home improvement statutes and therefore is strictly construed does not dictate a different result. All of the protections afforded to the consumer by virtue of the Home Improvement Act remain in place unaffected by the conversion of the sole proprietorship to a limited liability company. The plaintiff has all of the defenses afforded by that act against both the sole proprietor and the LLC. The LLC is entitled, as a matter of operation of law, to all of the contractual rights and obligations of its predecessor. The motion for summary judgment is therefore denied with respect to both the special defense to the third count of the plaintiff's amended complaint and as to the third court of the counterclaim.

Glossary

Alien corporation - Corporation formed in a country other than the United States

Articles of organization - Document filed with the state government to create an LLC

Assumed name (dba) form - Document filed so that a business can operate under an alias

Authorized shares - The number of shares appearing in the certificate of incorporation, the maximum amount of shares the corporation may sell

Blue sky laws - State securities laws

Board of directors - Fiduciaries who manage a corporation

Business judgment rule - Fiduciary standard for corporate directors

Bylaws - General rules that govern a corporation's day-to-day activities

Certificate of dissolution - Document filed with the state government to terminate a corporation

Certificate of incorporation - Document filed with the secretary of state to create a corporation

Certificate of limited partnership - Document filed with the state government to create a limited partnership

Certificate of registration - Document filed with the state government to create an LLC

Class - Group of stock with rights different from the common stock rights

Contribution - Legal right of partners to have other partners share in financial liability

Corporation - Artificial entity used as a business organization, owned by shareholders and managed by directors

Dividend - Profit of a corporation distributed to the shareholders

Domestic corporation - Corporation formed in the state in question

Foreign corporation - Corporation formed in a state other than the state in question

General partnership - An association of two or more persons who engage in business for profit as co-owners

Goodwill - The reputation of a business

Incorporator - Person who forms a corporation

Issued shares - Corporate stock available for purchase

Joint and several liability - Liability for partners in a tort action

Joint liability - Liability for partners in a contract action

Limited liability company (LLC) - Business organization used to afford limited liability for its owners

Limited partner - Owner in a limited partnership that has limited liability and no management control

Limited partnership - An association of two or more persons engaged in business for profit as co-owners, with one or more general partners and one or more limited partners

Limited partnership agreement - Contract between limited partners that must be agreed to to form the limited partnership

Member - Owner of an LLC

Outstanding shares - Corporate stock owned by a shareholder

Partnership agreement - Contract between partners

Partnership rights (interests) - The right to the assets, the right to manage, and the right to the income and profits

Pierce the corporate veil - Court doctrine permitting the assets of a corporation's shareholders to be reached to satisfy corporate creditors

Preferred stock - Stock with rights different from the common stock rights

Seal - An imprint that is used to indicate authorized corporate acts

Securities laws - Law designed to protect business investors

Self-dealing - Violation of a fiduciary duty stating that a fiduciary may not make a profit that should go to its principal

Shares of stock - Intangible personal property that represents ownership interests in a corporation

Sole proprietorship - Business owned and managed by just one person

Uniform Limited Partnership Act - Model law governing limited partnerships

Uniform Partnership Act (UPA) - Model law governing general partnerships

Exercises

1. List several factors to consider in determining the appropriate format for a business.

2. Obtain a copy of a certificate of incorporation for your state from your library or the Internet and analyze its provisions.

3. Explain why shareholders and limited partners have limited liability.

4. Obtain a copy of a general and limited partnership agreement from your library or the Internet and analyze their provisions.

5. Research your state law for its provisions for the creation of LLCs. Obtain a copy of a certificate of registration.

Chapter Nine

EMPLOYMENT LAW

Introduction

Every commercial enterprise that operates with employees must be aware of the various federal laws that regulate the employer-employee relationship. Since the Great Depression of the 1930s, the federal government has been increasingly involved in guaranteeing certain basic rights for all persons in the workforce. The modern business must be concerned not only with making a profit but also with seeing that all of its obligations as an employer are fulfilled.

Historically, all employment relationships were considered to be **employment at will** situations, meaning that both the employer and the employee were free to terminate the relationship without any notice or cause. However, the tremendous growth in the number of persons being employed, rather than self-employed, that burgeoned with the arrival of the Industrial Revolution demanded that the government respond to the needs of the general working population. The legislative response to these needs falls into two broad categories: financial accountability and the right to nondiscriminatory treatment in the workplace. This chapter will explore these two areas of federal regulation of employment. Be aware that, co-existent with this general employment law, there is a body of law referred to as **labor law** that applies exclusively to labor unions and collective bargaining, a subject that is too extensive for the purposes of this text. However, the entrepreneur must realize that the law regulating labor unions is vastly different from the general federal employment laws discussed in this chapter, even thought unions are still subject to federal employment laws as well.

Financial Accountability

Many of the laws dealing with the general labor force have been enacted during the twentieth century, and the regulation of employees' wages and pensions developed during the Great Depression. Because of the large number of suddenly unemployed people, the federal response was to enact legislation designed to guarantee persons who had worked all of their lives that they would still receive an income when they were no longer capable of working. The first piece of legislation dealing with this problem was the **Social Security Act**, which provides a governmental pension and retirement plan for all persons who work a certain number of years and who contribute to the general Social Security fund. This section of this chapter will discuss the Social Security Act and the major statutes that followed in its wake: the Fair Labor Standards Act, the Equal Pay Act, and the Employee Retirement Income Security Act.

The Social Security Act

The **Social Security Act (SSA)** was enacted in 1935 as one of the first of the New Deal programs formulated to address the financial needs of a workforce in crisis. Pursuant to this statute, the federal government levies a tax on both the employee and the employer, the proceeds of which go into a general fund used to provide retirement income to qualified individuals. The Social Security fund is administered by the **Social Security Administration**.

To qualify for Social Security benefits, the employee must have been employed for at least 40 quarters (3-month periods) during which the Social Security tax was credited to his or her account, and the worker must have attained the age of 62. If both of these requirements have been met, the employee is considered to be **fully insured**.

> *Example:* *A woman has worked on an assembly line for the past 30 years, ever since she graduated from high school at age 18. The woman has had Social Security taxes withheld throughout this entire period, which totals 120 quarters. However, because the woman is only 48 years old, she does not yet qualify as being "fully insured."*

The SSA also provides for benefits to persons who are or were dependent upon the worker's income for support, such as spouses and surviving spouses, minor children, and dependent parents. Spouses who are not employed are entitled to various benefits based on the working spouse's benefits, including surviving spouses of deceased workers, provided that they had been married for at least ten years.

If the fully insured spouse dies, the surviving spouse may claim benefits based on the deceased spouse's rights once he or she has attained the age of 60, or at age 50, if he or she is disabled. Further, children of deceased workers are entitled to benefits until they reach the age of 18 (19 if they are students or 21 if they are disabled).

> *Example:* *A single mother who was fully insured dies, leaving a disabled child who is 18 years old. The child is entitled to benefits based on his mother's earnings until he reaches the age of 21, at which point he may be entitled to benefits in his own right.*

Dependent parents of a deceased contributor may be entitled to benefits if the following requirements are satisfied:
- The parent is at least 60 years old.
- At least one-half of the parent's support came from the deceased child.
- The parent does not receive benefits in his or her own right or from a spouse.

Persons who are self-employed are also entitled to receive Social Security benefits, provided that they contributed to the fund for the 40 quarters. The tax imposed on self-employed persons is higher than that imposed on employees because only one party is contributing to the fund, as opposed to the employee and the employer.

The amount of a person's benefit depends on the extent of the person's earnings during the period for which he or she contributed to the fund. These benefits may be increased if the person continues to work beyond the age of 65 without receiving benefits. If a person already received Social Security benefits and then re-enters the workforce, the benefits will be reduced according to the worker's new income.

Employment Law

> **Example:** *A woman continues working beyond the age of 65 without receiving Social Security benefits. When she retires at age 70, her total benefits will be higher to reflect her increased contribution to the fund.*

The Fair Labor Standards Act

The **Fair Labor Standards Act (FLSA)** regulates the maximum number of work hours and minimum wages of a worker. In order to fall within the FLSA, an employer's business must generate income exceeding $500,000 annually.

If the employer meets the statute's standard, all employees of the employer with the exceptions listed below, including independent contractors, are covered by the act. FLSA mandates that the maximum number of hours that an employee may work at the basic minimum wage is 40 hours per week, computed on a seven-day basis. The hours do not have to be in any set order. For all hours worked above 40 in the seven-day period, the employee is entitled to receive 1½ times the prevailing minimum wage for each additional hour.

> **Example:** *A forklift operator works 12-hour shifts. She works a full shift on Monday, Tuesday and Thursday. If she works a full shift again on Saturday, she is entitled to 1½ times the minimum wage for 8 hours, the number of hours exceeding the 40 that she worked during the seven-day period.*

The provisions of the FLSA do not apply to the following categories of employees:

- *Executives.* Their primary duty is to oversee the management of the business or one of its divisions. An executive can also supervise two or more workers, hire and fire personnel, and spends no more than 20% of his or her time on nonmanagement duties (40% for retail and service industries).
- *Administrative personnel.* Defined as persons who perform nonmanual work and exercise independent judgment. A person may be classified as administrative personnel if he or she spends no more than 20% of his or her time on nonadministrative duties (40% for retail and service industries).
- *Outside salespersons.* Persons who regularly work away from the employer's premises.
- *Professionals.* Persons who are defined as having advanced knowledge or training, and certified teachers and instructors.

If an employee falls into one of these four categories, he or she may be required to work more than 40 hours per week without receiving any additional compensation.

The Equal Pay Act

The **Equal Pay Act** was enacted in 1963 to ensure gender equality in the workplace. This act requires that persons who perform the same work in the same establishment for the same employer receive equal compensation. To maintain a claim of discrimination based on the Equal Pay Act, the employee must prove the work performed is equal to that of a person of the opposite gender, the work is performed at the same establishment as the person of the opposite gender, and there is a different compensation paid to the complainant and the worker of the opposite gender.

Equal work is defined as jobs, the performance of which requires equal skill, effort, responsibility, and which are performed under similar working conditions. Equal work also refers to similar surroundings, meaning that a worker who is employed at an outdated facility may be entitled to a pay differential to compensate for the modern surroundings of another worker. A pay differential may be permitted if one of the workers performs additional duties on a regular basis in addition to the work under scrutiny.

The **same establishment** refers to the surroundings where the work is performed. To determine whether the pay rate is unequal, the government and the courts will look at the total compensation paid, including leave, profit sharing, pensions, etc. A pay differential may be permitted for:
- different shifts
- temporary assignments, which permits a temporary pay differential
- temporary or part-time work
- if one employee has been hired from a different company where he or she was earning more money, salary matching
- extra training acquired by the employee.

The Employee Retirement Income Security Act of 1974

The **Employee Retirement Income Security Act of 1974 (ERISA)** was created to protect employees from having their private pension funds dissipated due to the mismanagement of those funds by their employers or their employers' agents. Under ERISA, pension fund managers are held to certain fiduciary standards and are required to make regular reports and detailed statements of account. The Department of Labor and the Internal Revenue Service enforce the provisions of ERISA.

Under ERISA, pension fund managers are required to invest the funds in the same fashion as a **reasonably prudent investor**, meaning that the funds must be continually monitored and the investments must be diversified to reduce the risk factor associated with single investments. The pension manager must file annual reports indicating the status of the funds invested and distributions made to the pensioners. ERISA requires that the pension fund be nondiscriminatory, meaning that it cannot favor upper-echelon employees to the detriment of the body of the workforce.

To satisfy the mandates of ERISA, an employer pension plan must be in writing and include a detailed statement of its procedures, indicate procedures to amend the plan if that should be necessary, indicate the basis upon which payments from the plan will be made, specify the procedures for processing claims for benefits, and indicate the minimum age and/or service required for employee eligibility.

It should be noted that ERISA does not apply to pension plans maintained by sole proprietorships and partnerships, church plans, government benefit plans, plans maintained outside U.S. soil, plans created exclusively for medical needs, or certain excess benefit plans provided for in section 415 of the Internal Revenue Code.

The purpose and impact of ERISA is to guarantee workers who contribute to employer pension plans that, when they retire, there will be sufficient funds in the plan to provide them with the benefits that had been promised to them.

In addition to the foregoing, states have enacted legislation to provide compensation to employees injured while on the job. All of the foregoing indicates the governmental response to the financial needs of the workforce.

Nondiscrimination in the Workplace

Since the 1960s, the federal government has been increasingly concerned with preventing employers from discriminating against certain categories of workers with respect to hiring, training, and firing. As a response to the civil rights movement, Congress has enacted several significant statutes that impact traditional concepts of employment at will, of which all employers must be aware.

The Civil Rights Act of 1964

The first major piece of legislation dealing with discrimination in the workplace was **Title VII** of the **Civil Rights Act of 1964**. This act enumerated five **protected categories**, groups of individuals whose rights to nondiscriminatory treatment in the workplace are guaranteed. Title VII applies to all employers who are in industries that affect commerce and who have 50 or more employees. Almost every business has been judicially determined to affect commerce, so virtually every employer meets that requirement. To be considered an employee, the person must have worked each workday for 20 or more calendar weeks in the current or previous year. The weeks do not have to be consecutive, nor does the employee need to be permanent staff. Title VII does not apply to membership clubs, the military, or Native American tribes.

The categories that are deemed protected categories under Title VII are race; color; national origin, referring to the country or national group from which the employee or the employee's family came; sex, which applies only to gender, not sexual preference; and religion, which has been interpreted to encompass not only traditional religions but also any ethical belief that the person so holds in the same fashion as adherents to the traditional religions.

Title VII is administered by the **Equal Employment Opportunity Commission (EEOC)** and mandates that an employer cannot discriminate in hiring, training, or firing an employee based on the employee's being a member of one of the protected categories. Discrimination includes not only giving preference to persons who do not fall into these categories but also harassing a person because of his or her membership in one of the categories. The EEOC investigates cases of alleged discrimination under Title VII. Cases under Title VII must be filed with the EEOC before a lawsuit can be filed.

One type of unlawful harassment that has received much media attention is that of **sexual harassment**, which is defined as unwelcome sexual advances, requests for sexual favors, and other forms of physical contact of a sexual nature. This conduct may occur between persons of the same or different genders. Sexual harassment may occur if submission to such conduct is a condition of employment (***quid pro quo* harassment**), requests are used as the basis of making employment decisions, or the conduct creates a **hostile work environment**, making the employee who is subject to the conduct uncomfortable in the workplace. Employers are required to provide for effective and confidential reporting procedures for any employee who feels that he or she is a victim of such conduct, provide training dealing with these issues, and have a written policy disseminated to employees prohibiting such conduct.

If it is determined that an employer had been discriminating against employees in the past who fall within one or more of the protected categories, the employer must create an **affirmative action plan** to eradicate this past discrimination. Any employee who feels that he or she has been unlawfully discriminated against because he or she is in a protected category may file a complaint with the EEOC office.

An employer who has been charged with unlawful discrimination under Title VII may defend against such charges by indicating a need to discriminate because of a **bona fide occupational qualification (BFOQ)**. To maintain such a BFOQ, the employer must prove the following:

- All, or substantially all, of the class cannot perform the essential tasks of the job, usually limited to physical ability.
- Hiring a protected class member engenders a risk to third persons.
- The nature of the job indicates a reasonable need to discriminate, such as being a religious teacher in a seminary.

Note that race is the only protected category that cannot be used as the basis for a bona fide occupational qualification.

Example: The manufacturer of a line of cosmetics marketed to African American women refuses to hire a Chinese model. The model files an unlawful discrimination complaint. Can the manufacturer defend a BFOQ by stating that a Chinese model lacks the physical characteristics to demonstrate the produc,t or is this hidden racial discrimination that cannot be used as the basis for a BFOQ defense?

The Age Discrimination in Employment Act of 1967

The **Age Discrimination in Employment Act of 1967 (ADEA)** was enacted shortly after Title VII to include, as a protected category, persons over the age of 40. The ADEA operates in a manner similar to Title VII but applies to employers who employ a minimum of 20 employees for the requisite 20-week period.

Firefighters and law enforcement officers, executives who earn over $44,000 a year and who are entitled to certain retirement benefits, elected officials, and bona fide apprenticeship programs are not covered by the ADEA.

An employer who is charged with unlawful discrimination under the ADEA may show that age discrimination is necessary for a bona fide occupational qualification or by demonstrating that the action was not based on age but on other factors such as education, job experience, etc.

The Pregnancy Discrimination Act of 1978

The **Pregnancy Discrimination Act of 1978** is primarily an interpretation of some of the provisions of Title VII. Prior to its enactment, woman filed complaints of unlawful discrimination based on sex under Title VII if they were discriminated against because of their pregnancies. This act provides greater protection for not only pregnant women but for fathers as well.

Under this statute, all employers, as defined by Title VII, must provide leave for the pregnancy and related needs of its employees, and cannot deny the employee training or promotion because of the pregnancy. Any employee who is unlawfully fired because of the pregnancy may seek reimbursement, back pay, and the return of any lost benefits.

The Americans with Disabilities Act of 1990

The **Americans with Disabilities Act of 1990 (ADA)** prevents an employer from discriminating against a person with a disability with respect to job application procedures, hiring, advancement or discharge of employees, employee compensation, and other terms, conditions, and privileges of employment. The purpose of the ADA is to enable persons with disabilities to earn a living and to be treated with respect in the workplace, as well as with public services and transportation, public accommodations, and telecommunication services.

Employers who are subject to the provisions of the ADA are identified in the same manner as under Title VII. Under the ADA, the term **disability** is defined as a physical or mental impairment that substantially limits one or more major life activities. **Physical impairment** is defined as a physical disease or condition, cosmetic disfigurement, or anatomical defect. **Mental impairment** is defined as any mental or psychological disorder. The definitions under the ADA are specifically left broad to encompass a wide variety of situations.

To be considered disabled, not only must the person have such impairment, but the impairment cannot be temporary and must *substantially* limit a major life activity. Further, the impairment must be documented by the individual to prove that the impairment exists. The ADA also covers people who are not actually disabled, but who are perceived as being so. To be entitled to relief, the disabled worker must also be able to demonstrate that he or she is otherwise qualified to perform the essential functions of the job. If the employee has met the above-indicated tests, the employer is required to make **reasonable accommodations** to assist the employee in fulfilling the job functions. Such accommodations include
- changing the physical surroundings to accommodate the needs of the disabled worker
- restructuring the job to accommodate the disabled worker
- providing readers and interpreters
- changing a work schedule to accommodate the disabled worker
- purchasing equipment to assist the disabled worker
- provide training
- making any other reasonable adaptation to assist the disabled worker.

An employer may be granted relief from making reasonable accommodation if the employer can demonstrate that making such accommodation would constitute an **undue hardship** based on the employer's financial resources, total number of employees, and the impact of the accommodation on the operation of the business. The determination as to whether a reasonable accommodation would be an undue hardship is made on a case-by-case basis. Persons who come with the provisions of the ADA are entitled to all the relief afforded under Title VII. The employment provisions of the ADA are administered by the EEOC.

The Family Medical Leave Act of 1993

The **Family Medical Leave Act** mandates that employers of 50 or more persons, including schools and government agencies, provide employees up to 12 weeks of paid or unpaid leave to cover the needs of birth, adoption, or care of an ill family member. Many states provide for such type of leave for employees who work for employers who employ fewer than 50 workers as well. During the period of leave, the employer must provide the employee with all health care benefits to which the employee would be entitled if actually at work, and the employee cannot be discriminated against in hiring, promotion, benefits, or training because of taking the permitted leave.

Chapter Summary

Although the United States still operates under the concept of employment at will, that concept has been severely modified by various federal statutes that have been enacted over the past century. In the current work environment, employers are held to a high degree of financial accountability for the wages, pensions, and other benefits that they provide for their employees. Also, employers are prohibited from discriminating in making employment decisions regarding hiring, training, and firing persons who belong to a protected category. The categories that are protected by statute against discrimination in the workplace are race, sex, national origin, color, religion, age, pregnancy, and persons with mental or physical impairments. The modern businessperson must be alert to all federal (and state) regulation of employment.

Edited Judicial Decisions

JAMES v. LOUISIANA LABORERS HEALTH AND WELFARE FUND
29 F. 3d 1029 (5th Cir. 1994)

This case arose as an action under section 502(a)(1)(B) of the Employee Retirement Income Security Act (ERISA), 29 U. S.C. §1132(a)(1)(B), to recover benefits allegedly due under the terms of ERISA employee benefit welfare plan. Plaintiff appeals from a summary judgment granted in favor of the Louisiana Laborers Health and Welfare Fund (the Fund). Plaintiff asserts that the plan administrators abused their discretion in denying his claim for benefits based on a provision that excludes medical benefits for "injuries sustained in the course or the commission of a felony." For the following reasons, we AFFIRM.

I. FACTS AND PROCEEDINGS

A. Background

The facts in this case are largely uncontested. The Louisiana Laborers Health & Welfare Fund is a multiemployer, jointly administered employee benefit welfare fund established and administered pursuant to §302(c)(5) of the Labor Management Relations Act, 29 U.S.C. §186(c)(5), on the basis of collective bargaining agreements entered into between various Locals of the Laborers International Union and employer members of the New Orleans Chapter of the Associated General Contractors of America, Inc. The Plan administrators are the fund's six trustees, three of whom are designated by contributing employers and three of whom are designated by participating Unions. The fund is self-insured and employs no outside insurer to underwrite its plan benefits. The plan explicitly gives the trustees discretion to interpret the plan and make determinations concerning claims.

On June 8, 1989, Ollie James, a participant in the plan, sustained injuries as a result of a gunshot wound to his chest. The facts surrounding the incident, which eventually led to the denial of benefits, come from the New Orleans Police Department Police Report.

Officers arrived at 9:10 a.m. and found the victim, Ollie James, lying on his back next to a fence in front of 5223 Tchoupitoulas. A woman, later identified as Irma Jackson, ran up to the officers and said, "Help him, he's dying. I shot him." Suspect was handcuffed and placed in the back seat of 292. Officer Aldridge interviewed the arrested subject after advising her of her rights, while Officer Curet tended the victim. EMS was ordered on a Code 3 as the victim had been shot in the chest and was losing consciousness.

Arrestee Jackson stated that she and her common law husband, who both reside at 5221 Tchoupitoulas with her grandfather, Sidney Gaulden (also a witness), had been arguing over money all morning. They had both been drinking earlier at F & M Patio Bar, Tchoupitoulas, and they went home after being ejected from the bar. She stated that she had left the house to get away from James because he had begun to hit her in the face and side. He followed her outside and grabbed her to keep her from walking off. He threw her to the ground directly in front of their house. He pulled a knife from his pants and began to threaten her with it. He kicked her in the left side and left leg as she tried to avoid the knife. A neighbor, later identified as Raymond Stewart, was walking to a store with his two daughters, and he approached the couple and tried to stop the fight.

The grandfather approached the two and had in his right hand a gun that he pointed at the victim, telling him to stop kicking the arrestee. The arrestee jumped up, grabbed the gun from her grandfather, and as the victim tried to grab the arrestee, she shot him in the stomach. She dropped the gun and ran across the street. The victim picked up the gun and chased the arrestee across the street and then back again to the sidewalk in front of 5223 Tchoupitoulas, where he collapsed. Aldridge then interviewed witness/neighbor, Raymond Stewart, 5109 Tchoupitoulas, who stated that he was walking with his two daughters to the store when he saw the arrestee and the victim fighting on the sidewalk. The victim was kicking the arrestee. Stewart stated he saw something clutched in victim's right hand but could not identify it. He said that he said to the victim, "Leave her alone." Victim replied, "The bitch took my money, she's on that coke." Stewart said, "Talk to her father." He then turned around and took his two girls home. When he was about 50 feet from the scene, he heard a popping sound, which he believed was a gunshot, and he hurried home, never looking back. Aldridge then interviewed grandfather, Sidney Gaulden, 5221 Tchoupitoulas, who stated that his granddaughter and her common law husband constantly fought. He saw them fighting in the house, and she ran outside to avoid being struck by victim. Victim found her outside. Gaulden stated he heard them fighting outside, so he took his 22-caliber revolver outside to scare off the victim. He saw the victim kicking the arrestee who was on the ground. He saw the victim had a knife in his right hand, and he told the victim to go away and leave the arrestee alone. The arrestee jumped up and grabbed the gun from his hand and fired one shot at the victim. Victim picked up gun after arrestee dropped it and ran across the street after her. Victim returned to house behind arrestee and collapsed on the sidewalk.

According to the police report, Jackson sustained scratches to her face and bruises to her left side. In connection with the incident, she was charged with attempted second-degree murder and subsequently pleaded guilty to aggravated battery. Ollie James was not arrested, charged, or convicted as a result of the incident. As a result of the gunshot wound, he required hospitalization and extensive medical treatment, but this injury was not fatal. On March 12, 1990, Jackson, while out on parole, stabbed and killed Ollie James in Bogalusa, Louisiana. James' claims are being advanced by his estate to pay unpaid hospital bills.

B. The Plan's Decisions

By letter dated February 20, 1990, the Plan Office confirmed receipt of medical claims submitted by Ollie James totaling in excess of $358,000 for injuries sustained on June 8, 1989. The medical claims submitted by James were for services rendered by various providers in the total amount of $359,005.52. By certified letter dated April 12, 1990, the Plan notified James of the denial of payment of all claims related to the June 8, 1989, injury, based on the Fund's exclusion for injuries sustained in the course of the commission of a felony. The denial letter concluded that Aggravated Battery (La.R.S. 14:34) and Second Degree Battery (La.R.S. 14:34. 1), both felonies, could reasonably have been at issue.

On September 27, 1990, Lawrence James, as executor of the Estate of Ollie James, appealed the Board's decision. However, the Trustees determined the appeal presented no additional evidence that would support reversal of its prior decision and affirmed its denial of benefits. The denial stated in pertinent part:

In this case, two witnesses and Ms. Jackson stated that Mr. James kicked Ms. Jackson during the incident. Jurisprudence has established that kicking a victim may constitute an aggravated battery. The courts have reasoned that shoes are considered a dangerous weapon within the meaning of the aggravated battery statute if it were found that in the manner they were used it is calculated or likely to produce great bodily harm.

C. Court Proceedings

Finding that the Fund denied James his benefits without conducting an investigation of the facts and circumstances of the alleged felony, the district court remanded the case back to the Fund on November 19, 1992. The court was again not satisfied with the diligence of the investigative effort of the Fund, when it attempted to support its findings through inferences drawn from the police report, and remanded for the second time on June 8, 1993. The Fund was ordered to undertake a more rigorous and thorough investigation, in keeping with the fiduciary duty owed to plaintiff. After finally complying with the district court's mandate, the Fund provided the findings of a private investigator to support its denial of benefits based on the felony exclusion.

The Board of Trustees finds that Ollie James kicked Irma Jackson, while standing above her and brandishing a knife, with hard-soled shoes, either dress shoes or steel-toed work boots, in a manner that was calculated and did result in great bodily harm to Irma Jackson who sustained bruises from approximately her breastbone to her hips on her left side, complicated by her diabetic condition.

Satisfied that the Fund had, although belatedly, gathered sufficient evidence to support its denial of James' benefit claim on the basis that the injuries were sustained in the course or commission of a felony, the district court held the Fund's decision to be legally correct, and granted summary judgment for the Plan.

II. DISCUSSION

The Plan gives the trustees of the Fund the express authority to determine questions of eligibility for benefits. As a result, we are bound to review the Fund's decision under an abuse of discretion standard. *Firestone Tire and Rubber Co. v. Bruch*, 489 U.S. 101, 115, 109 S.Ct. 948, 956-57, 103 L.Ed. 2d 80 (1989). In situations where the administrator is acting under a possible or actual conflict of interest, that factor must also be weighed in determining whether there is an abuse of discretion. *Id.* at 115, 109 S.Ct. at 956-57. Such a review involves two steps. First, this Court must determine whether the Fund's decision was legally correct. *Kennedy v. Electricians Pension Plan*, IBEW No. 995, 954 F.2d 1116, 1124 (5th Cir. 1992); *Batchelor v. International Brotherhood of Electrical Workers Local* 861, 877

F.2d 441, 442-43 (5th Cir. 1989). If the answer to this question is no, then the court must determine whether, even though legally incorrect, the decision amounts to an abuse of discretion. *Kennedy*, 954 F.2d at 1124. For the following reasons, we find the Fund's conclusion to be legally correct, and therefore need not address any abuse of discretion.

The *Kennedy* case instructs us that, in determining the legally correct interpretation of the plans, we should consider: (1) whether the interpretation is consistent with a fair reading of the plans; (2) whether there has been uniformity in construction of the plans; and (3) whether the interpretation results in any unanticipated costs to the plans. *Kennedy*, 954 F.2d at 1121.

Since the parties have not submitted evidence of other occasions where the Fund denied benefits based on the injury arising during the course of a felony, or that the denial of benefits on this basis results in substantial unanticipated costs, we will concern ourselves only with whether the Fund's reading of the Plan was fair and reasonable.

Under Louisiana law, aggravated battery is defined as "battery committed with a dangerous weapon." La.R.S. 14:34. A dangerous weapon is defined as any "substance or instrumentality, which, in the manner used, is calculated or likely to produce death or great bodily injury." La.R.S. 14:2(3).

The Fund found, after conducting its own investigation, that James used his shoes in a manner calculated or likely to cause death or great bodily harm when he stood above Jackson and kicked her left side as she lay on the ground. Such a finding comports with a fair and reasonable interpretation of the Plan in light of the Louisiana criminal cases finding shoes to be dangerous weapons. *Interest of Ruschel*, 411 So.2d 1216 (La. App. 4th Cir. 1982) (steel-toed boot used in brutal attack); *State v. Taylor*, 485 So.2d 117 (La. App. 2d Cir. 1986) (tennis shoes used to stomp victim with such force that shoe marks were left on face).

Appellant contends that by remanding the case twice, and allowing the Fund to gather decision-driven supplemental findings, the district court abused its discretion. Moreover, the appellant argues that the Plan administrators' actual conflict of interest influenced their decision, as reflected in the minutes of the board's meeting. Any inferences of bad faith or conflict of interest are weighed not in the determination of whether the decision was incorrect but in reviewing a possible abuse of discretion. *Firestone*, 489 U.S. at 113-15, 109 S.Ct. at 956. As previously mentioned, since we find the Fund's decision that James was injured during the commission of a felony to be legally correct, we need not address issues that address the manner in which the Fund arrived at its decision.

Appellant further asserts that James' conduct cannot be considered a felony since the legal authorities did not prosecute the matter. The failure of the state criminal justice system to prosecute an individual for alleged felonious activity by no means constitutes an affirmative finding that the individual is absolved of any crime. Unlike the Plan, the State has neither the resources nor the obligation to prosecute a suspect in connection with each and every felony, potentially or actually committed. Our brethren on the Seventh Circuit, who present an example "in which a Plan participant is killed during the commission of a felony, also criticized the illogic of this rule. As the state cannot prosecute a dead man, the trustees would be unable to deny benefits although the injuries were not covered by the Plan." *Berg v. Board of Trustees*, Local 705 International Bro. of Teamsters Health and Welfare Fund, 725 F.2d 68, 70 (7th Cir. 1984).

III. CONCLUSION

Appellant has not pointed to any evidence in the record to prove that the Fund's decision to deny benefits did not meet with the *Kennedy* criteria. They did not present any evidence of the Fund's treating other similar employees' claims differently. Appellant did not submit evidence that Fund's decision resulted in unanticipated costs to plaintiff. Moreover, we hold that the decision of the trustees complied with a full and fair reading of the Plan that the plaintiff's injuries were incurred while in the commission of a felony.

After reviewing the Fund's factual determination, including the Fund's investigative report, our own reading of the Plan, and after careful consideration of any potential or actual conflict of interests under which the Plan administrators were acting, we are persuaded that the Fund gave the Plan its legally correct interpretation. Accordingly, the Fund's decision to deny the plaintiff's benefits on the grounds that James was in the commission of aggravated battery at the time he sustained his injuries was not an abuse of discretion in either its factual or its legal determinations. The grant of summary judgment was proper.

AFFIRMED.

NICOL v. IMAGEMATRIX, INC.
773 F. Supp. 802 (E. D.Va. 1991)

This case presents the question whether a husband, who claims his employer discharged him because of his wife's pregnancy, has standing to sue under Title VII, 42 U.S.C. §2000e *et seq.*, as amended by the Pregnancy Discrimination Act (the Act).

I. BACKGROUND

Mr. and Mrs. Nicol worked for Imagematrix, Inc., as vice presidents from approximately April 1988 until their termination in November 1989. On October 3, 1989, the results of a blood test confirmed Mrs. Nicol's suspicion that she was pregnant. She promptly advised Mr. Eggleston, the president of Imagematrix, of this fact. Six weeks later, on November 15, 1989, Mr. Eggleston terminated Mrs. Nicol, citing declining sales in her department and a company cash flow problem. Later that same day, Mr. Eggleston discharged Mr. Nicol, citing the same cash flow problem. Mr. and Mrs. Nicol claim that Imagematrix, Inc. discharged them solely because of Mrs. Nicol's pregnancy.

On March 5, 1990, Mr. and Mrs. Nicol filed a discrimination complaint with the Equal Employment Opportunity Commission (EEOC). The EEOC issued a right-to-sue letter to Mr. and Mrs. Nicol with respect to Mr. Nicol's claim, in addition to other claims, on December 14, 1990. Subsequently, Mr. and Mrs. Nicol filed suit on March 14, 1991. Mr. Nicol claims he has standing to sue under Title VII, as amended by the Pregnancy Discrimination Act, because he was discriminated against on the basis of his sex due to his wife's pregnancy. This matter is now before the Court on defendant's motion for partial summary judgment on the issue of Mr. Nicol's standing to sue.

II. ANALYSIS

Analysis of the standing issue properly begins with the words of Title VII that define who can sue for discriminatory discharge. §2000e-2(a)(1) states:

> It shall be an unlawful employment practice for an employer to fail or refuse to hire or to discharge any individual or otherwise to discriminate against any individual with respect to his compensation, terms, conditions, or privileges of employment, because of such individual's race, color, religion, sex, or national origin.

42 U.S.C. §2000e-2(a)(1) (emphasis added).

Thus, Title VII, by its terms, confers standing to sue on persons who claim they were discharged because of their gender. Mr. Nicol fits this category. He claims his discharge was the result of discrimination on the basis of his sex. More specifically, he argues that defendants terminated him for a reason that a female employee could never be terminated. A woman could never be terminated due to her employer's animus against a pregnant spouse because her spouse could not be pregnant. Therefore, defendants allegedly treated Mr. Nicol, a male employee, "in a manner which but for [his] sex would be different." *Los Angeles Dept. of Water & Power v. Manhart*, 435 U.S. 702, 55 L.Ed.2d 657, 98 S.Ct. 1370 (1978). This alleged difference in treatment affords Mr. Nicol standing under Title VII. Whether Mr. Nicol can prove at trial that defendants were prejudiced against pregnant women and fired him because he was married to a pregnant woman is another matter.

Defendant's argument focuses not on Title VII's basic language but on the expansion of that language as a result of the Pregnancy Discrimination Act. In that Act, Congress expanded the meaning of sex to include pregnancy. The Act states in pertinent part: "The terms 'because of sex' or 'on the basis of sex' include, but are not limited to, because of or on the basis of pregnancy, childbirth, or related medical conditions." 42 U.S.C. §2000e(k). Distilled to its essence, defendant's argument is that Mr. Nicol has no standing to sue for discriminatory discharge because he is not the pregnant employee. Put another way, defendants claim that the Act limits standing to a person discriminated against on the basis of such person's pregnancy, childbirth, or related medical conditions. This argument founders on the statutory language itself. The first clause of the Act plainly states: "The terms 'because of sex' or 'on the basis of sex' include, but are not limited to on the basis of pregnancy, childbirth, or related medical conditions." §2000e(k) (emphasis added). Although this Act expands Title VII's scope of prohibited discriminatory conduct to include an employee's pregnancy, the words "but are not limited to" in the Act indicate that the original prohibition in Title VII against discrimination on he basis of an employee's own sex still exists. See *Newport News Shipbuilding and Dry Dock Co. v. EEOC*, 462 U.S. 669, 684, 77 L.Ed.2d 89, 103 S.Ct. 2622 (1983) ("By making clear that an employer could not discriminate on the basis of an employee's pregnancy, Congress did not erase the original prohibition against discrimination on the basis of an employee's sex "). Therefore, under the terms of the Act itself, Mr. Nicol need not be the pregnant employee to have standing.

Defendants also point to the legislative history of the Pregnancy Discrimination Act, much of which indicates that the main purpose of the Act was to protect working women against all forms of employment discrimination based on sex. This alone, however, is not a basis on which defendants can argue that only pregnant, female employees have standing to sue under the Act. Congress may have focused on female employees when passing the Pregnancy Discrimination Act, but this emphasis "does not create a 'negative inference' limiting the scope of the [Pregnancy Discrimination] Act to the specific problem that motivated its enactment." *Id.* at 679. Furthermore, "proponents of the [Pregnancy Discrimination Act] stressed throughout the debates that Congress had always intended to protect all individuals from sex discrimination in employment—including but not limited to pregnant women workers." *Id.* at 680. Therefore, the legislative history points to no limitation in the Act that would preclude Mr. Nicol's standing.

Though not directly on point, *Newport News* squarely supports the result reached here. There, the Supreme Court held that an employer's health insurance plan providing female employees with pregnancy related benefits but not providing the same benefits to the spouses of male employees, discriminated against the male employees in violation of Title VII, §2000e(k). 462 U.S. at 684. In reaching this result, the Court explicitly recognized that male employees could recover under §2000e(k) even though they could not become pregnant themselves. *Id.* at 682-685. The Court reasoned that "the meaning of the first clause [of the Pregnancy Discrimination Act] is not limited by the specific language in the second clause, which explains the application of the general principle to women employees." *Id.* at 679 n. 14.

Newport News, therefore, establishes that Title VII's prohibitions cover discrimination against pregnant spouses. As Justice Stevens explained, discrimination against pregnant spouses is in essence discrimination against male employees because the sex of the spouse and the sex of the employee are always opposite. *Id.* at 684. Thus, even though Mr. Nicol is not a pregnant employee, he has standing to sue under Title VII because he was allegedly discharged and discriminated against on the basis of his own sex.

Also instructive here are the Title VII interracial relationship cases; Mr. Nicol's claim is analogous to claims of discrimination based on interracial relationships and courts have consistently and sensibly recognized that discrimination on the basis of interracial marriage or association and discrimination on the basis of race are one and the same. See *Parr v. Woodmen of the World Life Ins. Co.*, 791 F.2d 888, 892 (11th Cir. 1986) ("Where plaintiff claims discrimination based upon an interracial marriage or association, he alleges, by definition, that he has been discriminated against because of his race."); *Reiter v. Center Consol. School Dist. No. 26-JT*, 618 F.Supp. 1458, 1460 (D. Colo. 1985) (same); *Gresham v. Waffle House, Inc.*, 586 F.Supp. 1442, 1445 (N.D.Ga. 1984) (same); *Whitney v. Greater New York Corp. of Seventh Day Adventists*, 401 F.Supp. 1363, 1366 (S.D.N.Y. 1975) (same). In other words, a white employee who is discharged because his spouse is black is discriminated against on the basis of his race, even though the root animus for the discrimination is an anti-black prejudice. Similarly, the root animus here may be an anti-pregnancy prejudice, but the resulting discrimination is against Mr. Nicol's gender, for only males can have pregnant spouses.

Parr illustrates the relevance of the interracial relationship cases. There, a white male job applicant alleged that he had been denied employment by the defendant because of his marriage to a black woman. The Eleventh Circuit held that the plaintiff had been discriminated against because of his race. The Court found that the plaintiff had stated a claim as a white man who had been discriminated against because of his own race and the racial prejudices against white men who are married to black women. The root animus is, of course, an anti-black prejudice. This is analogous to Mr. Nicol's situation. Mr. Nicol has stated a claim as a married man who has allegedly been discriminated against because of his own sex and the prejudices of the defendant against men who are married to pregnant women. Thus, just as the plaintiff in *Parr* was discriminated against because of his race, Mr. Nicol has been discriminated against because of his sex.

Defendants contend that Mr. Nicol is asserting third party standing on the basis of his wife's pregnancy and that such derivative standing is not contemplated under Title VII. This Court agrees; third party standing is not adequate for a prima facie Title VII claim. But this argument misses the point, for Mr. Nicol is asserting standing on the basis of his own sex. Thus, in recognizing Mr. Nicol's standing, this Court has not opened the door to other derivative suits under the Pregnancy Discrimination Act. For example, a discharged employee who is also a parent could not state a *prima facie* Title VII claim under the Act based on his or her daughter's pregnancy, because the status of a parent is not gender-based. Parents are both male and female. Thus, discharge because of a daughter's pregnancy would not be discrimination against the employee based on his or her sex. The result would be the same for a sibling or a neighbor. The status of a husband, however, is distinctly gender-based. Therefore, Mr. Nicol was discriminated against on the basis of his sex if defendants indeed discharged him due to his wife's pregnancy.

For the reasons stated above, Mr. Nicol has standing to sue under Title VII, as amended by the Pregnancy Discrimination Act. Thus, the Court DENIES defendant's motion for partial summary judgment on the issue of Mr. Nicol's standing.

An appropriate order will be entered.

Glossary

Age Discrimination in Employment Act of 1967 (ADEA) - Federal statute protecting workers over the age of 40 from being discriminated against in employment

Affirmative action plan - Requirement under Title VII to make up for past discrimination

Americans with Disabilities Act of 1990 (ADA) - Federal statute protecting workers with disabilities from employment discrimination

Bona fide occupational qualification (BFOQ) - Specific work situation that would permit an employer to discriminate against a worker in a protected category

Civil Rights Act of 1964 - Title VII

Disability - Mental or physical impairment that affects a major life activity

Employee Retirement Income Security Act of 1974 (ERISA) - Federal statute designed to protect employees of private pension plans

Employment at will - Doctrine that permits an employer or employee to hire or leave without notice or cause

Equal Employment Opportunity Commission (EEOC) - Government agency that administers various anti-discrimination employment statutes

Equal Pay Act - Federal statute that guarantees equal pay for equal work regardless of gender

Equal work - Jobs performed under similar working conditions that require equal skill, effort, and responsibility

Fair Labor Standards Act (FLSA) - Federal statue mandating maximum work hours and a minimum wage

Family Medical Leave Act - Federal statute permitting a worker up to 12 weeks of unpaid leave to take care of a family emergency

Fully insured - Entitled to Social Security benefits

Hostile work environment - Form of sexual harassment in which an employee is made uncomfortable in the workplace

Labor law - The law regulating labor unions

Mental impairment - Any mental or psychological disorder

Physical impairment - Any disease or defect that impairs a major life activity

Pregnancy Discrimination Act of 1978 - Federal statute protecting employees from job discrimination based on pregnancy

Protected categories - Race, color, religion, sex, and national origin

Quid pro quo **harassment** - Sexual harassment in which employment decisions are based on granting sexual favors

Reasonable accommodation - Employers must make changes to assist a disabled worker to work provided that those changes do not constitute an undue hardship for the employer

Reasonably prudent investor - Fiduciary standard under ERISA

Same establishment - The surroundings where the work is performed

Sexual harassment - Making any unwelcome sexual overture in the workplace

Social Security Act - Federal statute guaranteeing a governmental pension and retirement plan for all persons who work a certain number of years and who contribute to the general Social Security fund

Social Security Administration - Government agency that administers Social Security

Title VII - Federal statute that prohibits job discrimination for workers in protected categories

Undue hardship - Determining that making reasonable accommodation would create an unfair financial burden for the employer in a given situation

Exercises

1. How should a manager deal with sexual harassment in the workplace? Discuss. Obtain a copy of your employer's policy regarding sexual harassment in the workplace.

2. What is your opinion of government interference with employment at will? Discuss.

3. Many statutes, such as workers compensation and Social Security, specify ailments and disabilities in order to qualify for benefits, but the ADA does not. Why not, and what is your opinion of the ADA approach?

4. What is your opinion of the efficacy of affirmative action plans? Discuss. Obtain a copy of your employer's affirmative action plan and analyze its provisions.

5. Discuss what other categories should be included as an exemption to the FLSA.

Chapter Ten

BANKRUPTCY

Introduction

At some point, a commercial enterprise may find itself faced with the prospect of invoking the protection of the federal bankruptcy legislation, either as a debtor or as a creditor. Despite what many lay persons believe, the principal objective of bankruptcy is not to discharge all of a debtor's financial obligations; rather, the primary goal of bankruptcy is to assist the debtor in reorganizing his, her, or its finances to pay off all obligations. Unfortunately, in many instances, this result is not possible, and for a business, the outcome of the bankruptcy proceeding may be the termination of the business.

All bankruptcy proceedings are handled pursuant to federal law, the **Bankruptcy Code** under title 11 of the United States Code. Pursuant to this statute, all bankruptcy proceedings must be filed in federal district court in a division generally referred to as the **bankruptcy court**. The specifics of the proceedings are determined by the nature of the debtor. **Chapter 7** bankruptcy, often refereed to as **straight bankruptcy**, is available for individual debtors who wish to have their financial obligations discharged. This form of bankruptcy is often referred to as **liquidation** because the debtor's assets are sold to discharge his or her obligations. If a debtor wishes to have his or her finances reorganized, rather than discharged, so that the debtor may be able to pay off all of the obligations, the debtor may seek to reorganize his or her finances under **Chapter 13**. This form of bankruptcy is available for debtors who have a regular income. Commercial enterprises operating as sole proprietorships (Chapter Eight) may seek protection under either chapter.

Commercial enterprises that wish to reorganize may submit a reorganization plan (see below) pursuant to **Chapter 11**, and family farms utilize the reorganization process of **Chapter 12**. For businesses, total discharge is the last resort of the bankruptcy court—reorganization of its financial structure is the court's predominant objective. Governmental entities utilize **Chapter 9**.

A commercial enterprise may find itself in bankruptcy court as
- a debtor who has voluntarily petitioned the court for protection
- a debtor who has been taken into court involuntarily by action of its creditors
- a creditor who seeks repayment pursuant to the bankruptcy court's power over the debtor.

Voluntary Bankruptcy

A commercial enterprise will seek protection under the federal bankruptcy law if its income is insufficient to meet its current obligations, and its total debts exceed its total assets. When this occurs, it becomes impossible for the debtor to discharge its obligations, and continuing its operations would probably engender greater debt for the enterprise.

A **voluntary bankruptcy** proceeding begins when the debtor files a petition seeking bankruptcy protection in the federal district court where the debtor operates, owes debts, or is domiciled. It must be noted that although the substantive and procedural laws governing bankruptcy are federal, each federal district court formulates its own specific local rules that must be followed with respect to filing, service, and mechanical matters. Each court's rules must be individually analyzed.

When filing for bankruptcy, the debtor is required to serve notice on all persons who must be notified that a bankruptcy petition has been filed. Persons who should be notified of the proceeding but who are not served may be exempt from the court's discharge, meaning that the obligations to those persons may survive the discharge.

The debtor, codebtors, debtor's counsel, and all of the business partners of the debtor should be served with copies of the court's documents. In addition, members of any committee appointed by the **United States Trustee,** a person appointed to oversee the assets of the debtor; their counsel; any other trustee appointed in the case, such as an individual appointed to protect the interests of minor government agencies who may need notification; any person who files a **notice or appearance**—a court document indicating a wish to participate in the proceedings; the 20 largest creditors; and any other person who the debtor believes should receive notification should be served.

While engaged in a bankruptcy proceeding, the debtor may be involved in another lawsuit that would have an effect on the bankruptcy proceeding, such as a tort or contract claim. In such instance, the parties to the separate suit may seek to have the matter adjudicated by the bankruptcy court in conjunction with the bankruptcy proceeding. The case may be included in the bankruptcy proceeding by a process called **removal** in which the other court is served with a petition and, if deemed appropriate, the matter will be transferred to the bankruptcy court.

> *Example:* A debtor corporation has filed for bankruptcy protection. The corporation is currently involved in a breach of contract suit with another corporation. The other company may seek to have the matter removed to the bankruptcy court so its financial rights can be decided in one proceeding.

Once the petition is filed, the debtor's assets are considered to be a part of the debtor's estate. At this point, all actions against the debtor are halted under the automatic stay provisions of the bankruptcy code, and the creditors are permitted to file claims against the debtor's estate in bankruptcy court. For Chapter 11, 12, and 13 proceedings, the debtor is required to file a plan for satisfying some or all of its obligations, and the creditors are permitted to examine the accuracy of the statement of financial affairs after it has been filed with the court.

The debtor must provide
- name, including any aliases or trade names it has used in the past six years
- Social Security or tax ID number
- mailing address
- location and description of its principal assets, including their current value
- county of its office or principal place of business
- type of debtor and description of its business
- names and addresses of all creditors, including whether they are secured or unsecured and the amount owing to each
- any prior bankruptcy filing
- financial statement and balance sheet for the past five years

- all loan agreements, security agreements, and deeds of trust
- accounts receivable and payable
- all current contracts
- names of all employees
- names of all equity holders—stockholders, limited partners, members, etc.
- names of all bondholders
- pending or anticipated litigation that the debtor is or will be a party to.

Finally, the debtor must file a **mailing matrix** with the court that includes the names and addresses of all creditors and other persons who must receive notice of the bankruptcy proceeding (see above).

To evidence the debtor's financial position, the debtor must file an official Statement of Assets and Liabilities. The Schedule must be prepared according to the following format:

- *Schedule A: Real Property.* The debtor must specify all realty in which he or she has any interest, including leaseholds and equitable interests. The Schedule must include a detailed description of the property, its current market value, and the value of any secured claim against the property.
- *Schedule B: Personal Property.* The debtor must prepare a detailed description of all personal property in which the debtor has an interest and indicate its current value. This Schedule includes all property that does not specifically appear in one of the other schedules.
- *Schedule C: Exempt Property.* This Schedule only applies to individuals who keep certain property enumerated in the statute, such as a personal residence up to a specific value, tools of the trade, etc. Corporations and partnerships are precluded from exempting any assets from creditors' claims.
- *Schedule D: Creditors Holding Secured Claims.* This Schedule details all of the debtor's secured creditors and must include the legal description of collateral subject to this security interest, plus its current market value.
- *Schedule E: Unsecured Creditors Holding Priority Claims.* This list includes all persons who are entitled to a priority under §507 of the Bankruptcy Code and includes employees' claims for wages not exceeding $2,000 per employee earned within the preceding ten days, pension and employee benefit plans, and tax claims.
- *Schedule F: Unsecured Creditors Holding Nonpriority Claims.* This group includes all other creditors.
- *Schedule G: Executory Contracts and Unexpired Loans.* This Schedule is of prime importance for commercial enterprises, and these agreements must be listed regardless of the debtor's position under the contracts. All particular terms of the agreement must be indicated.
- *Schedule H: Codebtors.* This list includes all persons who may be held jointly liable for the debtor's obligations.
- *Schedule I: Current Income of Individual Debtors.* Self-explanatory
- *Schedule J: Current Expenditures of Individual Debtors.* Self-explanatory.

The amounts that appear in this schedule will bind all creditors of the debtor unless the creditor files a proof of claim for a different amount.

> **Example:** *A debtor files a Schedule indicating that it owes Acme Corp., as an unsecured creditor, $50,000. Acme fails to file a proof of claim. In discharge, the bankruptcy court awards Acme $50,000. In fact, Acme is owed $75,000, but because it failed to file a proof of claim, it is entitled only to receive the $50,000 that appeared on the schedule, and the debtor is completely discharged from this obligation.*

Within 15 days of filing the petition, the debtor must file a **Statement of Financial Affairs** that indicates its operations and financial transactions. All debtors must file this Statement.

Individual debtors who file under Chapter 7 must also file a **Statement of Intention**, which indicates the debtor's intention to surrender, redeem, or retain through reaffirmation his or her own assets. **Reaffirmation** means that the debtor wishes to retain the property subject to a secured claim the debtor gives to do, which maintains the financial obligation so that it will not be discharged in bankruptcy.

> **Example:** *An individual debtor wishes to retain his car, which is secured to a finance company. The debtor owes $2,500 on the automobile. The debtor, by filing a reaffirmation, may keep the car but also keeps the debt of $2,500 that will survive any discharge that may be forthcoming by means of the bankruptcy proceeding. To secure the reaffirmation, the debtor may have to give the finance company additional security,*

Between 20 and 50 days after the petition is filed, the U.S. Trustee schedules a **creditors meeting** that must be attended by the debtor or the debtor's representative. The purpose of the meeting is to allow the creditors to examine the debtor regarding the debtor's conduct, property, operations, and other related matters. The meeting is presided over by the trustee and is taped for future review.

For corporations filing under Chapter 11, the corporate debtor, **debtor in possession**, actually possesses the property that is subject to the creditors' claims and must close all of its books, records, and bank accounts, and open new ones at an authorized financial institution. The new accounts, which must indicate on their faces that are coming from a debtor in possession, must include a general operating account to maintain the function of the business, a payroll account to protect employees, and a tax account to protect the government. Further, business debtors and individual debtors who reorganize under Chapter 13 must file monthly reports with the trustee.

A debtor in possession is permitted to use, sell, or lease property in its accounts for maintaining the ordinary operations of the business without court approval. If the debtor in possession attempts to use, sell, or lease property it does not ordinarily use, it must first seek the approval of the bankruptcy court.

> **Example:** *The debtor operates a flower shop and uses a van to make deliveries. The debtor may continue to use the van to make regular deliveries without obtaining court approval but may not sell the van without such authority.*

Certain property of the estate, including any income it generates, may be subject to a lien held by a secured creditor. Income that is received from such property is called **cash collateral**, and the debtor may not use, sell, or lease cash collateral unless the secured creditors agree and the court authorizes the sale or lease. Cash collateral includes cash, negotiable instruments, securities, and other cash equivalents (see Chapters Four and Eight).

> ***Example:*** *A debtor owns a commercial building secured by a mortgage. The debtor may not sell this property unless the mortgagee and the court agree.*

Commercial debtors and individuals who seek to reorganize under Chapter 13 are required to prepare and file a **Reorganization** or **Restructuring Plan** with the court. The purpose of this plan is to indicate how the debtor intends to reorganize to pay off its debts. Chapter 11 debtors (corporations) must also file a **disclosure statement** in addition to the plan that includes:
- a history of the business and the factors that led to the bankruptcy proceeding
- a description of all assets and their value
- the accounting method used by the corporation
- the present condition of the corporation
- a list of all claims against the corporation
- anticipated future of the business
- estimated expenses to date
- the probability of collecting on sums owed to the corporation
- potential litigation
- potential risk factors involved in the reorganization.

The bankruptcy court must affirm the debtor's plan, and the creditors have the right to review, accept, or reject the plan.

After the preceding procedures have been completed, the court will authorize the distribution of the debtor's assets, and the debtor will be discharged from further obligation.

Involuntary Bankruptcy

Involuntary bankruptcy results when the debtor's creditors petition the court to have the debtor's estate supervised by a trustee. Except for the fact that the creditor files the petition, in this instance, the procedures are identical to the various procedures discussed above. However, individuals are only subject to the voluntary bankruptcy proceedings of Chapter 7 of the Bankruptcy Code.

In addition to the initiation of the proceedings, the debtor's creditors, who filed pursuant to Chapter 11, 12, or 13, may seek to have the proceeding converted to a Chapter 7 proceeding. The purpose of this conversion is to entitle the creditors to attach the personal assets of the debtor. Chapter 7 conversion is not permitted for Chapter 11 cases that involve a nonprofit business unless the debtor consents to the conversion.

Creditors Rights

The commercial enterprise may find itself the creditor of a person or entity who has filed or been forced into bankruptcy court. In this instance, the objective of the creditor is to attach as much money or property from the debtor as possible.

In order to protect the creditor's interests, the creditor must file a **proof of claim** with the court that represents its rights to payment from the debtor. The Proof of Claim includes the person who is making the claim, called the **claimant;** the nature and amount of the claim; a statement indicating whether the claim is secured or unsecured; and any other information that is relevant to the assertion of the claim. The Proof of Claim must be signed by the claimant and include documentary evidence of the claim, such as a promissory note or contract of sale.

If the creditor had initiated court proceedings before the debtor filed for bankruptcy protection, that court proceeding is automatically stayed. A creditor may make a motion to the court to have the stay lifted so that the litigation may proceed despite the bankruptcy proceedings. To acquire relief, the creditor must assert a lack of adequate protection in the bankruptcy court, the debtor's lack of equity in the property in question, and that the property is not needed for an effective bankruptcy reorganization.

If the creditor is included in the bankruptcy proceeding, the creditor has the right to examine the debtor and to challenge all documents, statistics, schedules, and plans submitted by the debtor the court. However, if the debtor qualifies as a small business under Chapter 11, the court may conditionally approve a debtor's statement without offering the creditor the opportunity to object until the plan's confirmation hearing. For Chapter 11 cases, the creditor can vote to accept or reject the restructuring plan. For Chapter 12 and 13 cases, the creditor may object to the classification of certain property as being exempt from creditors' claims. However, once the objection has been made and heard and the court has rendered its decision, the debtor is discharged according to the provisions of the court's order. A creditor whose debts have been discharged loses all future objections unless the debtor has reaffirmed the obligation.

Chapter Summary

The purpose of the provisions of the Bankruptcy Code are to enable a debtor to have a fresh start, free of most financial obligations, and to provide for an equitable distribution of the debtor's assets to all of the debtor's legitimate creditors. Bankruptcy law is actually beneficial for commercial enterprises because it permits debtor businesses to continue their operations pursuant to the plan of reorganization and enables creditor businesses to receive funds or property to which they are entitled.

The Bankruptcy Code divides itself into four categories: Chapter 7 to discharge the financial liabilities of individuals; Chapter 11 to reorganize corporations, Chapter 12 to reorganize family farms, and Chapter 13 to reorganize (and discharge) debtor individual businesses. Bankruptcy proceedings are handled in the federal court in the district in which the debtor resides, operates, or owns property. Debtors must provide a detailed statement indicating all of their assets and liabilities, and creditors have the right to examine debtors to ascertain the validity of the financial statement and to challenge the value of the debtor's assets or the amount identified as owing to them. Bankruptcy proceedings may be initiated voluntarily by the debtor or involuntarily if brought by the creditors.

Unless a debtor specifically reaffirms a financial obligation, once the bankruptcy proceedings are concluded, the debtor is discharged from any further financial obligations to all creditors who have been notified and/or participated in the bankruptcy proceedings.

Edited Judicial Decisions

TOIBB v. RADLOFF
501 U.S. 157, 111 S. Ct. 2197, 115 L.Ed. 2d 145 (1991)

OPINION BY: BLACKMUN

In this case, we must decide whether an individual debtor not engaged in business is eligible to reorganize under Chapter 11 of the Bankruptcy Code, 11 U.S.C. §1101 *et seq.*

From March 1983 until April 1985, petitioner Sheldon Baruch Toibb, a former staff attorney with the Federal Energy Regulatory Commission, was employed as a consultant by Independence Electric Corporation (IEC), a company he and two others organized to produce and market electric power. Petitioner owns 24 percent of the company's shares. After IEC terminated his employment, petitioner was unable to find work as a consultant in the energy field; his family and friends have largely supported him since that time.

On November 18, 1986, petitioner filed in the United States Bankruptcy Court for the Eastern District of Missouri a voluntary petition for relief under Chapter 7 of the Code, 11 U.S.C. §701 *et seq.* The Schedule of Assets and Liabilities accompanying petitioner's filing disclosed no secured debts, a disputed federal tax priority claim of $11,000, and unsecured debts of $170,605. Petitioner listed as nonexempt assets his IEC shares and a possible claim against his former business associates. He stated that the market value of each of these assets was unknown.

On August 6, 1987, the Chapter 7 trustee appointed to administer petitioner's estate notified the creditors that the Board of Directors of IEC had offered to purchase petitioner's IEC shares for $25,000. When petitioner became aware that this stock had such value, he decided to avoid its liquidation by moving to convert his Chapter 7 case to one under the reorganization provisions of Chapter 11.

The Bankruptcy Court granted petitioner's conversion motion, App. 21, and on February 1, 1988, petitioner filed a plan of reorganization. *Id.*, at 70. Under the plan, petitioner proposed to pay his unsecured creditors $25,000 less administrative expenses and priority tax claims, a proposal that would result in a payment of approximately 11 cents on the dollar. He further proposed to pay the unsecured creditors, for a period of six years, 50 percent of any dividends from IEC or of any proceeds from the sale of the IEC stock, up to full payment of the debts.

On March 8, 1988, the Bankruptcy Court on its own motion ordered petitioner to show cause why his petition should not be dismissed because petitioner was not engaged in business and, therefore, did not qualify as a Chapter 11 debtor. *Id.*, at 121. At the ensuing hearing, petitioner unsuccessfully attempted to demonstrate that he had a business to reorganize. Petitioner also argued that Chapter 11 should be available to an individual debtor not engaged in an ongoing business. On August 1, the Bankruptcy Court ruled that, under the authority of *Wamsganz v. Boatmen's Bank of De Soto*, 804 F.2d 503 (CA8 1986), petitioner failed to qualify for relief under Chapter 11. App. to Pet. for Cert. A-17 and A-19.

The United States District Court for the Eastern District of Missouri, also relying on *Wamsganz*, upheld the Bankruptcy Court's dismissal of petitioner's Chapter 11 case. App. to Pet. for Cert. A-8 and A-9. The United States Court of Appeals for the Eighth Circuit affirmed, holding that the Bankruptcy Court had the authority to dismiss the proceeding sua sponte, and that the Circuit's earlier *Wamsganz* decision was controlling. In re *Toibb*, 902 F.2d 14 (1990). Because the Court of Appeals' ruling that an individual nonbusiness debtor may not reorganize under Chapter 11 clearly conflicted with the holding of the Court of Appeals for the Eleventh Circuit in In re *Moog*, 774 F.2d 1073 (1985), we granted certiorari to resolve the conflict. 498 U.S. 1060 (1991).

In our view, the plain language of the Bankruptcy Code disposes of the question before us. §109, 11 U. S. C. §109, defines who may be a debtor under the various chapters of the Code. §109(d) provides: "Only a person that may be a debtor under chapter 7 of this title, except a stockbroker or a commodity broker, and a railroad may be a debtor under chapter 11 of this title." §109(b) states: "A person may be a debtor under chapter 7 of this title only if such person is not—(1) a railroad; (2) a domestic insurance company, bank, . . .; or (3) a foreign insurance company, bank, . . . engaged in such business in the United States." The Code defines "person" as used in Title 11 to "include [an] individual." §101(35). Under the express terms of the Code, therefore, petitioner is "a person who may be a debtor under chapter 7" and satisfies the statutory requirements for a Chapter 11 debtor.

The Code contains no ongoing business requirement for reorganization under Chapter 11, and we are loath to infer the exclusion of certain classes of debtors from the protections of Chapter 11, because Congress took care in §109 to specify who qualifies—and who does not qualify—as a debtor under the various chapters of the Code. §109(b) expressly excludes from the coverage of Chapter 7 railroads and various financial and insurance institutions. Only municipalities are eligible for the protection of Chapter 9. §109(c). Most significantly, §109(d) makes stockbrokers and commodities brokers ineligible for Chapter 11 relief but otherwise leaves that Chapter available to any other entity eligible for the protection of Chapter 7. Congress knew how to restrict recourse to the avenues of bankruptcy relief; it did not place Chapter 11 reorganization beyond the reach of a nonbusiness individual debtor.

The *amicus curiae* in support of the Court of Appeal's judgment acknowledges that Chapter 11 does not expressly exclude an individual nonbusiness debtor from its reach. He echoes the reasoning of those courts that have engrafted an ongoing-business requirement onto the plain language of §109(d) and argues that the statute's legislative history and structure make clear that Chapter 11 was intended for business debtors alone. See, *e.g., Wamsganz v. Boatmen's Bank of De Soto*, 804 F.2d at 505 ("The legislative history of the Bankruptcy Code, taken as a whole, shows that Congress meant for chapter 11 to be available to businesses and persons engaged in business, and not to consumer debtors"). We find these arguments unpersuasive for several reasons.

First, this Court has repeated with some frequency: "Where, as here, the resolution of a question of federal law turns on a statute and the intention of Congress, we look first to the statutory language and then to the legislative history if the statutory language is unclear." *Blum v. Stenson*, 465 U.S. 886, 896, 79 L. Ed. 2d 891, 104 S. Ct. 1541 (1984). The language of §109 is not unclear. Thus, although a court appropriately may refer to a statute's legislative history to resolve statutory ambiguity, there is no need to do so here.

Second, even were we to consider the sundry legislative comments urged in support of a congressional intent to exclude a nonbusiness debtor from Chapter 11, the scant history on this precise issue does not suggest a "clearly expressed legislative intent . . . contrary . . ." to the plain language of §109(d). See *Consumer Product Safety Comm'n v. GTE Sylvania, Inc.*, 447 U.S. 102, 108, 64 L. Ed. 2d 766, 100 S. Ct. 2051 (1980). The *amicus* does point to the following statement in a House Report:

> "Some consumer debtors are unable to avail themselves of the relief provided under chapter 13. For these debtors, straight bankruptcy is the only remedy that will enable them to get out from under the debilitating effects of too much debt." H. R. Rep. No. 95-595, p. 125 (1977).

Petitioner responds with the following excerpt from a later Senate Report:

> "Chapter 11, Reorganization, is primarily designed for businesses, although individuals are eligible for relief under the chapter. The procedures of chapter 11, however, are sufficiently complex that they will be used only in a business case and not in the consumer context." S. Rep. No. 95-989, p. 3 (1978).

These apparently conflicting views tend to negate the suggestion that the Congress enacting the current Code operated with a clear intent to deny Chapter 11 relief to an individual nonbusiness debtor.

Finally, we are not persuaded by the contention that Chapter 11 is unavailable to a debtor without an ongoing business because many of the Chapter's provisions do not apply to a nonbusiness debtor. There is no doubt that Congress intended that a business debtor be among those who might use Chapter 11. Code provisions like the ones authorizing the appointment of an equity security holders' committee, §1102, and the appointment of a trustee "for cause, including fraud, dishonesty, incompetence, or gross mismanagement of the affairs of the debtor by current management . . .," §1104(a)(1), certainly are designed to aid in the rehabilitation of a business. It does not follow, however, that a debtor whose affairs do not warrant recourse to these provisions is ineligible for Chapter 11 relief. Instead, these provisions—like the references to debtor businesses in the Chapter's legislative history—reflect an understandable expectation that primarily debtors with ongoing businesses would use Chapter 11; they do not constitute an additional prerequisite for Chapter 11 eligibility beyond those established in §109(d).

Although the foregoing analysis is dispositive of the question presented, we deal briefly with *amicus'* contention that policy considerations underlying the Code support inferring a congressional intent to preclude a nonbusiness debtor from reorganizing under Chapter 11. First, it is said that bringing a consumer debtor within the scope of Chapter 11 does not serve Congress' purpose of permitting business debtors to reorganize and restructure their debts in order to revive the debtors' businesses and thereby preserve jobs and protect investors. This argument assumes that Congress had a single purpose in enacting Chapter 11. Petitioner suggests, however, and we agree, that Chapter 11 also embodies the general Code policy of maximizing the value of the bankruptcy estate. See *Commodity Futures Trading Comm'n v. Weintraub*, 471 U.S. 343, 351-354, 85 L. Ed. 2d 372, 105 S. Ct. 1986 (1985). Under certain circumstances, a consumer debtor's estate will be worth more if reorganized under Chapter 11 than if liquidated under Chapter 7. Allowing such a debtor to proceed under Chapter 11 serves the congressional purpose of deriving as much value as possible from the debtor's estate. Second, *amicus* notes that allowing a consumer debtor to proceed under Chapter 11 would permit the debtor to shield both disposable income and nonexempt personal property. He argues that the legislative history of Chapter 11 does not reflect an intent to offer a consumer debtor more expansive protection than he would find under Chapter 13, which does not protect disposable income, or Chapter 7, which does not protect nonexempt personal assets. As an initial matter, it makes no difference whether the legislative history affirmatively reflects such intent, because the plain language of the statute allows a consumer debtor to proceed under Chapter 11. Moreover, differences in the requirements and protections of each chapter reflect Congress' appreciation that various approaches are necessary to address effectively the disparate situations of debtors seeking protection under the Code.

Amicus does not contend that allowing a consumer debtor to reorganize under Chapter 11 will leave the debtor's creditors in a worse position than if the debtor were required to liquidate. See Tr. of Oral Arg. 29-31. Nor could he. §1129(a)(7) provides that a reorganization plan may not be confirmed unless all the debtor's creditors accept the plan or will receive not less than they would receive under a Chapter 7 liquidation. Because creditors cannot be expected to approve a plan in which they would receive less than they would from an immediate liquidation of the debtor's assets, it follows that a Chapter 11 reorganization plan usually will be confirmed only when creditors will receive at least as much as if the debtor were to file under Chapter 7. Absent some showing of harm to the creditors of a nonbusiness debtor allowed to reorganize under Chapter 11, we see nothing in the allocation of burdens and benefits of Chapter 11 that warrants an inference that Congress intended to exclude a consumer debtor from its coverage. See Herbert, *Consumer Chapter 11 Proceedings: Abuse or Alternative?*, 91 Com. L. J. 234, 245-248 (1986).

Amicus also warns that allowing consumer debtors to proceed under Chapter 11 will flood the bankruptcy courts with plans of reorganization that ultimately will prove unworkable. We think this fear is unfounded for two reasons. First, the greater expense and complexity of filing under Chapter 11 likely will dissuade most consumer debtors from seeking relief under this Chapter. See S. Rep. No. 95-989, at 3; see also Herbert, *supra*, at 242-243. Second, the Code gives bankruptcy courts substantial discretion to dismiss a Chapter 11 case in which the debtor files an untenable plan of reorganization. See §1112(b) and 1129(a).

Finally, *amicus* asserts that extending Chapter 11 to consumer debtors creates the risk that these debtors will be forced into Chapter 11 by their creditors under §303(a), a result contrary to the intent reflected in Congress' decision to prevent involuntary bankruptcy proceedings under Chapter 13. In particular, he suggests that it would be unwise to force a debtor into Chapter 11 reorganization, because an involuntary debtor would be unlikely to cooperate in the plan of reorganization—a point that Congress noted in refusing to allow involuntary Chapter 13 proceedings. See H.R. Rep. No. 95-595, at 120.

We find these concerns overstated in light of the Code's provisions for dealing with recalcitrant Chapter 11 debtors. If an involuntary Chapter 11 debtor fails to cooperate, this likely will provide the requisite cause for the bankruptcy court to convert the Chapter 11 case to one under Chapter 7. See §1112(b). In any event, the argument overlooks Congress' primary concern about a debtor's being forced into bankruptcy under Chapter 13: that such a debtor, whose future wages are not exempt from the bankruptcy estate, §1322(a)(1), would be compelled to toil for the benefit of creditors in violation of the Thirteenth Amendment's involuntary servitude prohibition. See H.R. Rep. No. 95-595, at 120. Because there is no comparable provision in Chapter 11 requiring a debtor to pay future wages to a creditor, Congress' concern about imposing involuntary servitude on a Chapter 13 debtor is not relevant to Chapter 11 reorganization.

The plain language of the Bankruptcy Code permits individual debtors not engaged in business to file for relief under Chapter 11. Although the structure and legislative history of Chapter 11 indicate that this Chapter was intended primarily for the use of business debtors, the Code contains no ongoing business requirement for Chapter 11 reorganization, and we find no basis for imposing one. Accordingly, the judgment of the Court of Appeals is reversed.

It is so ordered.

CUTLER v. CUTLER
165 B.R. 275 (1994)

This case is before the Court on Cross-Motions for Summary Judgment filed by Lawrence Cutler, Howard Cutler and Candette Cutler (Cutlers), on the one hand, and Robert J. Davis, Trustee (Trustee) for the Chapter 7 estate of Randy Scott Cutler (Debtor), on the other. At issue is the complex and often tortuous interaction between the Bankruptcy Code, state partnership law, and a general partnership agreement entered into pursuant to such law. Each motion is granted in part and denied in part.

I. FACTS

The Debtor and the Cutlers are siblings. On May 30, 1978, they formed a general partnership called Four Seas Investment Company (Four Seas) by executing a partnership agreement (Agreement). The assets of Four Seas are parcels of real property bequeathed to the four Cutler siblings by their parents. Some of the real property owned by Four Seas was owned by the Cutler siblings' grandparents and has been in the Cutler family for nearly four decades.

The Agreement contains provisions intended to govern the rights of the partners in certain circumstances, including the bankruptcy, death, disability, or withdrawal of one of the partners. The rights are materially different depending on the precipitating event. They include the following

1. In the event a partner files bankruptcy, paragraph 11 provides that the other partners will have the option, for a stated period of time, to purchase the interests of the debtor partner for an amount equal to the balance of the debtor partner's capital and income accounts at the time the option was exercised.

2. In the event of the death of a partner, paragraph 12.2(a) provides the remaining partners three options

a. They may continue the partnership with the personal representative of the decedent as a substituted partner

b. They may purchase the entire interest of the decedent

c. They may allow the interest of the decedent partner to be sold to a third party.

If the remaining partners choose to continue the partnership, the substitute partner would have no right to participate in management but would share in the profits and losses of the partnership, provided that he or she would not be obligated for partnership losses which would reduce his or her capital account below the amount at the time of the death of the decedent. If the remaining partners choose to purchase the partnership interest of the deceased partner, the price would be equal to the capital and income accounts of that partner "except that the book value of the capital and income accounts shall be adjusted by substituting the fair market value as of the date of the decedent's death, in place of book value, of any property and securities owned by the partnership."

3. In the event of a partner's disability or incompetence, Paragraph 12.3 gives the same rights to the remaining partners as in the event of death.

4. In the event of withdrawal, Paragraph 12.4 gives the remaining partners the same rights as with death or disability, with the proviso that the price payable is to be 87.5% of the fair market value of the withdrawing partner's interest.

Thus, the partners, at the time of formation of the partnership, intended substantially different results in the event of the bankruptcy of one of the partners than in the event of the death, disability or withdrawal of one of the partners. Although one can never be sure in these turbulent times, it is safe to assume that the parties believed that the fair market value of the property at a future date would be substantially higher than the book value of the assets. While the partners are given three choices in the context of death, disability, or withdrawal, there is no choice in the event of bankruptcy, with the apparent intent to yield the least favorable result for the estate of the filing partner and the most favorable result for the remaining partners.

Upon the debtor's bankruptcy, the Cutlers attempted to exercise the book value "buy-out option," engaging a certified public accountant to determine the balance of the capital and income accounts, less expenses, and tendering a check to the Trustee for $31,814.47, the amount calculated by the accountant. At first, the Trustee seemed inclined to accept this amount and sought Court approval of the disposition of the estate's interest in the partnership in exchange for the payment of $31,814.47. An objection was filed by a creditor and, at the hearing, the Court denied the Motion without prejudice.

Upon reflection, the Trustee determined that accepting the option price would not be in the best interests of the estate and instead sought to have the underlying assets of the partnership sold, the partnership terminated, and the proceeds divided pro rata among the three remaining partners and the estate.

The Cutlers objected and brought this action seeking an order compelling the Trustee to comply with the terms of the "buy-out option" and determining that the estate has no specific interest in the underlying assets of the partnership. The Trustee answered and counterclaimed, seeking an order vesting in the estate an undivided 25% interest in each asset of the partnership, thereby in effect allowing the Trustee to force the liquidation of those assets, the termination of the partnership, and the pro-rata distribution of the proceeds.

II. DISCUSSION AND ANALYSIS

The resolution of this case turns on the nature of the estate's interest in the general partnership in which the debtor was a partner prior to his filing a Chapter 7 bankruptcy petition. The Cutlers' view is that the Agreement is an executory contract and that the buy-out clause is enforceable under §365, the Trustee's rights are wholly controlled by state partnership law, and the Agreement that the Trustee has no interest in the underlying assets of the partnership, and the Trustee has no standing to force a liquidation of the partnership and those assets. The Trustee, on the other hand, claims that the buy-out clause is void, that the estate is entitled to one-quarter of the profits and interests of the partnership, and that the Trustee has standing to seek a judicial winding-up of the partnership. By this last point, the Trustee means that this Court, upon the Trustee's request, has the authority to force the immediate sale of the real property owned by the partnership, thereby liquidating the partnership's assets for the purpose of distribution, in equal shares to the three remaining partners and the estate.

Despite these seriously conflicting positions, there is much upon which both parties agree. For example, both parties agree that state partnership law defines the bundle of rights held by a general partner in a general partnership. Ariz.Rev.Stat.Ann. §29-224 n4 defines those rights to include

1) A partner's rights in specific partnership property

2) A partner's interest in the partnership

3) A partner's right to participate in the management of the partnership.

Under Arizona law, therefore, both parties agree that the estate, as successor to the debtor, does not have any rights in specific partnership property other than rights arising as a result of tenancy-in-partnership. Further, the Trustee does not seek the right to participate in the management of the partnership, except to the extent that he seeks a winding-up of the partnership pursuant to Ariz.Rev.Stat.Ann. §29-237. Both parties agree that the debtor's interest in the partnership is property of the estate, 11 U.S.C. §541, and that the Trustee, as representative of the estate, is the party holding that interest. Likewise, the parties do not dispute that some or all aspects of a partnership agreement may have the characteristics of an executory contract that is subject to the strictures of 11 U.S.C. §365, although the parties have significantly different views as to the significance of §365 in this case.

§31(5) of the U.P.A., codified in Arizona as Ariz.Rev.Stat.Ann. §29-231(E), provides that the bankruptcy of a general partner causes the dissolution of the partnership. The dissolution of a partnership is not the same as its termination. Rather, the term simply means that the partnership in which the debtor held an interest no longer exists in its former state, and that the affairs of that partnership need to be wound up. The winding up process does not necessarily mean that the assets of the partnership must be liquidated, although that is one option. One common method of winding up, contemplated by U.P.A. §41, is the reconstitution of the partnership by the remaining partners with the withdrawn partner retaining an economic but not a management interest in the new partnership.

Thus, upon the filing of this Chapter 7 bankruptcy, the Four Seas partnership was dissolved and the Trustee, as representative of the estate, succeeded to the economic interests of the debtor in the partnership pursuant to §541(a)(1). The nature of that interest is further refined by 11 U.S.C. §541(c)(1)(B), which provides that the "interests of the debtor in property," (*i.e.*, the Debtor's partnership interest) "becomes property of the estate . . . notwithstanding any provision in an agreement . . . that is conditioned . . . on the commencement of a case under this title . . . and that effects . . . a forfeiture, modification, or termination of the debtor's interest in property."

It is the duty of the Chapter 7 trustee to "collect and reduce to money the property of the estate for which such trustee serves." 11 U.S.C. §704(1). As one means of accomplishing this task, the Trustee has the power under §363(b)(1) to sell property of the estate out of the ordinary course of business. As stated above, §541(c)(1)(B) vests that property, here the partnership interest, in the estate, free and clear of any restriction or modification that is triggered by the debtor's having filed bankruptcy. Further, §363(1) provides that, subject to the provisions of §365, the trustee may sell such property "notwithstanding any provision in a contract . . . that is conditioned . . . on the commencement of a case under this title concerning the debtor . . . and that effects . . . a forfeiture, modification, or termination of the debtor's interest in such property."

Read together and applied to these facts, these provisions lead to the conclusion that the Trustee has the right and the obligation to liquidate the debtor's partnership interest and that he may do so notwithstanding any provision in the Agreement which purports to limit or modify that right.

In the only case to consider these issues at the Circuit level, the Tenth Circuit in In re *Manning*, 831 F.2d 205 (10th Cir. 1987), came to the same conclusion. *Manning*'s facts are very similar to this case. The Debtor was a general partner in a five-person partnership. After the debtor filed his Chapter 7, the Trustee brought an action against the partnership and the nondebtor partners seeking authority to sell the real estate of the partnership and to disburse the net proceeds among the four remaining partners and the estate. The nondebtor partners objected, contending that the Trustee had the right to sell only the debtor's interest in the partnership and that the nondebtor partners had the right to purchase that interest in accordance with the terms of the partnership agreement. That agreement, like the one at issue here, contained a special buy-out clause authorizing the purchase of the debtor's interest for an amount equal to 75% of the value of his capital account in the partnership. The Tenth Circuit stated §541(c) and 363(1) protect, respectively, the debtor's interest in and the trustee's right to sell property of the estate "notwithstanding any provision" that is "conditioned" on bankruptcy proceeding and that effects a modification or forfeiture of the debtor's interest in the property. We note that the 25% discount imposed on the amount payable would seem to effect a least a modification of the debtor's property of the estate, which is illegal under both these sections. Furthermore, valuing the bankrupt's interest, not at appreciated fair market value, as is typically done upon the death or incompetency of partner, but at book value produces not only a modification but also the added effect of requiring *Manning* to virtually forfeit his interest in his tenancy-in-partnership, which would seem to be equally repugnant under the two sections cited. *Id.* at 211. Here, the Agreement's clear modification of the debtor's interest in the partnership is expressly conditioned on bankruptcy. As in *Manning*, that modification becomes potentially punitive to the point of forfeiture because of the book value limitation put on the valuation of the interest.

This result is consistent with the Ninth Circuit's interpretation of §541(c)(1) in *In re Farmers Markets, Inc.*, 792 F.2d 1400 (9th Cir. 1986). There, the Court noted that while §541(c)(2) did not invalidate a provision of state law requiring that sales taxes be paid as a condition of transferring a liquor license from the estate to a third party, it would invalidate a restriction that would prohibit transfer of the license from the debtor to the estate. That is precisely what is at issue here: if the buy-out clause were to be given effect, the interest of the debtor in the partnership that transferred to the estate would be materially different from that interest when in the debtor's hands. For example, Randy Cutler, pre-bankruptcy, would have been free to assign the interest as collateral for a loan, sell his economic interest for cash or to withdraw from the partnership and be paid 87.5% of the fair market value of the interest. The buy-out clause reduces the estate's options to one: sale to the remaining partners at a pre-determined bargain price. This is precisely the type of modification or forfeiture that §541(c)(1) was intended to prevent.

The Cutlers argue that §365(e)(2)(A) compels a different result. The courts have generally assumed that partnership agreements are, at least in part, executory contracts. The issue presented by the Cutlers is whether the Trustee can assume the contract, thereby succeeding to the debtor's rights in all respects, and/or assign that interest to a third party. If not, the Cutlers argue, the buy-out clause should be held to be enforceable.

§365(e)(1) generally invalidates an "*ipso facto*" clause, *i.e.*, a clause which modifies or terminates the rights of the trustee, as successor to the debtor, as a result of the debtor's bankruptcy filing. §365(e)(2)(A), however, carves out from the general effect of §365(e)(1) those kinds of contracts where "applicable law excuses a party, other than the debtor, to such contract or lease from accepting performance from or rendering performance to the trustee or to an assignee of such contract . . . and where such party does not consent to such assumption or assignment." The Cutlers argue, and the Court agrees, that the relationship among partners, and the provisions of the Uniform Partnership Act, fit within the parameters of §365(e)(2) and therefore such restrictions are enforceable to the extent the relationship is an executory contract.

However, unlike the Court in *In re Catron*, 158 Bankr. 629 (Bankr. E.D. Va. 1993), heavily relied upon by the Cutlers, this Court believes that the §365(e)(1) and (2) inquiry is not dispositive of the issue. Stripped to its essence, those two sections, read together, mean that a trustee's rights under an executory contract may be terminated or modified as a result of the bankruptcy, so long as the contract is of the type where applicable law allows the nondebtor party to refuse to accept performance from a stranger. Since partnership is a wholly voluntary association, requiring the consent of all partners for the partnership to continue, a partnership agreement fits these criteria.

However, this generalized validation of *ipso facto* clauses in the executory contract context contrasts sharply with the specific invalidation of such provisions where the Code deals in §541 and 363(1) with the scope of and Trustee's right to sell property interests of the estate. Thus, while the application of executory contract principles may make sense in connection with management issues, it does not make sense in the definition of property interests.

The Court agrees with the analysis in a leading treatise, which suggests that the partnership relationship be viewed as an amalgam.

(1) A property interest in the profits and surplus of the partnership, with the property interest surviving any termination of the agreement upon the partner's bankruptcy; and

(2) An executory contract with respect to the governance of the partnership property.

If courts that have determined to enforce bankruptcy termination provisions in partnership agreements were to adopt this view, they would apply §365 to the executory contract elements of the agreement, but would not affect the original grant to the debtor of its economic interest in the partnership nor the Trustee's continuing economic rights in the partnership and its property. The continuation of the Trustee's economic interest in the partnership would render inapplicable any involuntary buy-out provisions, and obviate the need for a determination as to whether a particular buy-out price is fair.

Cherkis & King, Collier Real Estate Transactions and the Bankruptcy Code, P 4.07[1], pp. 4-72.3-73 (Matthew Bender 1992). See also *In re Priestley*, 93 Bankr. 253 (Bankr. D.N.M. 1988).

Therefore, the Court holds that the debtor's one-quarter interest in the profits and surplus of the Four Seas partnership is property of the estate and may be sold by the Trustee, free and clear of the restrictions contained in the buy-out clause.

The Trustee, however, wants more. While claiming that he is not asking to succeed to any management rights of the debtor, he nevertheless seeks to compel the liquidation of the underlying assets of the partnership and a distribution of all of the proceeds, with the resulting termination of the partnership. A right of this nature usually lies uniquely with a partner and not with an outsider.

While the Trustee does not claim that his authority to compel liquidation of the partnership assets derives from §363(h), an examination of that provision is instructive. §363(h) provides that the Trustee may sell both the estate's interest and the interest of a co-owner in property under certain limited circumstances. The Trustee sought to invoke this provision in the *Manning* case. The Tenth Circuit held, and this Court agrees, that §363(h) was inapplicable because the estate's property was the partnership interest, not the real estate owned by the partnership. The only interest of the partners in the partnership property is as "tenants-in-partnership;" that interest is not sufficiently specific to the underlying property to trigger the application of §363(h).

The Trustee in this case, however, has focused instead upon what he believes his state law rights to be, relying upon Ariz.Rev.Stat.Ann. § 29-237. That statute provides, "Unless otherwise agreed the partners who have not wrongfully dissolved the partnership or the legal representative of the last surviving partner, not bankrupt, has the right to wind up the partnership affairs; provided, however, that any partner, his legal representative or his assignee, upon cause shown, may obtain winding-up by the court." (emphasis added). As the holder of the debtor's economic interest in the partnership, the Trustee claims that he is the debtor's assignee within the meaning of A.R.S § 29-237 and that, therefore, he is entitled to "winding-up by the Court," presuming he can show cause.

It is this Court's view that the Trustee is not an assignee, as that term is used in Ariz.Rev.Stat.Ann. § 29-237. Further, even if the Trustee could be viewed as an assignee, the Court does not believe he has shown or can show cause why the assets of the partnership should be sold and that the partnership terminated.

Ariz.Rev.Stat.Ann. § 29-227 (§27 of the U.P.A.) deals with the assignment of a partner's interest in the partnership. That section provides

A conveyance by a partner of his interest in the partnership does not of itself dissolve the partnership, nor, as against the other partners in the absence of agreement, entitle the assignee, during the continuance of the partnership, to interfere in the management or administrative of the partnership business or affairs or to require any information or account of partnership transactions, or to inspect the partnership books; but it merely entitled the assignee to receive in accordance with his contract the profits to which the assigning partner would otherwise be entitled.

Ariz.Rev.Stat.Ann. § 29-227 is designed to deal with voluntary transfers, such as an assignment given as security for a debt, or an assignment in consideration for the transfer of property to the assignor, or an assignment in satisfaction of an antecedent debt. This consensual nature of assignments is underscored by the language "a conveyance by a partner" and is meaningful when juxtaposed with Ariz.Rev.Stat.Ann. §29-228, the section under which a partner's interest may involuntarily become subject to a charging order in favor of a judgment creditor. Further, Ariz.Rev.Stat.Ann. §29-231 makes clear that the bankruptcy of a partner does dissolve the partnership, while the same is not true with the assignment of a partner's interest.

Read as a whole, therefore, the U.P.A. does not contemplate that a trustee in bankruptcy, as the holder of the estate's interest in the debtor's interest in the partnership, becomes an assignee for purposes of Ariz.Rev.Stat.Ann. § 29-237. The Supreme Court of Washington, while not construing this provision of the U.P.A., came to the same conclusion in *Stickney v. Kerry*, 55 Wash. 2d 535, 348 P.2d 655 (1960), where it said:

It is true that, as the plaintiff says, while the filing of a petition in bankruptcy works an immediate dissolution of the partnership, the trustee in bankruptcy does not acquire jurisdiction of the partnership property for purposes of winding-up the partnership affairs if one or more of the partners is solvent. That the partner or partners who wind-up the business, and account for the property, have no right to distribute any part of the interests of the bankruptcy partner, once the partnership liabilities have been paid and that interest determined. The Supreme Court of the United States has made this clear: "Bankruptcy, it is said, when decreed by a competent tribunal, dissolves the copartnership, but the joint property remains in the hands of the solvent partner or partners, clothed with a trust to be applied by him or them to the discharge of the partnership obligations and to account to the bankruptcy partner or his assignees for a share of the surplus. *Amsinck v. Bean*, 22 Wall. 395, 89 U.S. 395, 22 L. Ed. 801 [1874]. 55 Wash. 2d at 537-38, 348 P.2d 656-657.

To allow the Trustee to liquidate the underlying assets of the partnership would be to grant to him management prerogatives where he has none. To have such management prerogatives, the Trustee would have needed to assume the contract. That is not possible in this case for two reasons:

1) This is a Chapter 7 case and 60 days have passed since the Order for relief, thereby causing automatic rejection (§365(d)(1).

2) §365(c)(1) would prohibit assumption by the Trustee of the management function for the same reasons as set forth in the discussion of §365(e)(2) above.

The interest of the Trustee in the debtor's interest in the partnership is not unlike that of a creditor with a charging order. The Trustee is entitled to receive his full one-quarter share of all surplus and profits, if and when such surplus and profits are realized. The remaining partners are free to re-form the partnership and to continue it in business and to manage the business consistent with their fiduciary obligations. At such time as there may be surplus and profits from the operation of the partnership, from whatever source, including liquidation of the underlying assets, the Trustee is entitled to receive the estate's one-quarter share at the same time and upon the same terms as each of the Cutlers. In the meantime, the Trustee is free, pursuant to §363(1), to sell the estate's interest to the highest bidder. Given the nature of the partnership, the highest bidder(s) may be the Cutlers, but that is not necessarily so. It is not inconceivable that a third party, based upon an examination of the economic viability of the underlying assets of the partnership, would wish to buy the right to receive distributions at a future time from those assets, based upon such buyer's determination that the projected future proceeds would yield a satisfactory internal rate of return on the investment to justify the cash investment to date.

That choice belongs to the Trustee and, once made, is to be executed pursuant to §363. Any agreement made with the Cutlers or a third party will be subject to the receipt of higher or better offers, if such may be received, at a sale supervised by the Court.

THEREFORE, IT IS ORDERED:

1. Granting the Motion for Summary Judgment of the Trustee, in part, and denying the same, in part

2. Granting the Motion for Summary Judgment of the Cutlers in part, and denying the same in part

3. Declaring that Paragraph 11 of the Four Seas Partnership Agreement is unenforceable

4. Declaring that the Estate does not have an interest in the underlying assets of the Four Seas Partnership

5. Declaring that the Trustee does not have standing to pursue the winding up of the Four Seas partnership

6. Authorizing the Trustee to sell the estate's interest in the Four Seas partnership pursuant to §363, notwithstanding the restrictions of Paragraph 11 of the Agreement.

Glossary

Bankruptcy Code - Federal law governing bankruptcy

Bankruptcy court - Federal court that administers bankruptcy proceedings

Cash collateral - Income derived from property held by a debtor in possession

Chapter 7 - Bankruptcy proceedings for individuals

Chapter 11 - Reorganization for corporations

Chapter 12 - Reorganization for family farms

Chapter 13 - Reorganization for individually owned businesses

Claimant - Person who seeks relief from the court

Creditors meeting - A meeting that allows creditors to review the debtor's conduct, property, operations, and other related matters

Debtor in possession - Debtor who has actual possession of estate assets and uses them to operate a business

Disclosure statement - Document filed indicating all assets

Involuntary bankruptcy - Bankruptcy proceedings instituted by creditors

Liquidation - Chapter 7 proceeding

Mailing matrix - Document indicting all persons who must be notified of bankruptcy proceedings

Notice of appearance - A court document indicating a wish to participate in bankruptcy proceedings

Proof of claim - Document filed by creditors to indicate debts owed to them

Reaffirmation - Statement of a debtor that it will not have the debt discharged so as to keep an asset of the estate

Removal - The change of a legal case from one court to another

Reorganization or **restructuring plan** - A plan indicating how the debtor intends to reorganize to pay off its debt

Statement of financial affairs - A statement identifying all assets and liabilities

Statement of intent - Document filed indicating the wishes of a debtor with respect to the property

Straight bankruptcy - Chapter 7 proceeding

United States trustee - Person appointed to oversee the assets of a debtor

Voluntary bankruptcy - Debtor petitions for bankruptcy protection

Exercises

1. Obtain a copy of the court rules for your local bankruptcy court.

2. Discuss why you think the proceedings should vary according to the local court rules.

3. Discuss the factors that a commercial enterprise should consider before forcing a debtor into bankruptcy.

4. Discuss why bankruptcy courts are more concerned with reorganization than discharge.

5. Obtain several examples of a plan of reorganization and analyze their provisions.

Chapter Eleven

ADMINISTRATIVE LAW

Introduction

Inevitably, either in its formation, its operation, or both, a commercial enterprise will be faced with the prospect of dealing with an administrative agency. Administrative agencies exist at both the federal and state levels and are responsible for regulating a wide legal spectrum.

Administrative agencies are those bodies that are created either by the executive or the legislative branch of government to assist in administering very specific areas of law. During the Great Depression, administrative agencies burgeoned as part of the New Deal, and this growth has continued. Commercial enterprises will typically become involved with these agencies of government when dealing with taxes, commerce, health and environmental protection, licensing, labor, and so forth. In many instances, a commercial enterprise is far more likely to have legal problems settled by the administrative process rather than the judicial system and, for this reason, a basic understanding of administrative law—those rules and regulations governing the administrative process, is imperative.

An administrative agency is bound by the provisions of the Administrative Procedure Act (APA) when it acts under its statutory authority. The APA is a federal statute, and a version of its provisions has been enacted by every jurisdiction to regulate state agencies. Its purpose is to ensure that all citizens are afforded the constitutional protections of due process when dealing with an administrative agency. Due process requires that a citizen be informed of all laws to which he or she must adhere, including all rules and regulations with respect to the administration and regulation of the laws, be afforded an opportunity to present arguments prior to an agency creating a rule or regulation, and be entitled to a fair hearing to present arguments if an agency asserts that a person has violated one of these rules.

Administrative agencies are required to effectuate their regulatory mandates, either through rule making or adjudication. When an agency creates rules or decides a dispute under its adjudicative process, it is acting in a quasi-legislative capacity. This chapter will examine the administrative process in both situations to determine how these actions directly affect commercial enterprises.

Administrative Rule-Making

A **rule** can be described as a prescribed guide for conduct or action. An **administrative rule** is a statement issued by an administrative agency that implements or interprets law or policy or indicates the practical procedural requirements of that agency. An administrative rule, by its very nature, is meant to be prospective in approach, meaning that it is created to provide guidance for a standard of conduct rather than to settle a legal dispute.

Administrative agencies regulate specific substantive statutes, such as the Internal Revenue Service to administer the federal tax laws (Internal Revenue Code). To accomplish this objective, administrative agency authority consists not only of the powers expressly granted to it pursuant to the statute that created it, known as its **enabling statute**, but also all powers that are incidental or necessary to carry out its statutory mandate. Courts have consistently construed this administrative authority in a manner that permits the fullest accomplishment of the legislative intent in creating the agency.

> ***Example:*** *In order to accomplish its goal of administering the federal tax laws, the Internal Revenue Service has the power to review and audit tax returns, assess fines and penalties, institute actions against the taxpayer, and attach taxpayer property. This broad grant of authority and discretion is necessary for the IRS to fulfill its function.*

The APA requires that the agencies initiate proceedings to determine facts in order to formulate rules that have appropriate application. To this end, agencies are required to hold public hearings in which all interested citizens are afforded the opportunity to be heard and present facts for the agency's consideration. Pursuant to §553 of the APA, federal agencies are required to follow specific procedures in fulfilling their rule-making functions. The agency must give a general notice of its proposed rule by having a notice printed in the ***Federal Register***, the official publication for all federal agency action. The notice must include

- the time, place, and nature of the public hearing
- a reference to the legislative authority under which the rule is mandated and the terms or statement of the proposed rule.

After notice, the agency must permit interested parties to make written submissions for the agency's consideration with respect to the proposed rule. After the agency considers these written submissions, it must include in the rule's adoption a general statement as to the basis of its version. The publication of the substantive rule adopted by the agency must be published at least 30 days prior to its effective date (certain exceptions to this rule are listed in the APA). Although not specifically required by the APA, agencies have the discretion to have public hearings where interested parties may make oral presentations to the agency prior to the final formulation of a rule.

> ***Example:*** *A federal agency is considering creating a rule to administer a new federal statute that it has been authorized to regulate. The agency formulates a proposed rule that it publishes in the* Federal Register. *The proposed rule will affect almost every small business in the country, and an overwhelming number of written submissions are received. Because of the pervasive aspect of the rule, the agency decides that it will hold a public hearing for oral presentation. After all submissions and oral presentations have been made, the agency promulgates the final version of the rule that it publishes in the* Federal Register *to take effect 30 days after publication.*

If a person is dissatisfied with an administrative rule, the person may seek to challenge the rule in court. Before an affected person may challenge an administrative rule or decision (and the person must actually be adversely affected by the rule, not just generally dissatisfied), the person must first **exhaust all administrative remedies**, meaning that the person must follow the agency's internal procedures for challenging its actions. Generally an agency's rule will be presumed to be legal unless it is clearly ***ultra vires*** on its face—beyond the agency's statutory powers. The burden of proof is on the person challenging the agency action, and the typical bases for challenging such actions are improper delegation, contrary to statutory authority, or procedural irregularities that violate the provisions of the APA. Also, agency action may be challenged on constitutional grounds, indicating that it violates due process or is unconstitutionally **vague**, meaning that the terms are too discretionary to provide specific guidance for their interpretation and administration.

Agency Adjudication

Not only do agencies have the authority to create rules, they also have the authority to adjudicate disputes that arise over the enforcement of their rules. In this context, the agencies are acting in a quasi-judicial manner, and the person challenging the agency action generally stands in the same position as a litigant in a lawsuit. Because such adjudication affects the rights of the individual, the United States Supreme Court has determined that certain constitutional safeguards must be afforded to persons whose rights may be adversely affected.

In order to meet the constitutional requirements of due process, an agency must adhere to the following procedures:

- The individual must be given a **notice** that the agency is terminating the person's right, with the grounds for such termination including:
  - time, place, and nature of the action
  - statutory basis
  - statement of facts on which the action is based
  - basis of the agency's jurisdiction.
- The individual must be allowed to confront any witnesses against him or her.
- The individual must be allowed an oral argument before a hearing officer, known as an **administrative law judge**.
- The individual must be permitted to cross-examine witnesses.
- The agency must provide any evidence it has against the individual.
- The individual has the right to be represented by an attorney.
- The ultimate decision must be based on the record and must include a statement of the reason for the decision.
- The administrative law judge must be impartial.

The actual hearing itself follows the form of a judicial lawsuit. The action commences with either a **pleading** or a **petition**, a written statement requesting the agency to reverse its original decision. This initial document must include the name and address of the complainant, a statement of the facts and laws giving rise to the challenge, and must request administrative action. Each agency has its own time limits specified with respect to filing such complaint and service of process.

The agency may file a **responsive pleading**, an answer to the matters asserted in the initial pleading. After these documents have been exchanged, the agency will schedule a hearing date, prior to which the parties are entitled to **discovery**—the right to ascertain facts and information the opposite side may have that affects the matters at hand. Typically, a **pre-hearing conference** will be held with the hearing officer to attempt to settle the matter or reduce the issues to be determined at the hearing.

The hearing itself follows the procedure of a trial, except that in an administrative hearing the parties are not bound by the federal rules of evidence. The administrative law judge may, on the interest of fairness, permit introduction of information that would be excluded at a judicial trial. The proceedings are maintained in verbatim record, either by a stenographer or by means of an audiotape. The parties may be represented by counsel and, if necessary, interpreters may be permitted at the party's own expense. At the conclusion of the presentation of both sides' evidence, the administrative law judge will render a decision. There is no right to a jury trial at an administrative hearing.

Judicial Review

If an individual is dissatisfied with the results of the administrative hearing, he or she has the right to seek **judicial review** of the matter unless the specific statute precludes such review. However, before a party may seek judicial review of agency action, the party must first exhaust all administrative remedies; i.e., follow any administrative procedures for internal agency review. The court will not adjudicate a case if the party seeking relief might be afforded such relief by the agency itself.

In seeking judicial review, the party applies directly to the appellate court; it is not necessary that the matter be relitigated at the trial level. Because this judicial review is appellate review, the scope of the matters that courts will review are limited to the interpretation of statutes, the jurisdiction of the agency, and the question of due process. The appellate courts will not retry facts—the finding of facts is left to the administrative hearing. Because the matter is now within the judicial process, the appellant follows the procedures of the appropriate state or federal court (Chapter One).

Chapter Summary

Most commercial enterprises probably have more frequent contact with administrative agencies than they do with the court system. In today's business world, many areas of law that affect the operation of a business are regulated by legislative and executive agencies.

Administrative agencies are regulated by their own rules and regulations, under guidelines promulgated under the Administrative Procedure Act. All internal agency rules are published in the *Federal Register*, at the federal level, and in similar publications at the state level for state agencies.

Administrative agencies are empowered with two specific functions: rule making, in which the agency determines standards of conduct prospectively for matters within its jurisdiction, and adjudication, in which the agency determines the rights of specific individuals who challenge particular agency action.

Administrative agency action is required to meet the standards of constitutional due process, affording persons the right to notice and a fair hearing of administrative matters. Further, actions of an administrative agency may be reviewed by appeal to the courts, but may only be judicially reviewed after all administrative remedies have been exhausted.

Although the legislatures enact the basic statutes that create the law, it is the administrative agencies that regulate and interpret those laws and have a significant and direct impact on commercial life.

Edited Judicial Decisions

NORDEN v. STATE OF OREGON
329 Ore. 641 (2000)

The issue in this case is the scope of the record on judicial review of an order in other than a contested case under Oregon's Administrative Procedures Act (APA), ORS 183.310 to 183.550. On judicial review under ORS 183.484, the circuit court took evidence both of what the agency knew at the time when it issued its order as well as evidence that the agency and petitioner had obtained after the agency issued its order. The court then made findings on that record and entered judgment in favor of petitioner. On appeal, the Court of Appeals held that the scope of the record that the circuit court had developed was correct under ORS 183.484, but that the circuit court had erred in setting aside the agency's order on the ground that it was not supported by substantial evidence in the record. *Norden v. Water Resources Dept.*, 158 Ore. App. 127, 135-38, 973 P.2d 910 (1999). We allowed review and affirm the decision of the Court of Appeals.

We begin with some background. Under the APA, agencies may issue orders in contested cases and orders in other than contested cases. See *Oregon Env. Council v. Oregon State Bd. of Ed.*, 307 Ore. 30, 36-37, 761 P.2d 1322 (1988) (explaining process). In either context, an order is "any agency action expressed orally or in writing directed to a named person or named persons." ORS 183.310(5). In contested case proceedings, "the agency must base its decision [or action] on a record of evidence that the contesting parties have an opportunity to develop, it must confine its decision to the evidence so developed, and it must explain how its decision complies with the law and is supported by the facts." Oregon Env. Council, 307 Ore. at 37; ORS 183.415 to ORS 183.470. Orders in contested cases are subject to review by the Court of Appeals, ORS 183.482 and that court reviews for legal error, abuse of agency discretion, and lack of substantial evidence in the record. ORS 183.482(8). Judicial review of orders in contested cases is confined to the record made in the hearing before the agency. ORS 183.482(7); Oregon Env. Council, 307 Ore. at 37.

This case involves judicial review of an order in other than a contested case proceeding, specifically, an order that the Water Resources Department (department) issued in November 1994, informing petitioner that she is not entitled to divert water from a spring that arises on her property without first obtaining a water right permit. The order was in the form of letter from Justus, a watermaster for the department.

Petitioner sought review of the order in the Umatilla County Circuit Court. ORS 183.484. As noted, the circuit court conducted a hearing at which the parties presented evidence both about the information that Justus had before him when he issued the order as well as evidence that the department and petitioner had obtained after Justus issued the order. Based on all the evidence, the circuit court found that there was not substantial evidence from which a reasonable person could conclude that the water arising from the spring on petitioner's property would flow off petitioner's property and into a nearby creek if petitioner did not divert it. The circuit court therefore entered a judgment reversing the order of the department. The judgment declared that petitioner had the right to use the water without first obtaining a water right permit. See ORS 183.486(1) (circuit court decision "may be mandatory, prohibitory, or declaratory in form and it shall provide whatever relief is appropriate irrespective of the original form of the petition"). The department appealed the judgment to the Court of Appeals. ORS 183.500.

Before the Court of Appeals, the department argued that, because Justus had issued an order in other than a contested case proceeding, the record on judicial review consisted of both the information on which Justus had relied in issuing the order and the evidence that the parties had developed after that time. Petitioner argued that the record on judicial review should be confined to the information that Justus had before him when he issued the order.

The Court of Appeals construed ORS 183.484 and agreed with the department. It reasoned that the legislature's intent regarding the scope of the record on judicial review in other than a contested case could be discerned by comparing the record making process in a contested case with that in other than a contested case. The court concluded that "the evident purpose of requiring petitions for judicial review of orders in other than contested cases to be heard by circuit courts—as opposed to appellate courts—is to enable the circuit courts to develop an evidentiary record against which to evaluate the agency's decision." *Norden*, 158 Ore. App. at 135.

Before this court, the first question is whether the Court of Appeals erred in holding that the record on judicial review in other than a contested case hearing is not limited to the information that the agency had before it when it issued its order. To answer that question, we must construe ORS 183.484. In determining the scope of the record on judicial review of an order in other than a contested case proceeding, we seek to determine the intent of the legislature. We are guided by the familiar methodology summarized in *PGE v. Bureau of Labor and Industries*, 317 Ore. 606, 610-12, 859 P.2d 1143 (1993). At the first level of analysis, we examine the text and context of the statute, giving words of common usage their plain, natural, and ordinary meaning. *Id.* At 611. Words that have a well-defined legal meaning are given that meaning. *Stull v. Hoke*, 326 Ore. 72, 78, 948 P.2d 722 (1997). Context includes other provisions of the same statute and other related statutes. *PGE*, 317 Ore. at 611. Case law interpreting the statute also is considered at the first level of analysis. *State v. Toevs*, 327 Ore. 525, 532, 964 P.2d 1007 (1998). If the intent of the legislature is clear at the first level of analysis, our inquiry is at an end. *PGE*, 317 Ore. at 611.

ORS 183.484 confers jurisdiction for judicial review of orders in other than a contested case on the Circuit Court for Marion County and the county in which the petitioner resides or has a principal business. ORS 183.484(1). A party seeking judicial review must file a petition for judicial review within a specified time, ORS 183.484(2), and the petition shall state, among other things, "the ground or grounds upon which the petitioner contends the order should be reversed or remanded." ORS 183.484(3). The circuit court may "affirm, reverse or remand" the agency's order and, if it finds that the agency erroneously has interpreted a provision of law, then it must set aside or modify the order or remand the case to the agency for further action under a correct interpretation of the provision of law. ORS 183.484(4)(a). ORS 183.484 also provides:

(4)(c) The court shall set aside or remand the order if it finds that the order is not supported by substantial evidence in the record. Substantial evidence exists to support a finding of fact when the record, viewed as a whole, would permit a reasonable person to make that finding.

(5) In the case of reversal, the court shall make special findings of fact based upon the evidence in the record and conclusions of law indicating clearly all aspects in which the agency's order is erroneous.

ORS 183.484 contains several references to the "record" on judicial review and requires the circuit court to make findings of fact if it reverses the agency. Although the statute does not define it, the word "record" has a well-understood legal meaning, namely, "a report of something that occurred that is memorialized or kept track of, whether by print or electronic means." *State v. K.P.*, 324 Ore. 1, 8, 921 P.2d 380 (1996). The legal meaning of the phrase "finding of fact" also is well established: "Determinations from the evidence of a case, either by court or an administrative agency, concerning facts averred by one party and denied by another." *Black's Law Dictionary*, 632 (6th ed 1990); accord *Maeder Steel Products Co. v. Zanello*, 109 Ore. 562, 570, 220 P. 155 (1924).

Although ORS 183.484 contemplates a record for review in all circumstances, and findings of fact based on that record when the circuit court reverses the agency, nothing in the APA directs an agency in other than a contested case proceeding to make a record or to make findings of fact before issuing its order. See *Oregon Env. Council*, 307 Ore. at 37 (APA says little about "that large body of agency actions" that are orders in other than contested cases). Circuit courts are record making, fact-finding courts. We conclude that the reference in ORS 183.484 to the "record" is to the record that is made before the circuit court and that the reference to "findings of fact" in ORS 183.484(5) is to the findings that the circuit court makes based on the evidence in that record when it reverses the agency.

The absence of a requirement that the agency, in other than a contested case proceeding, make a record or findings of fact before issuing its order means that the first opportunity that a party might have to present evidence is before the circuit court. Although the text of ORS 183.484 is not explicit regarding the scope of the record on review, the text suggests that the legislature did not intend to limit the scope of the record on judicial review only to the evidence that the agency had before it when it issued its order.

ORS 183.484(4) provides additional support for that conclusion. As noted, judicial review of an order in other than a contested case includes review for substantial evidence in the record as a whole. ORS 183.484(4)(c). This court has held that review for substantial evidence in the record, as a whole under the APA, requires a court to consider all the evidence in the record. *Younger v. City of Portland*, 305 Ore. 346, 356, 752 P.2d 262 (1988). Whole record review means consideration of whatever evidence the record may contain that would detract from as well as support the agency's order. *Id.* at 354 (citing *Universal Camera Corp. v. Labor Bd.*, 340 U.S. 474, 71 S. Ct. 456, 95 L. Ed. 456 (1951)). In other than a contested case proceeding, the first opportunity that a party might have to make a record of the evidence that would detract from an agency's order is on judicial review. Limiting the scope of the record to the evidence that was available to the agency when it issued its order would undermine the whole record review required by ORS 183.484(4)(c).

The context of ORS 183.484, describing the process for contested cases, also is instructive regarding the legislature's intent. ORS 183.415(1) provides that, in a contested case, all parties "shall be afforded an opportunity for hearing after reasonable notice" and that the record developed at the hearing must reflect "a full and fair inquiry into the facts necessary for consideration of all issues properly before the presiding officer in the case." ORS 183.415(10). ORS 183.415(11) and (12) identify what the record in a contested case "shall include," such as pleadings, motions, intermediate rulings, evidence received or considered, questions and offers of proof, objections and rulings thereon, proposed findings, and a verbatim record of all motions, rulings and testimony. A final order that is issued after a contested case hearing "shall be accompanied by findings of fact and conclusions of law." ORS 183.470(2).

Those statutes reveal that, in a contested case, the legislature has imposed on agencies the requirement of trial-like proceedings that culminate in a record, findings of fact, and conclusions of law that must accompany the agency's final order. Judicial review of an order in a contested case is conferred on the Court of Appeals, and its review is "confined to the record" that was made before the agency. ORS 183.482(7). See ORS 183.482(5) (Court of Appeals may order agency to take additional evidence under specified circumstances). ORS 183.482(8)(c), like ORS 183.484(4)(c), provides for review for substantial evidence of the whole record. In the contested case context, the agency has made the record by the time that judicial review occurs. In other than contested case proceedings, there may be no record to review, or only so much record as support's the agency's order, until a record is made before the circuit court. We find no suggestion in the APA that the legislature intended the record in other than a contested case proceeding to be less complete or well developed than the record in a contested case proceeding.

For the foregoing reasons, we agree with the Court of Appeals that the legislature's intent is clear, based on an examination of the text and context of ORS 183.484. On judicial review of an order in other than a contested case proceeding, ORS 183.484 affords the parties the opportunity to develop a record like the one that parties are entitled to develop at an earlier stage in a contested case proceeding.

That conclusion does not expand the circuit court's role in reviewing the record on review in other than a contested case proceeding, however. As noted, ORS 183.484(4)(c) and 183.482(8)(c) both provide that the circuit court's review of the record is review for substantial evidence. The court's evaluation of the record is limited to whether the evidence would permit a reasonable person to make the determination that the agency made in a particular case. See *Garcia v. Boise Cascade Corp.*, 309 Ore. 292, 295, 787 P.2d 884 (1990) (describing substantial evidence review).

The next question is whether, on the record in this case, substantial evidence exists from which a reasonable person could conclude that the water that arises from the spring on petitioner's property would run off her property if it were not diverted. We conclude that it does. The department produced both documentary and testimonial evidence that a significant quantity of water arises from the spring on petitioner's property and that, if that water were not diverted by a ditch and obstructed by a dike, then it would flow off petitioner's property and into a neighboring creek. Although petitioner was able to muster evidence to the contrary, the record, when viewed as a whole, would permit a reasonable person to find that the water would flow off the property and, accordingly, that petitioner is required to obtain a water right permit. See *Erck v. Brown Oldsmobile*, 311 Ore. 519, 528, 815 P.2d 1251 (1991) (substantial evidence standard of review in APA does not require reviewing court to explain away conflicting evidence).

The decision of the Court of Appeals is affirmed. The judgment of the circuit court is reversed. The order of the Water Resources Department is affirmed.

IN THE MATTER OF ALCA INDUSTRIES, INC.
92 N.Y.2d 775, 686 N.Y.S.2d 356 (1999)

In this case, Alca Industries petitions to have the Office of General Services (OGS) return its $11,800 bid security. As required by the OGS bid advertisement for an oil separator project and in conjunction with its bid, Alca had provided this security in the form of a bid bond. The day after OGS opened the bids, however, it became apparent that Alca had failed to include an allowance for "washwater treatment equipment," a component specified in the project manual accompanying the bid advertisement. Alca immediately requested that it be allowed to withdraw its bid and that OGS return its bid security. OGS considered this request in light of the bid withdrawal criteria set forth in the instructions and determined that Alca had failed to show that the mistake occurred in "the absence of negligence in the preparation of the bid." As a result, OGS retained the bid security.

In the petition seeking to overturn OGS's determination, Alca argued that the OGS bid withdrawal criteria and procedures were "rules" within the meaning of article 2 of the State Administrative Procedure Act and, absent promulgation in compliance with the State Administrative Procedure Act, could not be enforced (see, State Administrative Procedure Act §202; see also, NY Const, art IV, §8 [requiring rules to be filed with Secretary of State]). OGS contended that no policy or regulation mandated that these same withdrawal criteria be used in the future. They were not rules, OGS argued, but were contractual provisions to which Alca became bound by placing its bid. Both the Supreme Court and the Appellate Division agreed with Alca. We now reverse.

Key to our reversal is the distinction between ad hoc decision making based on individual facts and circumstances, and rulemaking, meaning "any kind of legislative or quasi-legislative norm or prescription which establishes a pattern or course of conduct for the future" *People v. Cull*, 10 NY2d 123, 126. The State Administrative Procedure Act defines a rule as "the whole or part of each agency statement, regulation or code of general applicability that implements or applies law, or prescribes a fee charged by or paid to any agency or the procedure or practice requirements of any agency" State Administrative Procedure Act §102 [2] (emphasis added). Choosing to take an action or write a contract based on individual circumstances is significantly different from implementing a standard or procedure that directs what action should be taken regardless of individual circumstances. Rulemaking, in other words, sets standards that substantially alter or, in fact, can determine the result of future agency adjudications.

The case law illustrates this distinction. Administrative orders establishing a speed limit were rules required to be filed with the Secretary of State because they "plainly establish[ed] a general course of operation to be effective for the future" *People v. Cull, supra*, 10 NY2d, at 127. Similarly, a blanket requirement regarding where and when service of a suspension for an infraction must be made was a rule subject to the State Administrative Procedure Act's rule-making procedures. *Matter of Cordero v Corbisiero*, 80 NY2d 771. Likewise, a Department of Labor procedure, uniformly applied, which required that previous overpayments of unemployment insurance benefits always be recouped by deducting 50% of the amount of future payments, was a rule. *Matter of Schwartfigure v Hartnett*, 83 NY2d 296.

In contrast, agency penalty guidelines that "vest inspectors with significant discretion, and allow for flexibility in the imposition of penalties, all with the view of imposing the appropriate sanction for the individual offense and offender in the particular case" are not rules under the State Administrative Procedure Act or the New York Constitution. *Matter of New York City Tr. Auth. v New York State Dept. of Labor*, 88 NY2d 225, 229; see also, *Matter of Roman Catholic Diocese v New York State Dept. of Health*, 66 NY2d 948, 951, rev'g on dissent below 109 AD2d 140, 146 (Levine, J., dissenting in part). Conceptually similar to the current case, *Matter of Williams v Smith* held that conditions of parole cannot be considered rulemaking because they do not establish general standards of conduct, but instead find their "force and authority ... [by] incorporation in a particular individual's parole agreement" 72 NY2d 939, 940.

In light of the distinction drawn in the cases, there can be little doubt that OGS was not acting in its quasi-legislative rule making capacity when it decided to include the withdrawal criteria in its bid advertisement for this project but rather in its discretionary capacity. Far from setting a general standard of conduct, the withdrawal criteria only purported to cover the bidding for a particular contract. Nothing in the record indicates that these same bid withdrawal criteria were required for any and all contract bidding. To the contrary, the bid withdrawal procedures were selected each time to be a part of each bid package. As is true for each project, and as evidenced by the project manual in this case, OGS must determine what specifications and requirements are necessary for each project.

Unlike *Matter of J. D. Posillico, Inc. v Department of Transp.* (160 AD2d 1113), in which the Honest Error Review Unit of the Department of Transportation applied fixed standards for all contract bidding, the "force and authority" of the bid withdrawal procedures stem solely from the fact that OGS selected them for this bid invitation, which Alca agreed to when it submitted its bid. See, *Matter of Williams v Smith, supra*. Since Alca's rights and remedies were entirely determined on the basis of bidding conditions to which it had assented, no policy of OGS can be said to have been "completely conclusive of the rights and remedies of the affected party," requiring promulgation as a rule. *Matter of Roman Catholic Diocese v New York State Dept. of Health, supra*, 109 AD2d, at 147 (dissenting in part opn), revd on dissenting opn below 66 NY2d 948.

Although OGS might have followed the course taken by the Department of Transportation in Posillico and adopted fixed bid withdrawal standards, nothing compelled it to do so. Indeed, the statute authorizing OGS to take bids on public work contracts grants discretion in determining what should be contained in bid advertisements see, *Public Buildings Law*

§ 8 [2]. In this case, OGS exercised the discretion given to it by statute to include other matters relevant to bidding on the particular contract and not its rule-making authority. Moreover, inclusion of the bid withdrawal standards appears wholly in line with the overarching authority granted OGS to "best promote the public interest" by awarding contracts to the "lowest responsible and reliable bidder." *Public Buildings Law* §8 [6].

Nor does our decision deprive contractors of notice. To be sure, one of the principal problems addressed by the filing requirements of the State Administrative Procedure Act and the New York Constitution was that there were "no public rules or regulations of the departments of which the public generally ha[d] any notice" (2 Revised Record of Constitutional Convention of 1938, at 1429 [Statement of Senator Fearon]). Here, Alca could conform its bid to OGS expectations and standards, and it knew precisely what circumstances would result in forfeiture of its bid deposit. Appearing at the beginning of the bid instructions, the bid withdrawal procedures were there for any contractor interested in the project to read. Having submitted the bid based on this invitation, Alca cannot complain about a lack of notice of the conditions contained within it.

As the Supreme Court expressly did not review the remaining contentions in Alca's petition, we remit to that court.

Accordingly, the order of the Appellate Division should be reversed, with costs, and the matter remitted to Supreme Court for further proceedings in accordance with this opinion.

Glossary

Administrative agency - Legislative or executive body that administers specific laws

Administrative law judge - Hearing examiner

Administrative Procedure Act (APA) - Statute governing administrative agencies

Administrative rule - Standard of conduct enunciated by an administrative agency

Discovery - The right to ascertain facts and information from the opposing party, which may be pertinent to the case

Enabling statute - Statute that creates an administrative agency

Exhaust administrative remedies - Requirement prior to seeking judicial review

Federal Register - The official publication for all federal agency action

Judicial review - Court review of administrative action

Notice - Method of informing the public of a prospective rule; Constitutional requirement

Petition - Document to start a challenge to government action

Pleadings - Documents used to start a judicial or administrative process

Pre-hearing conference - Meeting to limit issues or settle a case

Responsive pleading - Answer to a complaint

Rule - A prescribed guide for conduct or action

Ultra vires - Beyond the scope of one's powers

Vague - Terms that are too discretionary to provide specific guidance for their interpretation and administration

Exercises

1. Describe the difference between agency rule making and adjudication.

2. What is the function of judicial review?

3. Define and discuss the concept of exhausting administrative remedies.

4. Locate and analyze the APA version adopted by your jurisdiction.

5. Indicate the particular state administrative agencies that would have a direct effect on a commercial enterprise in your state.

Chapter Twelve

BANKING

Introduction

One of the two types of negotiable instruments is a draft, a three-party instrument involving a drawer, a drawee, and a payee. For most transactions, the bank customer is the drawer; the bank is the drawee/payor; and a third person, to whom the drawer is financially obligated, is the payee.

A business's ability to flourish depends on its on-hand cash and its credit worthiness, both of which rely on the business' ability to issue and deposit checks. If the bank refuses to honor the checks drawn by the business, the business's credit will decline. If a bank disclaims a check drawn to the business, the business will lack ready cash. Consequently, the banking relationship is one of paramount importance to a commercial enterprise.

Articles 3 and 4 of the Uniform Commercial Code (UCC) define the law with respect to a bank's payment procedures. This chapter will explore the relationship between a payor bank, its customer, and the bank's collection process. Understanding these concepts is important for the commercial enterprise's financial cash flow.

The Business Customer and the Payor Bank

The relationship between a customer and its payor bank is regulated under the provisions of Article 4 of the UCC. This relationship is established when the business deposits funds with a bank, typically in the form of a checking account. This relationship is based on a contract (Chapter Three) in which the bank agrees to pay on checks drawn by the business, based on funds the business has deposited with the bank.

> ***Example:*** *Acme, Inc., opens up a checking account with First City Bank. Acme deposits $9,000 in cash in its checking account and signs a signature card that describes the relationship between the parties as customer-depositor and bank. The bank issues blank checks to Acme that Acme then uses to pay its bills. This check is an example of a draft. Acme, the drawer, writes the check that requires the bank, the drawee/payor, to pay from Acme's funds the specified amount to a payee. The bank, by contract, has accepted this role as drawee-payor.*

A bank is obligated to charge against its customers' accounts any checks that are drawn *properly payable* under §4-401(1) of the UCC. Under this section, properly payable is defined as payable at any time when the customer has sufficient funds in its account to meet the obligation. If a bank refuses to pay on a check that is properly payable, the bank is automatically liable to the business customer for any loss the customer suffers based on the dishonor. The term **honor** refers to a bank properly paying on an instrument, and dishonor refers to the bank's refusal to make such payment. Further, a bank will be automatically liable to its customer for honoring a check if the signature on the check was forged, the check was altered after the customer signed it, or a necessary signature was forged.

> **Example:** The treasurer of a company is carrying the corporate checkbook when she has her pocketbook stolen on a city bus. The pickpocket prints a check for himself, forging the signature of the treasurer. If the corporation's bank honors the check, the bank is liable to the corporation for the funds it deducted from the corporation's account.

> **Example:** A small business owner pays one of his suppliers by check. The amount of the check is $100. Prior to presenting the check to the business owner's bank, the supplier adds another zero to the amount and changes the word "hundred" to "thousand." If the business owner's bank pays on this check, the bank is liable to the business for $900, the difference between the amount the business owner actually authorized and the amount that was collected.

However, despite the foregoing, there are certain instances in which the bank will not suffer absolute liability. These circumstances arise when the customer has failed to meet its obligations with respect to the instrument.

- If the customer is negligent in the manner that the check is drawn and the instrument can be altered or the signature forged, the customer's negligence has contributed to the alteration so the bank will not be liable.

> **Example:** In making out a check, a business owner leaves blank spaces surrounding the dollar amount. The space enables the payee to insert extra digits, thereby having the check read for a larger amount than what was intended. Because of the customer's own negligence, the customer will be liable for the damages.

- If the customer executed an incomplete instrument and authorized someone to complete the check, the bank will not be liable to the customer for the payment on the completed instrument.

> **Example:** A business owner signs a blank check and tells his employee to fill in the amount for supplies when the supplies are received. The cost of the supplies is $50, but the employee fills out the check for $200, and the supplier pays the employee the difference. In this instance, the bank will not be held liable to the customer when it honors the check presented by the supplier.

- If the customer makes out a check to an imposter, the bank will not be liable.

> **Example:** A man enters a store and represents himself as one of the store's suppliers. The storeowner has never met the supplier and fails to ascertain the man's true identity. If the storeowner makes out a check to the imposter who then cashes it, the bank will not be liable to the storeowner because the owner's negligence caused the injury.

- If the customer makes out a check to a **fictitious payee**—a person who he knows does not exist—the bank will not be liable to the customer for payment.

> **Example:** *A company's bookkeeper, who is authorized to make out checks on behalf of the company, makes out a check to a person who does not exist. The bookkeeper then goes, with false identification, to the bank and presents himself as the payee. Because the company was negligent in supervising its agent, the bank will not be liable to the customer for the money withdrawn from the customer's account to honor this check.*

- If a customer fails to discover any forgery or altered instrument appearing on the statement issued to it from the bank, and the bank reasonably and in good faith paid on the instrument, the bank will not be liable. A customer has a duty to inform the bank promptly of any error that appears on his statement; if the customer fails to do so, the bank is relieved of liability.

> **Example:** *A bank sends its customer an itemized statement of checking activity every month. A small business owner received this statement but was too busy to examine it closely for about three months. When he does examine the statement, he discovers that one of the checks he issued was altered. Because the customer did not notify the bank promptly, the bank is not liable for the payment it made on the altered instrument, provided that the payment was reasonable and made in good faith.*

If the bank paid on a forged or altered instrument, and the forgery or alteration could have been discovered if the bank exercised reasonable care, the bank will remain liable regardless of the customer's negligence. Therefore, even if the customer left sufficient space on the check so that the amount could be altered, if a reasonable inspection of the check would indicate different ink and penmanship, the bank may remain liable to the customer for its failure its exercise due care.

As long as the bank is authorized, it is permitted to make payment on the customer's check. However, a customer may terminate or suspend this authority.

If a customer decides that he or she issued a check in error, or has a dispute with the payee, the customer may issue a **stop payment order** to the bank. An oral stop payment order is effective for two weeks, and a written stop payment order is effective for six months.

Checks are considered to be stale after six months, meaning that a bank is under no duty to honor a check that is dated more than six months prior to **presentment**. However, the bank is not totally precluded from honoring such checks and may pay on these instruments and deduct the amount from the customer's account, provided that the bank in good faith makes payment (§4-404 of the UCC).

If a customer dies or becomes incompetent, the customer's bank may still honor checks, provided that it does not know of the customer's death or disability. However, checks drawn by a customer may be honored up to ten days after the customer's death even if the bank is aware of the customer's demise (§4-405 of the UCC).

If a customer seeks bankruptcy protection, the customer may still issue checks unless precluded from so doing by the court or the trustee (Chapter Ten) or the bank has notice of the customer's bankruptcy.

Pursuant to the various circumstances stated above, a bank may lawfully dishonor an instrument without being obligated to its customer. However, if the bank **wrongfully dishonors** an instrument, *i.e.*, refuses to make payment for no lawful reason, the bank will remain liable to the customer for all damages that are proximately caused by the wrongful dishonor (Chapter Two). Generally, it is considered a breach of contract if the bank wrongfully dishonors the obligation.

The Bank's Collection Process

If the customer drawer and the payee both use the same bank, the bank can simply transfer the funds from one account to the other; however, in most situations, the drawer customer and the payee will use different banks. In these instances, the payee will deposit the check into his or her account with his or her own bank, known as the **depository bank**, and the depository bank must then seek payment on the check from the drawee bank.

When the physical locations of the customer and the payee are different, other banks may become involved in the collection process. For example a business customer in New York issues a check drawn on his New York bank, the drawee-payor bank, to a supplier located in Los Angeles. The supplier deposits the check drawn on the New York bank in his local bank, which is the depository bank. This bank may then transfer the check to a Federal Insurance Bank in California in order to obtain cash on the check immediately. This bank will then transfer the check to a Federal Insurance Bank in New York. These banks are referred to as **intermediary banks** or **clearing banks**. The bank that eventually presents the check to the drawee bank in New York, in this instance the Federal Insurance Bank in New York, is called the **presenter bank**. Until the drawee-payor bank actually pays on the check, all of the banks in the clearing process make provisional payments to the affected accounts. If the payor bank dishonors the check, all of the credits to the intermediary banks are revoked. Note that once a bank credits an account on a negotiable instrument, the bank may become a holder in due course (see Chapter Four).

An item is considered to be paid by the drawee bank when the drawee-payor bank pays on the check in cash, the drawee-payor bank makes a **final settlement**—settles on the check without retaining a right to revoke—the drawee-payor bank does not revoke a provisional settlement within a specified time, or the drawee-payor bank places the item on the drawer's account. A bank remains accountable for the amount of the check until final payment of the item.

The process of collection is extremely important for a commercial enterprise. Until final payment of the check to the payee, the funds appear in its account, even though they have been allocated to the payee, and the underlying debt obligation is not discharged. Both of these circumstances have a direct effect on the business' cash on hand and its contractual obligations.

Chapter Summary

For the most part, a commercial enterprise operates financially by using and receiving checks. Checks are forms of drafts, known as commercial paper, and are intended to act as cash substitutes in order to promote the free flow of commerce. As such, the provisions of the UCC govern issuing checks and the bank's collection process.

The parties to a check are the drawer—the bank's business customer, the drawee-payor—the bank where the customer deposited funds to honor its drafts, and the payee—the person who the customer wishes to receive the funds. The relationship between the bank and its customers is based on contract, and the bank is obligated to honor all of its customers' drafts presented for payment. A bank remains liable to its customers for any injury proximately caused by its wrongful dishonor of a valid instrument drawn by the customer.

A bank may not be liable to its customer for honoring a check that has been forged or altered if the error can be traced to the customer's own negligence. Further, a customer is under a statutory duty to review all statements sent to it by its bank and to discover any error on it and then notify the bank of any discrepancies. The bank will not be liable for paying if it reasonably and in good faith made such payment without notice of any problem.

If the drawer and the payees use different banks, several intermediary banks may become involved in the collection process, which involves the process of actually receiving cash for the check. Any bank used by the payee's bank in this process is referred to as an intermediary bank, and the bank that eventually presents the instrument to the drawee bank is known as the presenter bank. Until the drawee bank makes final payment on the instrument, the customer remains obligated to the payee, and when final payment is made, the customer is discharged.

Edited Judicial Decisions

IN RE LOU LEVY & SONS FASHIONS, INC.
988 F.2d 311 (2d Cir. 1993)

This appeal involves a bank's liability under the Uniform Commercial Code for accepting for deposit into a defalcating employee's personal accounts checks bearing forged endorsements drawn payable to the employer corporation. First Fidelity Bank, N.A. New Jersey (Fidelity) appeals from a judgment of the district court for the Southern District of New York, Thomas P. Griesa, Judge, granting Lou Levy & Sons Fashions, Inc., Mod-Maid Imports, Inc., Donnybrook Fashions, Ltd., and Braeten, Inc. (Levy) summary judgment on a conversion claim and granting Levy, the employer, prejudgment interest from the date the claim was filed. The district court determined as a matter of law that Fidelity was barred from asserting any defenses based on Levy's own allegedly negligent conduct (failure to discover the defalcations) because Fidelity had acted in a commercially unreasonable manner. *In re Lou Levy & Sons Fashions, Inc., Litig.*, 785 F. Supp. 1163 (SDNY 1992). For the reasons set forth below, we affirm.

I. BACKGROUND

The following facts are taken from the district court opinion and are undisputed. Levy's accounts receivable bookkeeper, Michelina Romano, and Levy's sales manager, Lawrence Meltzer, forged Levy's corporate endorsement on 193 checks worth over $2 million during a five and one-half year period between late 1984 and January 1990. Meltzer or Romano endorsed 188 of these checks by writing or typing the name of the particular corporate payee and the account number of one of Meltzer's personal accounts. The remaining five checks were endorsed with Meltzer's or his wife's name without any corporate name. Meltzer deposited all of the checks in his personal checking and savings accounts at Fidelity. Over the five and one-half years during which Meltzer deposited corporate checks into his personal accounts, only once did a Fidelity teller challenge his authority to make deposits. Even then, Meltzer ultimately succeeded in making the improper deposit by going to another teller at a different branch of the bank.

Levy, an affiliation of New York corporations engaged in the business of manufacturing and selling women's clothing, brought suit in diversity against Romano, Meltzer, and Fidelity in the district court for the Southern District of New York on January 16, 1990. In response to a personal jurisdiction defense raised by Fidelity, Levy also brought suit in the District of New Jersey. The Judicial Panel on Multidistrict Litigation subsequently transferred the New Jersey suit to the Southern District of New York. In multidistrict litigation transfers, the law of the transferor district must be applied. *Stirling v. Chemical Bank*, 382 F. Supp. 1146, 1150 n.5 (SDNY 1974). Therefore, the district court followed New Jersey law in this case. New Jersey has adopted the Uniform Commercial Code (the UCC), found in Title 12A, Subtitle 1 of the New Jersey Statutes Annotated.

On October 1, 1990, the district court granted Levy's motion for summary judgment against Romano and Meltzer for conversion. *In re Lou Levy & Sons Fashions, Inc., Litig.*, No. 90 Civ. 0238, 1990 U.S. Dist. LEXIS 12881 (SDNY Oct. 1, 1990). Thereafter, Levy moved for summary judgment against Fidelity for conversion pursuant to N.J. Stat. Ann. §12A:3-419(1)(c) (West 1992). Levy's motion was granted. *In re Lou Levy & Sons Fashions, Inc., Litig.*, No. 90 Civ. 0238, 1991 U.S. Dist. LEXIS 16576 (SDNY Nov. 15, 1991). Following a motion for reconsideration, the district court reaffirmed its prior ruling, holding that Fidelity's commercially unreasonable conduct in accepting for deposit into personal accounts 193 checks drawn to the order of Levy estopped Fidelity from asserting the defense of contributory negligence or any other defense based on Levy's alleged negligence. On April 30, 1992, the district court issued a memorandum decision awarding Levy prejudgment interest against Fidelity from the commencement of the action, following New Jersey court rule 4:42-11(b), rather than from the dates of the accrual of the claim for relief, as required by N.J. Stat. Ann. §12A:3-122(4)(b) (West 1992). *In re Lou Levy & Sons Fashions, Inc., Litig.*, No. 90 Civ. 0238, 1992 U.S. Dist. LEXIS 6271(SDNY Apr. 30, 1992).

On appeal, Fidelity argues that the district court erred in not accepting its affirmative defense that Levy was contributorily negligent in not discovering Romano and Meltzer's fraud. Although Fidelity concedes that accepting checks payable to a corporate payee for deposit into a personal account is commercially unreasonable as a matter of law, Fidelity maintains that its behavior does not bar it from raising a defense of contributory negligence or equitable estoppel. Levy cross-appeals on the question of prejudgment interest, arguing that it should receive interest on the judgment from the date each check was converted.

We find neither Fidelity's appeal nor Levy's cross-appeal persuasive.

II. DISCUSSION

Resolution of Fidelity's appeal depends on the interpretation of two provisions of New Jersey law adopted from the UCC, N.J. Stat. Ann. §12A:3-404(1) (West 1992) (§3-404(1)) and 12A:3-406 (West 1992) (§3-406). §3-404(1), which covers the liability of parties in situations involving unauthorized signatures, provides:

Any unauthorized signature is wholly inoperative as that of the person whose name is signed unless he ratifies it or is precluded from denying it, but it operates as the signature of the unauthorized signer in favor of any person who in good faith pays the instrument or takes it for value.

Section 3-406 creates a defense in situations where a claimant's negligence substantially contributes to a forgery or alteration. Of particular concern to this case, §3-406 allows a bank to assert a claimant's negligence as a defense only if the bank can demonstrate that its conduct met reasonable commercial standards. Section 3-406 provides:

Any person who by his negligence substantially contributes to a material alteration of the instrument or to the making of an unauthorized signature is precluded from asserting the alteration or lack of authority against a holder in due course or against a drawee or other payor who pays the instrument in good faith and in accordance with the reasonable commercial standards of the drawee's or payor's business.

Fidelity argues that Levy negligently failed to discover Romano and Meltzer's conversion scheme and, according to §3-404(1), is thereby "precluded from denying" Meltzer's authority to deposit the 193 checks. Fidelity challenges the district court's opinion on the grounds that the district court erred by applying the §3-406 commercial reasonableness test to §3-404(1) even though "§3-404(1) contains no provision expressly authorizing plaintiffs to set up commercial unreasonableness as a bar to the defenses of estoppel, laches, and negligence." *In re Lou Levy & Sons, Fashions, Inc., Litig.*, 785 F. Supp. At 1167 In short, Fidelity argues that §3-404(1) should be read independently of §3-406, and, therefore, the commercial reasonableness test found in §3-406 should not prevent it from avoiding liability.

The district court was correct in reading §3-404(1) and §3-406 together and in concluding that the §3-406 commercial reasonableness test applied to §3-404(1). Individual sections of the UCC should be interpreted as part of an entire statutory scheme, not as isolated statutes each standing on its own, as Fidelity insists. The interdependence of each section of the UCC is made clear in the official Comments to the UCC. The Comments state that "the text of each section should be read in the light of the purpose and policy of the rule or principle in question, as also of the Act as a whole . . . ." N.J. Stat. Ann. §12A:1-102 (West 1992) (UCC Comments). The UCC was adopted by New Jersey in its entirety and made to take effect on January 1, 1963. See N.J. Stat. Ann. §12A:10-106 (West 1992). The purpose in adopting the UCC was "to simplify, clarify, and modernize the law governing commercial transactions" and "to make uniform the law among the various jurisdictions." N.J. Stat. Ann. §12A:1-102(2)(a), (c) (West 1992).

The general principle guiding the UCC's allocation of losses from forged endorsements on checks is to place the loss on the party in the best position to avoid the loss. See Donald J. Rapson, *Loss Allocation in Forgery and Fraud Cases: Significant Changes Under Revised Articles 3 and 4*, 42 Ala. L. Rev. 435, 435 (1991); George G. Triantis, *Allocation of Losses from Forged Indorsements on Checks and the Application of §3-405 of the Uniform Commercial Code*, 39 Okla. L. Rev. 669, 669 (1986). As a result, the UCC typically places the burden of loss on the person who dealt with and took the instrument in question from the forger as "such person is presumed to have been in the best position to thwart the attempted fraud and thereby prevent the loss." Triantis, *supra*, at 670. More specifically and relevant to this appeal, the "depositary bank is assumed to have been in the best position to prevent the fraud by taking steps before cashing the check to verify the genuineness of the indorsement and to ascertain the identity of the wrongdoer presenting the check for payment." *Id.* at 671-72 (footnote omitted).

The UCC, however, supplements the general principle of allocating losses to the party who accepts a forged check with certain defenses that take into account the culpability of the parties. Section 3-404(1) provides for two categories of defenses: ratification and estoppel against the person whose name is signed. Fidelity's claim is limited to this second category and relies exclusively on allegations that Levy was negligent in allowing the conversion scheme to go unhindered for so long.

Although §3-404(1) does not reiterate the commercial reasonableness Provision found in §3-406, as we commenced by saying, the official Comments to the UCC, which are also included in the New Jersey statute, indicate that §3-404(1) is to be read in conjunction with §3-406. Comment 4 to §3-404 states that the "words 'or is precluded from denying it' are retained in subsection (1) to recognize the possibility of an estoppel against the person whose name is signed . . . and to recognize the negligence which precludes a denial of the signature." N.J. Stat. Ann. §12A:3-404 (West 1992) (UCC Comments). The Comment section lists §3-406 as the cross reference for this Comment.

Moreover, it is difficult to understand what purpose would be served by treating negligence differently under §3-404 than it is under §3-406. Fidelity suggests that §3-406 applies to negligence, which contributes to the making of an unauthorized signature whereas §3-404(1) addresses situations where negligence allows the improper conduct to continue. However, Fidelity provides no basis in the text, purpose, logic, commentary, or case law of the UCC for this proposition.

In fact, the case law on this issue uniformly supports the application of the commercial reasonableness test to §3-404. In *Trust Co. of Georgia Bank of Savannah, N.A. v. Port Terminal & Warehousing Co.*, 153 Ga. App. 735, 266 S.E.2d 254 (Ga. Ct. App. 1980), the Georgia Court of Appeals found that §3-404(1) "does not establish a separate and distinct estoppel by negligence defense for a payor who pays an instrument over a forged endorsement." *Id.* At 257. Likewise, in *American Mach. Tool Distrib. Ass'n v. National Permanent Fed. Sav. & Loan Ass'n*, 464 A.2d 907 (D.C. 1983), the District of Columbia Court of Appeals looked first at official Comment 4 of §3-404 and then determined that §3-406 "complements §3-404(1) and defines the circumstances in which one may be precluded from denying the authority of the one making an unauthorized signature." *Id.* at 911. The District of Columbia Court of Appeals reiterated this conclusion five years later in *American Sec. Bank, N.A. v. American Motorists Ins. Co.*, 538 A.2d 736, 738 (D.C. 1988).

Fidelity offers one additional argument for interpreting §3-404 without the §3-406 commercial reasonableness test. Like §3-404, N.J. Stat. Ann. §12A:3-405 (West 1992) (§3-405) contains no provision expressly authorizing plaintiffs to set up commercial unreasonableness as a bar to the defenses of estoppel, and the majority of jurisdictions have not read the commercial reasonableness test into §3-405. See, *e.g.*, *Shearson Lehman Bros., Inc. v. Wasatch Bank*, 788 F. Supp. 1184, 1193-94 (D. Utah 1992). Fidelity argues by analogy that §3-404 should also be understood as not containing the commercial reasonableness test. The interpretive treatment of §3-405 is not properly extended to §3-404. Unlike §3-404, §3-405 does not make specific reference to negligence and §3-406 within the official Comments. Section 3-405 establishes a definite and predictable rule covering a carefully circumscribed set of cases, where the drawer issues a check to an imposter or fictitious payee. In these cases, it is presumed that the drawer is in the best position to discover and prevent fraud. See Brian P. McCarthy, Note, *Section 3-405 of the Uniform Commercial Code: Time for a Negligence Standard?*, 37 Ala. L. Rev. 199 (1985). The New Jersey Study Comments to §3-405 support the view that §3-405 cases are treated differently from other forgeries intentionally. As Comment 1 states, "it should be noted that one case, frequently thought of as a forgery situation under the NIL, is specially handled by the Code §3-405 in a way that removes it from the conversion rule of §3-419 . . . ." N.J. Stat. Ann. §12A:3-405 (West 1992) (N.J. Study Comment 1). Thus, §3-404 includes the commercial reasonableness test, whereas §3-405 does not.

Both Levy and Fidelity object to the district court's determination of damages. Levy contends that the district court should have applied N.J. Stat. Ann. §12A:3-122(4) (§3-122(4)), which measures prejudgment interest from the date of accrual of the cause of action, rather than New Jersey court rule 4:42-11(b), which measures prejudgment interest from the date of the institution of the claim. On the other side, Fidelity argues that the district court applied the correct rule but should have held an evidentiary hearing to determine whether this was an exceptional case under rule 4:42-11(b) not requiring prejudgment interest.

Neither of these arguments is persuasive. In applying rule 4:42-11(b), the district court followed the only judicial decision applying New Jersey law on point, *McAdam v. Dean Witter Reynolds, Inc.*, 896 F.2d 750 (3d Cir. 1990). The *McAdam* court found that the UCC did not provide for prejudgment interest on conversion claims brought under §3-419. *Id.* at 773-74. As a leading commentator on the UCC has stated:

The Code makes no provision relating to the recoverability of prejudgment interest in an action based on UCC §3-419. As such action is tortious in character, the recoverability of prejudgment interest will be governed by the pre-Code law relating to the recovering of such interest in tort actions.

6 Ronald A. Anderson, Anderson on the Uniform Commercial Code §3-419:33 at 434 (3d ed. 1984).

We have no reason to take issue with the Third Circuit on this point, and, accordingly, we find that the district court applied the correct rule in determining prejudgment interest.

Fidelity's argument that the district court erred in charging any prejudgment interest is also meritless. Decisions by trial courts regarding the suspension of prejudgment interest are given great deference and reviewed under an abuse of discretion standard. See *Kotzian v. Barr*, 81 N.J. 360, 408 A.2d 131, 133 (N.J. 1979). Fidelity bases its claim on the fact that the district court did not allow an evidentiary hearing on whether exceptional circumstances could be shown. There is nothing in rule 4:42-11(b) to suggest that a party has the right to an evidentiary hearing concerning this issue, and, therefore, a denial does not give grounds for reversal.

III. CONCLUSION

Accordingly, the judgment of the district court is affirmed.

MUTUAL SAVINGS AND LOAN v. NATIONAL BANK OF DETROIT
185 Mich. App. 591 (1990)

The check was processed through the normal banking channels and received by NBD on October 26, 1987. A provisional settlement was made in favor of Mutual, and NBD's account was debited accordingly. NBD claims that it orally dishonored the check before expiration of the midnight deadline of October 27. Teresa Gokey, an employee of Mutual, stated in her deposition that an NBD employee told her sometime between October 27 and 29 that the check was being returned. Then, in a subsequent affidavit, she stated that she did not receive oral notice until October 29. NBD actually returned the check to the Federal Reserve Bank on November 3. Plaintiff received it November 10.

On appeal, NBD claims the court erred in granting Mutual's motion for summary disposition. It insists the oral notice of dishonor was timely and sufficient to satisfy the midnight deadline.

Articles 3 and 4 of the Uniform Commercial Code govern transactions relating to bank deposits, collections and commercial paper. MCL 440.3101 et seq.; MSA 19.3101 *et seq.* Section 4-302 provides that a payor bank must take action within a prescribed time period in order to avoid liability for the amount of a cashier's check. It states: In the absence of a valid defense such as breach of a presentment warranty (subsection (1) of §4207), settlement effected or the like, if an item is presented on and received by a payor bank the bank is accountable for the amount of

(a) A demand item other than a documentary draft whether properly payable or not if the bank, in any case where it is not also the depositary bank, retains the item beyond midnight of the banking day of receipt without settling for it or, regardless of whether it is also the depositary bank, does not pay or return the item or send notice of dishonor until after its midnight deadline. [MCL 440.4302; MSA 19.4302.]

The midnight deadline is midnight on the next banking day following the banking day on which the payor bank receives the item. UCC 4-104(h), MCL 440.4104(h); MSA 19.4104(h).

In this case, the deadline was midnight on October 27. NBD claims it gave oral notice of dishonor prior to the deadline. The evidence does not support this contention. Ms. Gokey clarified her deposition testimony and indicated oral notice of dishonor was not received until October 29.

Even if there were a question of fact regarding the date of the oral notice, we conclude that, under the UCC, oral notice of dishonor is not sufficient.

There is no Michigan case law addressing the sufficiency of oral notice of dishonor under the UCC. Other jurisdictions have rendered decisions that differ on the issue. Oral notice was held insufficient in Utah in 1975 but sufficient ten years later in Indiana. *Valley Bank & Trust Co v First Security Bank of Utah*, 538 P2d 298 (Utah, 1975); *Yoder v Cromwell State Bank*, 478 NE2d 131 (Ind App, 1985).

The Code at §3-508 permits notice of dishonor to be oral or written. MCL 440.3508; MSA 19.3508. However §4-302(a) states that the payor bank must pay, return, or "send notice of dishonor" before the midnight deadline. The definition of send "in connection with any writing or notice means to deposit in the mail or deliver for transmission by any other usual means of communication with postage or cost of transmission provided for and properly addressed . . . ." UCC 1-201(38), MCL 440.1201(38); MSA 19.1201(38). This definition necessarily implies delivery of a written instrument. Thus we find a conflict between §3-508 and §4-302 with respect to the propriety of oral notice. In the event of a conflict, Article 4 provisions govern. UCC 4-102, MCL 440.4102; MSA 19.4102. Oral notice of dishonor is not permitted under §4-302. Thus NBD is liable for the amount of the check, unless it can establish a valid defense.

NBD alleges such a defense. It contends Mutual breached its presentment and transfer warranties under §4-207 by failing to obtain an authorized signature and by presenting an item outside the chain of title. MCL 440.4207; MSA 19.4207. It claims that Stantz Electronics, as remitter, was not a proper endorser of the cashier's check, that the actual owner was N.C. Servo.

A cashier's check is a bill of exchange drawn by a bank upon itself. The bank becomes the drawee and the drawer, rather than merely the drawee as in the ordinary check scenario. *Bruno v Collective Federal Savings & Loan Ass'n*, 147 NJ Super 115; 370 A2d 874 (1977); *Swiss Credit Bank v Virginia National Bank-Fairfax*, 538 F2d 587 (CA 4, 1976). A cashier's check, therefore, is accepted by the bank upon issuance and is a primary obligation of the issuing bank, rather than of the purchaser of the check. *Munson v American National Bank & Trust Co of Chicago*, 484 F2d 620 (CA 7, 1973); *Pennsylvania v Curtiss National Bank of Miami Springs, Florida*, 427 F2d 395 (CA 5, 1970). By issuing a cashier's check, the bank promises to draw the amount of the check from its own resources and to pay it upon demand. Consequently, this promise to pay ordinarily cannot be countermanded. *Florida Frozen Foods, Inc v National Commercial Bank & Trust Co*, 81 AD2d 978; 439 NYS2d 771 (1981); *Wertz v Richardson Heights Bank & Trust*, 495 SW2d 572 (Tex, 1973).

A cashier's check is generally acquired for the purpose of assuring a payee that the necessary funds contemplated by the transaction are available. *Gillespie v Riley Management Corp*, 59 Ill 2d 211; 319 NW2d 753 (1974). Until delivery of the cashier's check to the named payee, the purchaser remains the owner and retains the right to cancel. *Gillespie, supra*. Thus a bank is justified in relying on the presumptions of continued ownership and lack of delivery to the payee when presented with a cashier's check by the purchaser. These presumptions exist except when unusual circumstances raise a duty of inquiry.*Gillespie, supra*; *Bunge Corp v Manufacturers Hanover Trust Co*, 31 NY2d 223; 335 NYS2d 412 (1972); *Scharz v Twin City State Bank*, 201 Kan 539; 441 P2d 897 (1968).

The entitlement to rely on a presumption of continued ownership is necessary and appropriate, since a contemplated transaction sometimes fails to materialize. In such an event, the purchaser is left with a cashier's check that he no longer wishes to deliver. It would pose an unwarranted commercial burden to require the purchaser then to obtain the endorsement of the named payee in order to have the cashier's check honored or cancelled. *Gillespie, supra*. Therefore, until the check is placed in the stream of commerce, the purchaser must be able to cancel it. *Id.*

Extending this principle to cover the breadth of modern commercial transactions, it is desirable to permit the cashier's check to be honored at the bank of the purchaser's choice. It would be burdensome to require the purchaser instead to return the check to the issuing bank, cancel it, and receive a new check. It is far preferable to permit him, upon sufficient identification, to use the cashier's check at another bank for a purpose other than that which he originally intended. This extension is in keeping with the purpose and policies of the UCC. UCC 1-102, MCL 440.1102; MSA 19.1102. Only a limited burden is imposed on the drawee bank, as it already has received the funds to cover the check. Moreover the drawee bank accepted the check for payment upon issuance, thus obligating itself to make good the face amount upon demand.

Since the depository bank is entitled to rely on the presumption of the purchaser's continuing ownership, there can be no breach of warranty under §4-207 for lack of title. The only exception exists where an unusual circumstance gives rise to a duty on the part of the depository bank to inquire into the purchaser's ownership.

In this case, the cashier's check stated on its face that Stantz Electronics was the owner of the check. The check was endorsed "not used for intended purpose." There is no evidence of any unusual circumstance that should have indicated to Mutual that Stantz Electronics was not the owner, purchaser, and remitter of the cashier's check. Therefore, no duty arose to inquire as to the authority of Stantz to use the check for another purpose. There is nothing to indicate that Donald Stantz lacked authority to sign on behalf of his company and to divert the company's funds to his own account.

NBD failed to establish the existence of a valid breach of warranty defense under §4-207 sufficient to relieve it of strict liability for the amount of the cashier's check. The trial court did not err.

Affirmed.

Glossary

Clearing bank - An intermediary bank

Depository bank - Payee's bank into which the check is deposited

Dishonor - Refusing to pay on an instrument

Fictitious payee - Person who the drawer knows does not exist

Final Settlement The drawee-payor bank settles on a check without retaining the right to revoke

Honor - Making payment on an instrument

Intermediary bank - Any bank other than the drawee and depository bank involved in the collection process

Presentment - Bringing a draft to the drawee for payment

Presenter bank - Intermediary bank that presents the instrument to the drawee

Stop payment order - Suspension of bank's authority to pay on a draft

Wrongful dishonor - Refusing to pay on an instrument without a lawful reason

Exercises

1. Obtain a signature card and contract for opening up a bank checking account from your local bank.

2. Briefly discuss how a bank may become a holder in due course.

3. Differentiate between the banks that may be involved in the collection process.

4. Discuss the situations in which a customer's own negligence will preclude a bank being liable to the customer for honoring the customer's check.

5. Discuss the importance of the banking provisions of the UCC to a commercial enterprise.

INDEX

A

acceptance, 42
   defined, 41, 60
   determination of delivery of deed, 88
acceptor
   liability on negotiable instrument, 68
accession
   defined, 115, 124
accommodation party
   liability on negotiable instrument, 68
accord and satisfaction
   defined, 51, 60
actual cause
   defined, 18, 33
actual eviction
   defined, 92, 106
actual possession
   defined, 87, 106
adhesion contracts
   defined, 45, 60
adjudication
   defined, 2, 11, 193
administrative agency
   authority to carry out mandates, 193
   bound by Administrative Procedure Act, 193
   creation of rules, 193
   defined, 11, 202
administrative law
   defined, 1, 5, 11
administrative law judge
   defined, 195, 202
   permission of introduction of information, 195
   requirement of impartiality, 195
Administrative Procedure Act, 194
   defined, 5, 11, 202
   exceptions to publication rules, 194
   generally, 193
   initiation of proceedings, 194
   requirement of due process, 193
administrative rule
   defined, 193, 202
   dissatisfaction with rule, 194
administrative rule-making process
   generally, 193
adversarial
   defined, 11

adversarial system
   defined, 6
adverse possession
   defined, 87, 106
affirmative action plan
   defined, 164, 173
Age Discrimination in Employment Act of 1967
   application, 164
   defense of bona fide occupational qualification, 164
   defined, 173
   exceptions, 164
   generally, 164
agency adjudication
   elements of due process, 195
   generally, 195
   hearing process, 195
agency relationship
   purpose, 132
agent
   actual authority, 130
   apparent authority, 130
   authority by estoppel, 131
   authority to act, 130
   defined, 129, 138
   exercise of independent discretion, 129
   express authority, 130
   fiduciary duty to principal, 131
   implied authority, 130
   legal authority to bind, 129
   ostensible authority, 130
   self-dealing in contract, 131
alien corporation
   defined, 146, 155
allonge
   defined, 67, 78
ameliorative waste
   defined, 85, 106
Americans with Disabilities Act of 1990
   application to employers, 165
   application to perceived disabled, 165
   defined, 173
   generally, 165
   purpose, 165
   relief afforded under Title VII, 165
anticipatory repudiation, 50
   defined, 49, 60
apparent authority

defined, 130, 138
appeal
   defined, 27, 33
appellate court
   defined, 6, 11
arraignment
   defined, 26, 33
arrest
   defined, 33
arson
   defined, 25, 33
articles of organization
   defined, 155
assault
   as intentional tort, 15
   contrasted to battery, 16
   defined, 33
   elements, 15
   responsibility of employer, 15
assignee
   defined, 47, 60
assignment
   consideration, 47
   defined, 47, 60
   exceptions, 47
   right of enforcement, 48
assignment of lease
   generally, 92
assignor
   defined, 47, 60
assumed name (dba) form
   defined, 155
assumed name form
   defined, 142
assumption of risk
   as defense to negligence, 19
   defenses to negligence, 19
assumption of the mortgage
   defined, 90, 106
attempt
   defined, 23, 33
authority by estoppel
   defined, 131
authorized shares
   defined, 148, 155

B

bailee
   defined, 112, 124
   entitlement to absolute possession, 113
   liability for ordinary negligence, 114
   liability for unauthorized use of bailed item, 114
bailment
   defined, 112, 124
   express use, 113
   implied bailment with possession, 112
   implied use, 114
   incidental use, 114
   problems, 113
      bathhouses and retail stores, 113
      cloakrooms, 113
      parking lots, 113
      pledges, 113
      safe deposit boxes, 113
   requirement of physical transfer, 112
   transfer of right of bailee to possess, 112
bailor
   defined, 112, 124
   right to sue for breach of contract, tort, or conversion, 114
bank collection process
   generally, 208
bank liability
   exceptions, 206
      check made out to imposter, 206
      customer negligence, 206
      failure to discover forgery, 207
      incomplete instrument, 206
      known fictitious payee, 207
   failure to discover forgery, 207
bank statement rule
   defined, 70
bankruptcy
   customer ability to issue checks, 208
   debtor documents, 176
   effect on other proceedigns, 176
   lift of stay of other proceedings, 180
   roles of commercial enterprises, 175
   stay of other proceedings, 180
Bankruptcy Code, 177, 179
   defined, 191
   generally, 175
bankruptcy court
   defined, 175, 191
bargain and sale deed
   defined, 88, 106
battery
   as intentional tort, 15
   contrasted to assault, 16
   defined, 33
   elements, 16
battle of the forms
   defined, 41, 60
bearer

defined, 65, 78
bilateral contract
    defined, 42, 60
bill
    defined, 3, 11
block and lot index
    defined, 89, 106
blue sky laws
    defined, 155
    regulation of limited partnerships, 145
board of directors
    defined, 155
    management of corporation, 146
bona fide occupational qualification
    as defense against age discrimination, 164
    defined, 173
    elements, 164
    exclusion of race, 164
breach
    defined, 60
breach of contract
    bailments, 112
    compensatory damages, 52
    consequential damages, 53
    defined, 49
    determination of extent of breach, 52
    equitable remedies, 53
    injunction, 54
    legal remedies, 52
    liquidated damages, 53
    nominal damages, 53
    punitive damages, 53
    quasi-contract, 54
    remedies, 52
    rescission and restitution, 54
    specific performance, 53
bribery
    defined, 26
burglary
    defined, 25, 33
business judgment rule
    defined, 147, 155
business organizations
    generally, 141
bylaws
    defined, 147, 155
    variances from governing laws, 147

C

case
    defined, 6, 11
cash collateral
    defined, 179, 191
causation in fact
    defined, 18, 33
certificate of dissolution
    defined, 148, 155
certificate of incorporation, 148
    authorized shares, 148
    defined, 146, 155
    functions, 146
    preferred stock rights and obligations, 147
    variances from governing laws, 147
certificate of limited partnership
    defined, 155
    requirement by state, 145
certificate of registration
    defined, 149, 155
Chapter 11
    acceptance or rejection of restructuring plan, 180
    conversion to Chapter 7, 179
    defined, 175, 191
    disclosure statement, 179
    possession of property subject to claims, 178
    qualification as small business, 180
    requirement to file plan for satisfaction of debts, 176
Chapter 12
    conversion to Chapter 7, 179
    defined, 191
    defined, 175
    objection to classification of exempt property, 180
    requirement to file plan for satisfaction of debts, 176
Chapter 13
    conversion to Chapter 7, 179
    defined, 175, 191
    objection to classification of exempt property, 180
    reorganization or restructuring plan, 179
    requirement for monthly reporting, 178
    requirement to file plan for satisfaction of debts, 176
Chapter 7, 179
    conversion from other chapters, 179
    defined, 175, 191
    Statement of Intention, 178
Chapter 9
    defined, 175
chattel, 17
    defined, 17, 106
circuit court

defined, 6, 11
civil law, 13
   defined, 1, 11
Civil Rights Act of 1964
   defined, 173
   generally, 163
claimant
   defined, 180, 191
class
   defined, 155
clearing bank
   defined, 208, 215
closing
   defined, 87, 106
   transfer of property deed to grantee, 88
codification
   defined, 4, 11
collateral
   defined, 89, 108
collection guarantor
   defined, 78
   liability on negotiable instrument, 68
commercial paper
   as cash substitute, 66
   as intangible property, 111
   defined, 65, 78
   discharge of obligations, 70
   generally, 65
   negotiation or transfer, 67
   requirement for use as cash substitute, 67
common carrier
   defined, 115, 124
   insurer liability for goods, 116
   right to lien, 116
common law
   American legal system, 2
   benefits, 2
   conveyance of property, 88
   defined, 1, 11
common stock rights
   defined, 147
community property
   defined, 83, 106
comparative negligence
   as defense to negligence, 19
   defenses to negligence, 19
   defined, 15
compensatory damages
   defined, 52, 60
complaint
   criminal law, 26
   defined, 33

concurrent estates
   defined, 84, 106
condition
   defined, 49, 60
   excuse of
      generally, 49
   failure of, 49
condition concurrent
   defined, 49, 61
condition precedent
   defined, 49, 61
condition subsequent
   defined, 49, 61
confusion
   defined, 115, 124
consent
   as valid reason for tort, 17
consequential damages
   defined, 53, 61
consideration
   defined, 43, 61
conspiracy
   defined, 23, 33
constructive bailment
   defined, 112, 124
constructive eviction
   defined, 92, 106
contract, 42, 51
   bargain element, 43
   defined, 61
   definition of legal capacity, 45
   element of offer, 40
   elements, 39
   entry into valif contract, 44
   intent of parties, 45
   liability of principal, 132
   provisions, 49
   required specificity of terms, 40
   requirement for specific acceptance, 41
   requirement of mental ability to enter into
      contract, 45
   rules of construction, 49, 50
   special types, 41
   transfer of risk of loss, 87
contract rights
   assignment exceptions, 47
contractual capacity
   defined, 44, 61
contribution
   defined, 156
   to liability, 15
contributory negligence

Index

as defense to negligence, 19
defenses to negligence, 19
defined, 34
conversion
    defined, 17, 34
    in bankruptcy, 179
    relation to embezzlement, 24
conveyance
    defined, 86, 106
    requirement of writing, 86
    requirements, 86
    Statute of Frauds, 86
copyright
    defined, 111, 125
corporation
    alien, 146
    as legal entity, 146
    as separate entity, 148
    authorized shares, 148
    board of directors
        as agent, 147
        as fiduciaries, 147
        defined, 147
        election by shareholders, 147
        liability, 147
        management of business, 147
        prohibition against self-dealing, 147
        statutory minimum for directories, 147
        term of office, 147
    bylaws, 147
    defined, 146, 156
    dissolution, 148
    domestic, 146
    duration, 146
    foreign, 146
    formation, 146
    funding, 148
    generally, 146
    issued shares, 148
    liability of shareholders, 148
    management by board of directors, 146
    notice requirements for meetings, 147
    number of directors, 147
    outstanding shares, 148
    ownership by shareholders, 146, 147
    payment of dividends, 148
    preferred stock, 147
    purpose, 146
    registered office for service of process, 146
    regulation by securities laws, 148
    removal or replacement of directors, 147
    requirement for common stock rights, 147
    seal, 147
    secretary of state as agent for service of process, 146
    shares of stock, 147
    tax year, 147
    termination by government, 148
    total number of shares, 146
    unique name requirement, 146
    variance from governing laws, 147
counter-offer
    defined, 41
covenant
    defined, 49, 61
covenant against encumbrances
    defined, 88
covenant for further assurances
    defined, 88
covenant for quiet enjoyment
    defined, 88
covenant of right to convey
    defined, 88
covenant of seisin
    defined, 88
covenant of warranty
    defined, 88
covenant running with the land
    defined, 96, 106
cover
    defined, 53, 61
creditors meeting
    defined, 191
    purpose, 178
creditors rights
    generally, 180
criminal law, 22
    criminal liability of commercial enterprises, 22
    defined, 34
    generally, 13
    guilt of commercial enterprises, 22
cross-offer
    defined, 41
Cutler v. Cutler, 184

D

damages
    defined, 17, 34
    merchant traders under UCC, 53
debtor in possession
    defined, 191
    in Chapter 11, 178
    use of property for ordinary operations, 178
deed

defined, 87, 107
general warranty deed, 88
transfer when delivered to grantee, 88
types, 88
defamation
categories, 21
defenses
absolute privilege, 21
consent, 21
qualified privilege, 21
truth, 21
defined, 34
elements, 21
defamatory language
defined, 21, 34
defect in chain of title, 87
defendant
defined, 34
requirement of specific act or failure to act, 22
deficiency
defined, 107
delegation, 61
defined, 48
exceptions, 48
delegator
defined, 48, 61
Department of Labor, 162
depository bank
defined, 208, 215
Devereaux's Carpentry Services, LLC v. Ericson, 153
disability
defined, 165, 173
discharge of contractual obligations
accord and satisfaction, 51
agreement of parties, 51
breach of contract, 52
death or destruction, 51
excuse of conditions, 51
frustration of purpose, 52
generally, 50
impossibility of fulfillment, 51
mutual rescission, 51
novation, 51
performance, 51
release, 51
substituted agreements, 51
supervening illegality, 51
discharge of obligations
commercial paper, 70
act operating to discharge, 70
cancellation and renunciation, 70
delay in presentment, 70

fraudulent or material alteration, 70
impairment of recourse, 70
payment in satisfaction, 70
reacquisition, 70
tender of payment, 70
discipline of child
as valid reason for tort, 18
disclaimer
defined, 54, 61
disclosure statement
defined, 191
elements, 179
discovery
defined, 195, 202
dishonor
bank ability to dishonor without obligation, 208
bank liability on properly drawn checks, 205
defined, 68, 78, 215
distinguish
defined, 2, 11
district court, 6
bankruptcy proceedings, 175
defined, 6, 11
jurisdiction for bankruptcy, 175
dividend
defined, 147, 156
divisible contract
defined, 50, 61
doctrine of equitable conversion
defined, 87, 107
Uniform Vendors' and Purchasers' Risk Act, 87
domestic corporation
defined, 146, 156
dominant tenement
defined, 95, 107
draft
defined, 65, 78
dram shop act
defined, 14, 34
drawee
defined, 65, 78
liability on negotiable instrument, 68
drawer
defined, 65, 78
liability on negotiable instrument, 68
Dubin v. Hudson County Probation Department, 74
duress
defined, 45, 61
duty to mitigate damages
defined, 53

E

easement
  abandonment by holder, 95
  defined, 94, 107
  elements, 94
  express grant, 94
  implication, 94
  necessity, 95
  prescription, 95
  Statute of Frauds, 94
easement appurtenant
  defined, 95, 107
easement in gross
  defined, 95, 107
ejection
  defined, 87, 107
embezzlement
  defined, 24, 34
eminent domain
  defined, 96, 107
Employee Retirement Income Security Act of 1974, 162
  defined, 173
  exceptions, 162
  generally, 162
  purpose, 163
  requirements of employer pension plans, 162
employment at will
  and nondiscrimination, 163
  defined, 159, 173
enabling statute
  defined, 5, 193, 202
encumbrance
  defined, 87, 107
Equal Employment Opportunity Commission
  administration of ADA, 165
  cases filed, 164
  defined, 173
  generally, 163
  investigation of discrimination cases, 163
Equal Pay Act
  defined, 173
  generally, 161
  requirements for claim of discrimination, 162
equal work
  defined, 162, 173
equitable servitude
  contrasted to real covenant, 96
  defined, 96, 107
equitable waste
  defined, 85, 107
estate
  defined, 81, 107
  inclusion of debtor's assets, 176
eviction
  generally, 91
evidence, 195
  defined, 2, 6, 11
executive agency
  defined, 11
executory
  defined, 51, 61
exhaust administrative remedies
  defined, 194, 202
express authority
  defined, 130, 138
express warranty
  defined, 20, 34, 54

F

Fair Labor Standards Act
  defined, 173
  exceptions, 161
    administrative personnel, 161
    executives, 161
    outside salespersons, 161
    professionals, 161
  generally, 161
  maximum hours at minimum wage, 161
false imprisonment
  as intentional tort, 15
  as kidnapping, 24
  defined, 34
  elements, 16
false pretenses
  defined, 24, 34
Family Medical Leave Act
  benefits, 166
  defined, 173
  generally, 166
Federal Register, 194
  defined, 202
fee holder
  rights, 81
fee simple absolute
  defined, 81, 107
fee simple estates
  community property, 83
  concurrent estates, 84
  joint tenancy, 82
  tenancy by the entirety, 83
  tenancy in common, 82
  tenancy in partnership, 83
  tenancy in severalty, 81

types, 81
fellow servant exception, 128
  defined, 14, 34
felony
  defined, 25, 34
fictitious payee
  defined, 69, 215
final settlement
  defined, 208, 215
financial accountability of employers
  generally, 159
first impression
  defined, 2, 11
fixture
  defined, 86, 107
foreclosure
  defined, 90, 107
foreign corporation
  defined, 146, 156
forgery
  bank failure to exercise reasonable care, 207
  bank statement rule, 70
  certification, 70
  customer failure to discover, 207
  defined, 25, 34
  fictitious payee, 69
  generally, 69
  negligence, 69
four units
  defined, 107
fraud
  defined, 45, 61
freehold
  defined, 81, 107
freehold estate
  defined, 81
frolic of his own
  defined, 13, 34
  master-servant relationship, 128
fully insured
  defined, 160, 173
future covenants
  types, 88

G

general partnership
  contribution in liability, 144
  defined, 143, 156
  funding by partner contributions, 145
  joint liability in contract, 144
  liability of partners, 144
  partnership rights, 143

resemblance to sole proprietorship, 144
  several liability in tort, 144
general warranty deed
  defined, 88, 107
goods
  defined, 39, 61
goodwill
  defined, 144, 156
grantee
  defined, 86, 107
  later prevalence over earlier grantee, 89
grantor
  defined, 84, 86, 107
  requirement of marketable title, 87
grantor-grantee index
  defined, 89, 107
Great Depression, 159
Grover aka Guillermo Salinas v. Ragan, 9
guarantee
  defined, 44, 61
guilty
  defined, 22, 26, 34

H

holder
  defined, 67, 78
holder in due course
  defenses and claims, 68
  defined, 67, 78
  good faith test, 67
  shelter rule, 67
holdover doctrine
  defined, 91
holdover tenant
  defined, 91, 107
homicide
  defined, 24, 34
honor
  bank duty to honor without notification, 207
  defined, 205, 215
  no bank duty on stale check, 207
hostile work environment
  defined, 163, 173

I

Illinois v. Johnson, 27
illusory promise
  defined, 44, 61
implied authority
  defined, 130, 138
implied warranty

defined, 34
implied warranty of fitness for a particular use
    defined, 20, 54
implied warranty of habitability
    defined, 92
implied warranty of merchantability
    defined, 20, 54
In re Lou Levy & Sons Fashions, Inc., 209
In the Matter of Alca Industries, Inc., 200
inchoate crime
    attempt, 23
    conspiracy, 23
    defined, 23, 34
    solicitation, 23
incidental beneficiary
    defined, 47, 61
incorporator
    defined, 156
    role in formation of corporation, 146
indemnification
    defined, 138
    from liability, 15
    master-servant relationship, 129
independent contractor
    coverage under Fair Labor Standards Act, 161
    defined, 35, 132
    enterprise liability, 14
    liability of other parties, 132
        exceptions, 132
independent supervening force
    defined, 18, 35
indictment
    defined, 26, 35
indorse
    defined, 78
indorsements
    defined, 67
    types, 67
indorser
    defined, 67, 78
    liability on negotiable instrument, 68
information
    defined, 26, 35
injunction
    defined, 21, 35, 54
innkeeper
    defined, 115, 125
    liability, 115
    right to lien, 116
installment contracts
    defined, 50, 61
intangible

defined, 125
intangibles
    bank checks, 111
    commercial paper, 111
    defined, 111
    intellectual property, 111
intellectual property
    copyright, 111
    defined, 111, 125
    mark, 112
    patent, 112
    types, 111
intended beneficiary
    defined, 46, 61
    right to enforce contract, 47
intentional tort
    defined, 15
intermediary bank
    defined, 208, 216
Internal Revenue Code, 162, 193
Internal Revenue Service, 162, 193
involuntary bankruptcy
    defined, 192
    generally, 179
ironclad
    defined, 41, 61
issued shares
    defined, 148, 156

J

James v. Louisiana Laborers Health and Welfare Fund, 166
Jefferson Airplane & Afterthought Productions, Inc. v. Berkeley Systems, Inc., 117
Johnson v. Morgester, 9
joint and several liability
    defined, 156
joint committee
    defined, 4, 11
joint liability
    defined, 156
joint tenancy
    defined, 82
    requirements of four unities, 82
judicial review
    defined, 4, 11, 196, 202
    limits on administrative ability to act, 6
    process, 196
jurisprudence
    defined, 1, 11
jury
    and administrative hearing, 196

defined, 6, 11

K

kidnapping
  defined, 24, 35
K-Mart Corp. v. Balfour Beatty, Inc., 58

L

labor law
  defined, 173
  generally, 159
landlord
  duty to make premises safe, 93
    latent defects, 93
    public use, 93
    repair, 93
  duty to make premises short-term furnished residences, 93
  duty to mitigate damages, 91
landlord duties to tenant
  generally, 91
larceny
  defined, 24, 35
  distinguished from embezzlement, 24
  relation to robbery, 24
latent defects
  defined, 93
law of agency
  generally, 127
  independent contractor, 127
  master-servant relationship, 127
  principal-agent relationship, 127
lease, 92
  actions after termination, 91
  defined, 81, 90, 108
  termination after condemnation of property, 92
leasehold
  defined, 108
  surrender by tenant, 91
leasehold estate
  defined, 81
legal cause
  defined, 18, 36
legislative agency
  defined, 11
legislative process
  defined, 3, 11
Lensa Corporation v. Poinciana Gardens Association, Inc., 136
lessee

defined, 90, 107
lessor
  defined, 90, 108
liability on negotiable instrument
  acceptor, 68
  accommodation party, 68
  drawee, 68
  drawer, 68
  guarantors, 68
  indorser, 68
  maker, 68
  transferor, 68
liable, 13, 145
  as opposed to guilt, 22
  defined, 35
  employer for employee actions, 14
libel
  defined, 21, 35
license
  defined, 95, 108
lien
  as intangible personal property, 116
  common carrier, 116
  defined, 125
  of secured creditor in bankruptcy, 179
life estate
  categories, 84
  defined, 108
  reversion at termination, 84
  status as freehold estate, 85
life estate pur autre vie
  defined, 84, 108
limited liability company
  articles of organization, 149
  certificate of registration, 149
  creation, 149
  defined, 148, 156
  generally, 148
  liability of members, 149
  management, 149
  purpose, 149
  taxation, 149
limited partner, 177
  as investor, 145
  defined, 156
limited partners
  liability, 145
  role in limited partnership, 145
limited partnership
  advantages, 146
  creation by agreement, 145
  defined, 145, 156

Index 227

funding by selling limited partnership shares, 145
generally, 145
liability of limited partners, 145
management by general partner, 145
operation, 145
regulation by securities laws, 145
requirement of limited partner consent, 145
role of limited partners, 145
limited partnership agreement
defined, 145, 156
liquidated damages
defined, 53, 62
liquidation
defined, 175, 192
Lorbrook Corp. v. G. & T. Industries, Inc., 55

M

mailbox rule
defined, 41, 62
mailing matrix
defined, 177, 192
Maisch v. Hunt Midwest Mining, Inc., 99
maker
defined, 65, 78
liability on negotiable instrument, 68
malum in se
defined, 44, 62
malum prohibitum
defined, 44, 62
Statute of Frauds, 44
mark
defined, 112, 125
marketable title requirement, 87
master-servant relationship
concept in tort law, 128
defined, 127, 138
duration until termination of relationship, 129
material alteration
defined, 70
negligence, 70
material breach
defined, 52, 62
measuring life
defined, 84
meddling stranger
defined, 70, 78
material alteration of negotiable instrument, 70
member
defined, 156
mental impairment

defined, 165, 173
merchant
defined, 39, 62
minor
defined, 45, 62
minor breach
defined, 52, 62
mirror image rule
defined, 41, 62
misprision of felony, 26
misrepresentation
defined, 45, 62
mistake
defined, 46, 62
mitigation of damages
defined, 62
moot
defined, 6, 12
mortgage
assignment of interests, 89
deficiency after default, 90
defined, 89, 108
generally, 89
mortgagee
assignment of interests, 89
defined, 89, 108
relief in case of default, 90
mortgagor
assignment of interests, 89
default on loan, 90
defined, 89, 108
forestall of public sale, 90
motion
defined, 35
mutual mistake
defined, 46, 62
mutual rescission
defined, 51, 62
Mutual Savings and Loan v. National Bank of Detroit, 213
mutuality of consideration, 46
defined, 43, 62

N

necessaries
defined, 45, 62
necessity
as valid reason for tort, 18
negligence
defenses, 19
defined, 35
elements, 18

generally, 18
negligent hiring, 128
    defined, 14, 35
negligent misrepresentation
    defined, 19, 35
negotiable instrument
    defined, 65, 79
    forgery, 69
    material alteration, 70
    parties to instrument, 68
    party liability, 68
    requirements, 65
negotiation
    defined, 65, 79
Nicol v. Imagematrix, Inc., 170
nolo contendere
    defined, 26
nominal consideration
    defined, 44, 62
nominal damages
    defined, 53, 62
nonassignment clauses
    defined, 47
nonassignment provision
    defined, 62
nonconforming goods
    rejection of, 53
nondiscrimination in workplace
    generally, 163
Norden v. State of Oregon, 197
not guilty
    defined, 26
note
    defined, 65, 79
notice
    defined, 202
    in rule-making, 194
        elements, 194
    requirement of service on all creditors, 176
notice of appearance, 176
    defined, 192
notice of statutes
    defined, 89
novation
    defined, 48, 51, 62
nuisance
    defined, 35
    types, 21

O

offenses against habitation
    generally, 25

offenses against judicial procedure
    generally, 26
offenses against the person
    generally, 24
offer
    communication to offeree, 40
    defined, 40, 61, 62
offeree
    defined, 40, 62
offeror, 42
    defined, 40, 62
One Valley Bank of Oak Hill, Inc. v. Bolen, 71
order to pay
    defined, 66, 79
ordinary negligence
    liability of bailee, 114
ostensible authority
    defined, 130, 138
output contract
    defined, 41, 62
outstanding shares
    defined, 148, 156
overrule
    defined, 2, 12

P

parol evidence rule
    defined, 50, 63
    oral testimony exceptions, 50
partial eviction
    defined, 92, 108
partition
    defined, 84, 108
partnership agreement
    defined, 143, 156
    potential unenforceability if oral, 143
    requirement of filing with government, 143
    Statute of Frauds, 143
    termination by court order, 145
    termination by death or bankruptcy of partner, 145
    termination by operation of law, 145
    termination by partner agreement, 145
partnership interests
    defined, 143
partnership rights
    defined, 143, 156
    requirement that person be a partner, 144
    right to income, profits, and losses, 144
    right to manage and control business, 143
    right to physical assets of business, 143

rights personal to partners, 144
rights that can be assigned, 144
patent
    defined, 112, 125
pay differential
    elements for permitted differentials, 162
payable at a definite time
    defined, 66
payable on demand
    defined, 66
payable to bearer
    defined, 66
payable to order
    defined, 66
payee
    defined, 65, 79
payment
    requirements, 69
payment guarantor
    defined, 79
    liability on negotiable instrument, 68
payor bank
    relationship with customer, 205
periodic tenancy
    defined, 90
perjury
    defined, 26
permissive waste
    defined, 85, 108
personal property
    as chattel, 85
    categories, 111
    defined, 81, 108, 111, 125
    transfer, 112
personalty
    defined, 111, 125
petition
    defined, 195, 202
    for bankruptcy, 175
physical impairment
    defined, 165, 173
piercing the corporate veil
    defined, 148, 156
pleadings
    defined, 202
pledge
    defined, 113, 125
precedent, 2
    after establishment, 2
    authority to override, 3
    change by statute, 3
    defined, 1, 12

effect on statute application, 4
judicial
    defined, 6
pre-existing duty rule
    defined, 43, 63
    exceptions, 43
preferred stock
    defined, 147, 156
Pregnancy Discrimination Act of 1978
    defined, 173
    generally, 164
pre-hearing conference
    defined, 195, 202
preliminary hearing
    defined, 26, 35
presenter bank
    defined, 208, 216
presentment
    defined, 68, 79, 216
    requirements, 69
    stale checks, 207
pretrial
    defined, 26, 35
principal
    agent's fiduciary duty to, 131
    defined, 129, 138
    liability for agent's actual authority, 130
    liability for agent's apparent authority, 131
    liability for agent's authority by estoppel, 131
    need for contractual capacity, 129
    obligations to agent, 131
principal-agent relationship
    creation, 129
    creation by agreement, 129
    creation by estoppel, 130
    creation by ratification, 130
    defined, 129, 138
    termination, 132
        renunciation, 132
        revocation, 132
private necessity
    defined, 18, 35
private nuisance
    defined, 21
privilege
    as valid reason for tort, 17
probable cause
    defined, 26, 35
probation
    defined, 27, 35
probation officer
    defined, 27, 35
procedural law

defined, 22, 35
   for bankruptcy, 175
product liability
   defined, 20, 36
   theories of liability
      breach of warranty, 20
      intent, 20
      negligence, 20
      strict liability, 20
profit, 145
   defined, 96, 108
promise
   defined, 46, 63
promise to pay
   defined, 42, 66, 79
promisor
   defined, 46, 63
proof of claim
   defined, 177, 180, 192
property offenses
   generally, 24
protected categories
   affirmative action plans, 164
   defined, 174
   protection from discrimination and harassment, 163
   under Title VII, 163
proximate cause
   defined, 18, 36
public law
   defined, 4, 12
public necessity
   defined, 18, 36
public nuisance
   defined, 21
public use
   defined, 93
punitive damages
   defined, 53, 63

Q

quantum meruit
   defined, 54, 63
quantum valebant
   defined, 54, 63
quasi-contract
   defined, 44, 54, 63
question of fact
   defined, 12
question of law
   defined, 12
quid pro quo harassment

defined, 163, 174
quiet title
   defined, 87, 108
quitclaim deed
   defined, 88, 108

R

race statutes
   defined, 89
race-notice of statutes
   defined, 89
reaffirmation
   defined, 178, 192
real covenants
   defined, 96, 108
real property, 87
   defined, 81, 108
   financing, 89
   fixture, 85
   government infringements, 96
   record of transfers, 88
reasonable accommodation
   defined, 165, 174
   inclusions, 165
   relief under undue hardship clause, 165
reasonable person
   defined, 18, 36
reasonably prudent investor
   defined, 162, 174
receipt of stolen property
   defined, 25, 36
redemption
   defined, 90, 108
rejection, 42
   defined, 41, 63
release
   defined, 51, 63
remainder interest
   defined, 84, 108
removal
   defined, 192
   severance of additional value from original item, 115
   transfer of other litigation to bankruptcy court, 176
renunciation
   defined, 132, 138
reorganization or restructuring plan
   defined, 192
   purpose, 179
requirements contract

defined, 41, 63
rescission and restitution
  defined, 54, 63
respondeat superior, 14
  defined, 13, 36, 138
  exceptions, 128
    fellow servant exception, 128
    intentional torts, 129
    negligent hiring, 128
  master-servant relationship, 128
responsive pleading
  defined, 195, 203
reversion
  defined, 84, 108
revocation, 63
  defined, 132, 138
revoke or renounce
  defined, 42, 63
RICO
  defined, 26, 36
ripe
  defined, 12
robbery
  defined, 24, 36
royalty
  defined, 111, 125
rule
  challenge in court, 194
    burden of proof, 194
    improper delegation, 194
  creation by agency, 193
  defined, 193, 203
rule-making
  defined, 193
  under Administrative Procedure Act, 194
rules of construction
  defined, 63
  generally, 50

S

same establishment
  defined, 162, 174
Schedule C
  reporting sole proprietorship earnings, 142
seal
  defined, 147, 156
securities laws
  defined, 157
  regulation of limited partnerships, 145
security
  defined, 89, 108
self-dealing
  defined, 147, 157
self-defense
  as valid reason for tort, 17
sentence
  defined, 27, 36
service mark
  defined, 112, 125
servient tenement
  defined, 95, 108
sexual harassment
  conditions of employment, 163
  defined, 163, 174
  hostile work environment, 164
  quid pro quo harassment, 164
sham consideration
  defined, 44, 63
shareholder
  liability limited to shares, 147
shareholders
  limit to liability, 148
shares of stock
  defined, 147, 157
  different classes of stock, 147
  intangible personal property, 147
shelter rule
  defined, 67, 79
slander
  defined, 21, 36
Social Security, 176
  administration by Social Security Administration, 159
  benefits calculations, 160
  benefits for dependents, 160
  benefits for parents, 160
  benefits for self-employed, 160
  qualification for benefits, 160
Social Security Act, 159
  defined, 174
  generally, 159
Social Security Administration, 159
  defined, 174
sole proprietorship
  advantages, 142
  defined, 141, 157
  difficulty in funding, 142
  distinguished from general partnership, 143
  ease of formation, 142
  ease of management, 143
  exception from ERISA, 162
  few regulatory filing requirements, 143
  funding with owner assets, 142
  liability, 141

no liability for income taxes, 142
protection in bankruptcy, 175
rights and obligations, 141
tax on profit, 142
solicitation
    defined, 23, 36
special warranty deed
    defined, 88, 108
specific performance
    defined, 53, 63
stare decisis
    defined, 2, 12
    overrule by legislation, 3
state court system
    structure, 7
State of Alaska v. ABC Towing, 150
Statement of Assets and Liabilities
    codebtors, 177
    current expenditures of debtor, 177
    current income of debtor, 177
    executory contracts and unexpired loans, 177
    exempt property, 177
    generally, 177
    personal property, 177
    real property, 177
    Schedule A, 177
    Schedule B, 177
    Schedule C, 177
    Schedule D, 177
    Schedule E, 177
    Schedule F, 177
    Schedule G, 177
    Schedule H, 177
    Schedule I, 177
    Schedule J, 177
    secured claims, 177
    unsecured nonpriority claims, 177
    unsecured priority claims, 177
statement of financial affairs
    defined, 192
    generally, 176
Statement of Financial Affairs
    time limits, 178
statement of intent
    defined, 192
Statement of Intention
    defined, 178
Statute of Frauds
    contracts included, 44
    conveyancing, 86
    defined, 44, 63
    easements, 94

partnership agreement, 143
removal from Statute statys, 44
statutory right of redemption
    defined, 90, 109
stop payment order
    defined, 207, 216
straight bankruptcy
    defined, 175, 192
straw man
    defined, 84, 109
strict liability
    defined, 19
    elements, 19
strict or absolute liability
    defined, 36
subject to
    defined, 79
subject to the mortgage
    defined, 89, 109
sublease
    defined, 92, 109
subornation of perjury
    defined, 26
substantive law
    defined, 2, 22, 36
sum certain, 66
    defined, 66, 79
    requirements, 66

T

tangibles
    defined, 111, 125
tenancy at sufferance
    defined, 90, 109
tenancy at will
    defined, 90, 109
tenancy by the entirety
    defined, 83, 109
tenancy for years
    defined, 90, 109
tenancy in common
    defined, 82, 109
tenancy in partnership, 143
    defined, 83, 109
tenancy in severalty
    defined, 81, 109
tenant
    defined, 81
tenant duties
    generally, 91
    maintenance of property, 91

obligation to pay rent, 91
obligations after property destruction, 91
preclusion from illegal use, 91
tenant obligations to temporary visitors
duty of ordinary care, 94
generally, 93
invitees, 94
licensees, 94
trespassers, 93
testimony
defined, 6, 12
third-party beneficiary
defined, 46, 63
right to enforce contract, 47
third-party beneficiary contract
defined, 47, 63
third-party creditor beneficiary
defined, 46, 63
third-party donee beneficiary
defined, 46, 63
third-party rights
generally, 94
title, 83
check for validity, 89
defined, 81, 109
fixtures, 86
loss of marketability, 87
claim of adverse possession, 87
defect in chain of title, 87
encumbrance, 87
zoning violation, 87
use of indorsement to transfer, 67
title insurance
defined, 89, 109
faulty conveyance, 89
title search
defined, 89, 109
Title VII
administration by EEOC, 163
application to employers, 163
cases, 163
defense of bona fide occupational qualification, 164
defined, 174
exceptions, 163
generally, 163
persons over 40, 164
protected categories, 163
protection against pregnancy discrimination, 164
protection for disabled, 165
relief for disabled, 165
requirement for leave for pregnancy, 165

Toibb v. Radloff, 181
tort
defined, 13, 36
no liability of principal, 132
specific business torts, 19
tortfeasor
defined, 13, 36
intentional torts, 15
valid reasons for actions, 17
consent, 17
discipline of child, 18
necessity, 18
privilege, 17
self-defense, 17
tortious interference with contract
defined, 19, 36
Town of Stratford v. Mudre, 98
tract index
defined, 89, 109
trade fixture
defined, 86, 109
failure to remove, 86
trademark
defined, 112, 125
transferor
liability on negotiable instrument, 68
trespass to chattels
as intentional tort, 15
defined, 36
elements, 17
trespass to land
as intentional tort, 15
defined, 36
elements, 16
trial, 2
defined, 36
trial court
defined, 2, 6, 12
district court, 6
trier of fact
defined, 6, 12
Twin Books Corporation v. The Walt Disney Company, 121

U

ultra vires
agency rule presumed to be legal, 194
defined, 203
unconditional
defined, 79
unconditional promise to pay
defined, 66

undue hardship
  defined, 165, 174
Uniform Commercial Code
  accord and satisfaction, 51
  Article 2, 39
  Article 3, 65, 205
  Article 4, 205, 207
  bank statement rule, 70
  bank's obligation to pay properly drawn checks, 205
  damages for merchant traders, 53
  defined, 64
  discharge of contractual obligations, 50
  generally, 39
  holder in due course, 67
  indorsements, 67
  installment contracts, 50
  liquidated damages, 53
  no requirement for mirror image acceptance, 41
  parol evidence rule, 50
  regulation of sale of good, 39
  requirements for negotiation, 65
  requirements under Article 2, 40
  special issues, 54
  Statute of Frauds removal, 44
  types of warranties, 54
  written assurances, 50
Uniform Limited Partnership Act
  defined, 157
  generally, 145
Uniform Partnership Act
  defined, 157
  generally, 143
  termination of agreement, 145
  types of agreements requiring unanimity, 143
Uniform Vendors' and Purchasers' Risk Act
  defined, 87, 109
unilateral contract
  defined, 42, 64
unilateral mistake
  defined, 46, 64
United States Code
  defined, 4, 12
  Title 11, 175
United States Constitution
  authority to override precedent, 3
  defined, 12
  foundation of criminal procedure, 26
  generally, 3
  interpretation by Supreme Court, 7
United States Supreme Court
  defined, 7, 12
  safeguard to adversely affected individuals, 195
United States trustee
  defined, 192
United States Trustee
  defined, 176
  scheduling of meetings, 178
usual covenants
  defined, 88

V

vague
  defined, 203
variance
  contract variances, 41
  defined, 109
  in zoning, 97
verdict
  defined, 6, 12
veto
  defined, 4, 12
vicarious liability, 127
  as law of agency, 127
  defined, 36, 138
  generally, 13
  sharing of financial liability, 15
voidable
  defined, 45, 64
voluntary bankruptcy
  defined, 192
  generally, 175
  individual subjection, 179
  initiation of proceedings, 175
voluntary waste
  defined, 85, 109

W

waive
  defined, 50
waiver
  defined, 64
Walls v. Lombard Police Officers, 29
warranty
  defined, 37
  types, 54
warranty against infringement
  defined, 64
warranty of fitness for a particular use
  defined, 37
warranty of marketability

defined, 109
    real estate contracts, 87
warranty of merchantability
    defined, 37
warranty of title
    defined, 54, 64
waste
    defined, 109
    types, 85
workers compensation
    defined, 138
workers compensation law
    defined, 37
workers compensation statutes
    defined, 14
writ of certiorari
    defined, 7, 12

written assurances
    defined, 50, 64
wrongful dishonor
    bank liability for damages, 208
    defined, 216

Z

Zimmer v. Carlton County Co-op Power Association, 133
zoning
    defined, 97, 110
    effect on restructions and designations, 97
zoning board
    defined, 97, 110
zoning violation
    defined, 87